MATCHDAY
WHAT MAKES SATURDAY SPECIAL?

CHRIS GREEN

Published in 2005 by Highdown,
an imprint of Raceform Ltd
Compton, Newbury, Berkshire, RG20 6NL
Raceform Ltd is a wholly-owned subsidiary of Trinity Mirror plc

A CIP catalogue record for this book is available from the British Library.

ISBN 1-905156-17-0

Cover designed by Tracey Scarlett
Designed by Fiona Pike

Printed in Great Britain by William Clowes Ltd, Beccles, Suffolk

CONTENTS

ACKNOWLEDGEMENTS

It would have been impossible to carry out the research for this book without the unique assistance I have received from all kinds of people.

First, my profound thanks go to all the interviewees. Each has entered into the spirit of this book and opened their arms and sometimes their hearts to me. They have welcomed me, driven me and in some cases fed me, and I'm sure put up with me (though they have been too polite to say so). Generally, they have been as helpful as possible. I must also thank their partners who must, at times, have wondered why this strange bloke seemed so obsessed with what they do.

So a big thanks to Bob Marley, and Seb, Sam and Mandy; Brian Murdoch and his cooking crew at Kiddy; Dr Ralph Rogers and Liz Crane; Paul and Mel Taylor; Rob Bradley; John Baine (aka Attila the Stockbroker); Neil Williams and Josh; Paul Barnett; James Alexander Gordon; Stuart Hall; John and Anne Boyers; Neil Doncaster; Bill and Ann Berry; Phil Hamilton; Alison Geddes; Phil Robinson; Brian Tinnion; and Danny Coles.

Making the various arrangements for some of these interviews and observations would not have been possible without those who received some unusual requests for behind-the-scenes access at several football clubs. I would like to place on record my thanks to the following people: John Whitney, Jeff Bonser and Paul Merson at Walsall FC; Edward Stone at the FA; Terry Baxter and Samantha Kirk at Ipswich Town; Paul Camillan and Derek Allen at Brighton & Hove Albion; the woman at Gretna who packed a 'doggy bag' for me to take home; Brooks Mileson; Cyrille Regis (for finding a player for the book with much persistence); Mike Beardall and Rachel Porter at the Institute of Groundsmen; Michelle McDonald and all the staff at Bristol City; Geraint Parry at Wrexham FC; Nic Outterside from Clubs in Crisis; Phil Tooley of Supporters Direct; Rob Griffiths and Simon Johnson of the Wrexham Supporters Trust; Joe Ferrari at Norwich City; Lee Wellings and Audrey Adams at Radio Five Live Sport; and Amanda Duffy at Positive Futures.

Thanks also to the many, many people I met along the way who offered words of support and encouragement and good wishes. I fully appreciate all of your thoughts.

In the acknowledgements to his last book, *The Beautiful Game*, my journalist friend and colleague David Conn thanked me for the help and advice I gave and mentioned that he owed me a drink. I still haven't had it, but I guess, after the all-too-sensible advice I have received from David, we are now all square!

Particular thanks to the publisher of *Matchday*, Jonathan Taylor, who has been nothing less than 100 per cent supportive for what must, at first sight, have seemed a pretty unusual concept for a sports book, and to my literary agent, Robert Dudley, who has provided so much support in so many ways.

The idea of writing a book about the excitement of matchday and football as a national game played, watched and absorbed by so many people in so many different settings was spurred by a conversation with the photographer Stuart Clarke in his gallery in Ambleside in the Lake District. Stuart told me how, in order to ensure good radio reception, he often rowed a boat on to Coniston Water to listen to the football scores. What an enduring image! Of all the hundreds or thousands of fantastic photographs Stuart has taken to record the changing face of our national game in recent years, has he ever painted a more romantic one than that? He has also taken the cover photos for this book. He has my profound thanks. And I would urge you all to visit his gallery in Ambleside, and/or visit www.homesoffootball.com.

Hidden between the lines of my own love of football and links to *Matchday* are so many other people who deserve a special mention. First, my good, long-standing (and long-suffering!) friend Tim Lewis, with whom I have probably spent more matchdays than any other person.

Without the devotion and dedication of my grandparents Arthur and Edith Green, who took me on so many visits to Worcestershire County Cricket Club and Worcester City FC, I doubt if I would have developed such an early love for watching sport. Or my Uncle Jack, who took me to my first West Brom game at the age of eleven. More significantly, I thank with all my heart my parents, Kenneth and

Marjorie Green, who fostered a love of playing sport in both my brother Phillip and in me from an early age.

It is truly hard to convey my thanks to Bob Marley, the Worcester City director featured in this book, who, during a genuine hour of need, drove from Worcester to Carlisle and back to rescue me when I was stuck in floods far away from home. The tale is told here as an unusual aspect of *Matchday*. His effort in driving that distance at the end of a busy day was awesome. Words seem barely enough to express my gratitude, but thanks, Bob.

Lastly, although in my heart they will always come first, this book would not have been possible without the support and love of my wife Teresa, who has waved me out of the door each and every Saturday for the past four months and has cherished and looked after our son Nicholas, whom we both love so dearly, while I have been away. Magically, when I came home (late, again) after the last of these matchdays, Nicholas said, 'Daddy's back.' In my heart I was never away.

THE MEANING OF
MATCHDAY

Before you read this book, let me tell you something about the concept and narrative of *Matchday*. It is about the unfolding drama of football's matchday as told through the eyes of some eighteen people connected with the game. These are real people, and their stories are faithful accounts of the matchdays I spent with each of them between December 2004 and April 2005, with all the unpredictable consequences that can occur.

I have squashed them together into one narrative, a story that unfurls in chronological order, like concentric circles closing in and later extending outwards from the classic three o'clock kick-off time. It starts with the person who wakes first and ends with the last one to switch off the bedroom light. My own observations have been thrown in for good measure.

The only artistic licence I have taken, with the full agreement of all concerned, has been to adjust some of the start times to fit a uniform three o'clock kick-off. Sadly, it was not possible to find eighteen suitable traditional three p.m. kick-off matches and ensure the right spread of people. This has not affected any vital detail or altered the way in which anyone carries out their normal matchday functions.

Each of the characters featured here is special. I am not saying they are necessarily unique (although some are clearly outstanding individuals), or that they are more worthy than thousands of other people who make matchday happen, who might equally have been chosen for inclusion. But they have been selected because, in my eyes at least, they make a distinct contribution to British football. Some I knew from my previous work; others came on recommendation; many were simply people I was fascinated by and wanted to find out more about. They cover a wide spectrum of the modern game. This is no selection of jobsworths or group of industry professionals.

So what have we got? A chairman, a director, a chief executive, a manager, a player, a doctor, a referee, a groundsman, a chaplain, a PA announcer, a couple of media folks, a few fans and one person who basically does everything at his club. It doesn't, I know, sound much for being on the road every Saturday for four months – a journey, emotional at times, that has taken me to remote football outposts and the game's inner-city heartlands.

I have been marooned in a hotel surrounded by flood water and frozen beside junior football pitches; I have been inside steamy dressing rooms where nervous players have retched up phlegm; I have rubbed shoulders with Roman Abramovic and seen a seven-year-old boy with head-shaking health problems play his first match. Geographically this journey has taken me to Scotland, Wales and the west, east, north, south and Midlands of England. Although I have tried to avoid tokenism, for the record, the age spread of interviewees is 24 to late 70s, and there is one female interviewee (sadly women are under-represented in football) and two black people (ditto).

In some respects this is a snapshot of the 2004/05 football season, and I have tried to encompass many levels of the game from the Premier League down to the Hertfordshire Senior League. The doubling up of games for some of the interviewees – trebling up in one case – means several morning junior/youth matches are also included, and rightly so, for *Matchday* is about much more than the interests and whims of the adult professional game. Unless it is understood and developed at grassroots and junior level, there is no top-flight football, no social context, no understanding, no meaning.

Dozens of thought-provoking topics were raised. Some interviewees were selected with that in mind. Many told truly heart-rending stories and shed tears while describing their passion for this most beguiling of sports. I guess there is an element of Fantasy Football about this too: if I was putting an ideal football club together I would certainly want some of these fellas on board. Most would definitely suit a collective of football's good guys. I just hope I have done them justice. There are social issues too. The fight to save Wrexham FC from the bulldozers has been the big supporters issue of the season. The good work of the Positive Futures programme in using football as a force for good by helping youths in inner cities is to be applauded. These are topics that transcend the normal 'soap opera' of football's matchday.

Now let me tell what you won't find here. This book isn't about the rich and famous. Neither is it about hooliganism. There are no lurid, largely fictional tales written by members of 1980s fighting crews which have proliferated on bookshelves in recent years – no hooligan porn for football's *nouveau riche* fans who 'found' football in the 1990s and are obsessed with what they believe constitutes lad and ladette culture. If these readers had been there in the dark days they might have been sickened by the violence they now choose to read about for fun.

C'mon, guys, matchday is about much more than that. The British football culture is as intense as anywhere in the world. We, after all, invented the game. Saturday – matchday – is still, by and large, shaped the way it was when it was turned into a formalised and then commercialised sport in the late Victorian era. Built initially around the industrial week – Saturday afternoon was a half-day of leisure in what was a six-day working week – matchday was a creation. Football is our national game, and we should treasure it. Matchday is still special. Just listen to some of the interviewees for this book.

'It's my adrenalin, my drug,' said Phil Hamilton, a youth worker in Birmingham, with tears in his eyes. 'If I don't have football at least three or four times a week I'm desperate.'

'It's everything,' said Bob Marley, a director of Worcester City FC. 'It's judgement day.'

Ralph Rogers is an American sports physician also based in Birmingham: 'I'm raring to go on matchday, man. It's exciting. The passion for football is fantastic in England. Nothing anywhere in the world compares to it.' To some, matchday is put up or shut up day, one of fear and trepidation. Bristol City manager Brian Tinnion, interviewed during his first season in charge, observed, 'In management it's the worst day really because all week you can enjoy working with the players but it's the Saturday that counts. It is all about getting the three points. Take the Saturday out of management and it is really enjoyable.'

Paul Barnett, a groundsman with Gretna FC, doesn't sleep on Friday nights. 'No one thinks about the groundsman's nerves, but you never know what you will turn up to.'

For others matchday is one of perpetual optimism. 'If you've lost twenty on the trot it doesn't matter,' insisted Rob Bradley, the chairman of Lincoln City. 'If you win the twenty-first, the feeling is amazing because you've had to wait so long for it. There are always positives.' Bradley quit his role at the end of the 2004/05 season and described being in charge as 'a wonderful nightmare – a classic labour of love'.

For fans it can be a day of pride and passion. 'It is my life, my history and my identity,' said Neil Williams, a Cornwall-based Wrexham fan. He likens travelling to home games when the club's future is in doubt as 'a pilgrimage ... a calling ... losing the club would be like losing a part of your body, or a member of your family'.

Only a game that is truly special can engender this depth of feeling.

That legendary Radio Five Live reporter Stuart Hall, he of the erstwhile *It's a Knockout* giggles and quick turn of phrase, is still drawn by 'the theatre of football – the atmosphere, earnest endeavour, and smiling faces'.

But maybe Phil Robinson, a man who has been the driving force behind Afan Lido, a small community club on the South Wales seafront at Port Talbot whose first team plays in the Welsh Premier League, summed matchday up best: 'To me, Saturday is special. When summer comes and there is no football you just don't know what to do with yourself.' Casting his head to the sky he then laughed. 'The world changes.'

Matchday is about young boys in tears who have let their team-mates down; about professional players with crazy superstitions; about James Alexander Gordon's golden voice reading the classified football results; about sublime skills, precious penalty saves and lip-biting, last-minute winners; about the dedication of thousands upon thousands of willing workers who make it all happen. Matchday is about all these things, and more. And that is why it truly is special.

DAWN THOUGHTS

My first memory of football dates back to infants school, though it's hazy. I vaguely recall going to a female teacher to moan about some of the boys not letting me kick the ball. I was upset – crying probably. She sat me on her knee, gave me a cuddle and explained, 'You have to run after it and then kick it. You can't just wait until it comes to you.' Sometimes I wonder if all I have been doing ever since is chasing the ball.

5 A.M.: A NEW YEAR'S MORNING THOUGHT It had to be me. I had fully intended to start this book with someone with football coursing through their veins. They would have the honour of rising first, of featuring in this opening homage to matchday. But it is me climbing out of bed at five a.m. on New Year's Day morning. Drat. Now, I'm not for a moment claiming that my own efforts anywhere near match those hardy souls who routinely make Saturday special for hundreds of thousands of people across the country every week. It's just that, well, in terms of accuracy I did get up earlier than anyone. Honest. In days of yore, I would barely have got in from a night's partying by five a.m.

I'm out of the house within half an hour. This is the quietest time at which I have ever driven to London. There is barely another vehicle on the M5, the M42 and the M40 south, a journey often as torturous as anaesthetic-free dentistry. I'm making my way to the Hertfordshire home of referee Paul Taylor for a meeting; we will later head to Ipswich together for their New Year's Day footy match at the top of the Coca-Cola Championship with West Ham. On the distant horizon lies a layer of bright intermingling colours, a truly awe-inspiring sight of reds, golds and oranges, together symbolising warmth and a sense of optimism. I feel good. I feel energised. Euphoric.

And that is how I, and so many of the interviewees for this book, feel about each and every matchday. Excited. Expectant.

On this particular morning I think about my loving wife, Teresa, whose body warmth I have left behind, and our gorgeous two-year-old son Nicholas, whose last words to me had been 'Big hugs!' the night before (followed by the less-pleasing 'You haven't got much hair, Daddy' as he got into our bed for a very early-morning cuddle). I feel immensely lucky to have a job most people consider to be a hobby; to have the good fortune to be blessed with good health and happiness; to be able to look forward to researching and writing this book; to have the opportunity to make so many journeys and see so many people and matches in so many contrasting settings. I think, too, of the desperately sad disaster in southeast Asia. The full devastation of the tsunami that hit a few days ago is still sinking in.

Before long, however, I'm aware again of how excited I'm feeling at the prospect of the day ahead – childishly so, and at the age of 45! I am on the cusp of another unfolding matchday. But as I press my body firmly back against my seat and take a large, deep breath, I am jolted out of this serene moment. I bet the bloody Albion lose today …

5.30 A.M.: COFFEE AND TOAST ON THE HOOF It's half-past five, and Worcester City director Bob Marley (real name Kevin, but we'll come to that) wakes up. He's had two hours' sleep, having been up until three a.m. 'entertaining' former England and Manchester United star Paul Parker, who was the speaker at a function hosted by another local non-League club, Evesham United. Bob and Worcester City chairman Dave Boddy had gone along to show support, but after the question-and-answer session and obligatory autographs, Parker wanted some action. Where to go? Evesham is hardly Las Vegas, so a small entourage headed for Worcester (little better), some fifteen miles away. Bob, a non-drinker, became chauffeur for the night, and eventually got Parker (manager of southeast London club Welling) back to his hotel in Evesham.

He's at work by six a.m., having left the house within minutes: no shower, just a very quick wash and shave, and toast and coffee grabbed on the hoof. By eight he'll already have put in two hours' work. And that's 'work work', as Bob calls it: his day jobs include running a business-to-business mobile phone company and being a freelance venture capital adviser. He's a non-drinker so he's not hung over. He is tired, but being a prodigious drinker of coffee, his teetotal, caffeine-fuelled body doesn't waiver for a quaver. Indeed, until he goes to bed at eleven p.m. Bob will maintain a ferocious pace throughout this supposed day of leisure.

Football club directors are often accused of being in it for the kudos, the fame, the money, the chance to rub shoulders with famous footballers like Paul Parker; but this relative glory is meagre comfort compared to the hours accrued trying to steer a small non-League club along the straight and narrow. Welcome to the real world of a non-League director.

The day ahead isn't just an organisational feat, the schedule of a supremely confident man, it is a triumph of will. Bob keeps pushing. Our day together is literally one of mud, sweat and tears covering three games: two at junior level and, according to Bob, the least important one in the overall scheme of things, Worcester City's first-team match at home in the Nationwide Conference North League against Stalybridge Celtic. We will wade through water to reach a junior club Bob formed a few years ago, see a whole tier of youth football he has instigated in the Midlands and the progress or otherwise of a senior club in England's largest city without a Football League club.

All this has contributed to his marriage breakdown – which, given that the two junior games we will take in involve watching his youngest son Sam (9) and coaching Seb (11), makes the day emotionally challenging.

6 A.M.: 'CORNISH RED' RISES It's an early, cold, midwinter morning in Cornwall, one of those biting ones when the option of turning over and curling up next to a loved one beneath the duvet is all too tempting. The summer option of leaping out of bed, drawing back the curtains, opening the window and gulping in the bracing air sweeping in from the Atlantic is a distant memory. It is pitch black outside. And silent. There are no birds singing, nor even the faintest rattle of a milk float. For Neil Williams, who lives in an idyllic four-bedroom house overlooking the rolling hills of Cornwall's Lizard Point, there are no roaring motorways either, or intrusive street lighting. In fact, few distractions to tempt you away from under the eiderdown.

Neil is knackered. He hasn't been able to sleep, and at five a.m. was in that half-comatose state, wavering between the hope of sneaking a few extra winks of sleep and lying in bed frustrated by his mind not quite being able to relax. At six he reaches over to extinguish the sound of that damn alarm clock, gets out of bed with his eyes half-closed, and walks into the shower. No shave – there isn't time.

Neil is a man on a mission. He wakes his partner's sixteen-year-old son Josh, who is travelling with him to the match today, then reaches for his own clothes. He pulls on his precious crimson replica shirt, jeans and coat. There is only time for a cigarette and a quick cup of tea; breakfast will be grabbed on the way. He quickly checks he has the essentials – money, scarf, Welsh flag, hat, toy sheep – for the pressing priority is to get out of the house and on the road. At 6.28 he pulls the car out of the drive.

The issue worrying Neil most at the moment is the future of the football club he supports – Wrexham FC. Neil isn't directly involved in the football industry. He can't influence things from within. But fans like Neil and millions like him, are the lifeblood of the game. Without them there is no meaning to the sport. No value. No worth. No social context. Nothing. Just 22 men kicking a ball about.

Neil goes that extra mile. Well, 650 of them to be precise. The Wrexham shirt he proudly wears says it all: Cornish Red – the pseudonym he uses on the Red Passion supporters message board. Let me do the geography for you. Wrexham is in North Wales. Helston, where Neil lives, is on the western tip of Cornwall, just fifteen miles or so from Land's End. It takes more than an hour just to drive out of this vast county; reaching Wrexham involves a five-and-a-half-hour journey. That's a 650-mile round trip, eleven hours on the road, a 6.30 a.m. to 11.30 p.m. day. All for 90 minutes of League One football. One hell of a commitment.

And there isn't that much to cheer about this season. Quite the opposite in fact. The future of the club hangs in the balance. Wrexham is a club in crisis, and the owner wants to sell their ground. But all this has only encouraged Neil, the son of a Flintshire farmer who moved with his job to Cornwall, to make the trip more often. It may be, unthinkably for Neil, his club's last season.

Let's leave the politics for later. The most important thing at the moment is to get to Wrexham as soon as possible. As a keen member of the newly formed Wrexham Supporters Trust (WST), a fans' body fighting to keep the club afloat, today is a special day for Neil. Fans from other clubs are also beating a path to Wrexham to show their support for an ailing fellow club. The day is called Clubs in Crisis and is being organised by a group called Fans United. Neil wants to attend the pre-match rally. If he gets a wriggle on he'll make solid progress along the A30 and up the M5 before too many other vehicles hit the road. He can then stop for breakfast. He'll need to break the 325-mile journey to Wrexham and get some winter fuel to warm those cold bones.

6.30 A.M.: GOOD MORNING, DOCTOR In Birmingham Dr Ralph Rogers wakes, yawns, showers, slips on a tracksuit and heads downstairs to his study to deal with some early-morning paperwork. He glances out of the window of the two-storey Victorian house on Birmingham's busy Bristol Road that he and his long-standing partner Liz have converted into a home and workplace. They have a flat upstairs, Ralph's clinic is on the ground floor, and Liz's medical supplies business occupies the first floor.

It is a midwinter Saturday morning, a matchday – always a special one for Ralph, who is a sports physician and club doctor at Walsall FC. 'Put up or shut up day,' he says. 'I've always been an early riser,' he adds, staring out of the window at the early-morning traffic negotiating its way along this busy thoroughfare to the south of the city. The nocturnal amber lighting and the ever-changing red, gold and green of the traffic lights in this most urban of settings contrasts with the drab greyness of the tower blocks beyond.

Ralph, a tall native New Yorker, is a city creature. Being Walsall's doctor is only part of what he does. He runs his own sports medicine clinic called MOST (Medical Orthopaedic Sports Therapy). But matchday is special. 'I'm raring to go, man. It's the same buzz I used to get when I played university sport. It's all about game day. I still get butterflies even though I'm not playing. It's exciting. It's about competing. It's about winning. It's fun. I love being involved. The passion for football is fantastic in England. Nothing anywhere in the world compares to it. It's a good culture.'

When Ralph talks like this, you feel inspired. Imagine being treated by someone as effervescent as this. To be honest, it was touch and go whether I would include him in this book. For starters, being American, he is alien to the British football culture. He doesn't have football flowing through his veins. And he's a doctor – hardly the most high-profile position at British football clubs. But these are the very reasons for his inclusion. Ralph can make observations as an outsider, even though he is actively participating in British football. He also has some thought-provoking opinions to offer. His view of the role of the club doctor, for instance, contrasts with too much ingrained common practice in the game.

Let me explain. At most clubs the doctor's role is little more than an honorary title, a name nestled among the list of officials in the club programme, a mandatory appointment clubs are duty-bound to have available to treat players of both sides and anyone who suffers serious illness in the crowd. In reality, they are rarely needed; most turn up, enjoy the free hospitality and pocket their cheque. Sorted.

At Walsall, Ralph is much more than that. For starters, he is team physician. He oversees the medical treatment of players. That doesn't mean he runs around with a kit bag and a sponge, and he's not to be confused with the physiotherapist, who is more hands on and is sometimes given all-embracing powers to heal injuries beyond their medical expertise. It means Ralph diagnoses injuries and prescribes remedies and the precise form of treatment required (sometimes physiotherapy). But even that is not necessarily his first port of call. He also carries out regular blood tests to make sure the players are fit, well and responding to training, dietary regimes and medical conditions. It is unique for a club at Walsall's level (League One, the third rung of English football) to have someone of Ralph's expertise on board.

And he's part of the team. He is more than a matchday doc: Ralph makes himself available 24 hours a day, seven days a week, even though he is, technically, appointed part time. Available if and when needed. It's his personal ethos, but also part of his professional training as a sports medic – the way things are in many sports across Europe and North America where his work would be cherished and respected. In the UK it is frequently stolen by jobbing GPs with a passing interest in sport, employed by clubs that will spend thousands or millions of pounds on procuring players but penny-pinch when it comes to looking after their health and fitness. Madness.

But right now he has a crust to earn. Donning his white coat, he heads downstairs. He will see private patients in his clinic from nine a.m. to midday, but thereafter he is Walsall's for the day, where he has been doctor since 2001.

7 A.M.: GRETNA'S GROUNDSMAN GETS UP In the Scottish town of Dumfries Paul Barnett gets out of bed. He hasn't slept well. He never does the night before matchday. It isn't nerves, or even because he has a three-month-old-son, Jack, or for that matter another boy, three-year-old Cameron, who can also be an early-morning livewire. It's not knowing what the weather will bring.

Paul – 'Barney' to all and sundry – is groundsman at Gretna FC, the southernmost side in Scottish League football, which is running away with the Scottish Third Division title. The club is being financially backed by northern businessman Brooks Mileson, who, since Gretna moved out of the English non-League system to the north of the border, has developed a full-time playing squad and background staff. Barney was, according to Mileson, 'his most important signing', someone who could create a pristine pitch for Gretna to play on. He has worked for Mileson before, at his hometown club Scarborough, and at this level of football he is a rare full-time groundsman. Paul's wife, Annette, is a Dumfries girl, so making the decision to hop across the border wasn't difficult. But Paul is a worrier on matchday mornings.

'We have accurate forecasts these days,' he says, 'but you just never know what the weather will actually be like.' The possibilities have been whizzing around his mind all night. Yesterday evening, when a group of staff members gathered for an end-of-week drink, he told them he hated Fridays. 'They are a nightmare to me,' he says. 'You never sleep properly just in case you've got to get to the ground urgently. Hopefully, all goes well, but you can never quite be sure.'

He peers out of the window, up at the dark sky. All looks well. The wind is whistling in from the Solway Firth but there are no wet, glistening pavements, no white layer of frost to worry about. He's hoping it will be the same at Gretna, some 24 miles away, where he has concerns over one of the penalty areas. A heavy downpour could cause problems. Wisely, he cut the grass and marked the pitch yesterday. 'We try to get everything ready if we can,' he explains over an early-morning cuppa. 'Sometimes you can't.'

But this morning there is no need to make an urgent dash to save his precious pitch from the elements, which he's had to do many times already this season. A few weeks earlier, when the club had a romantic Scottish FA Cup tie lined up against Dundee United, an eagerly anticipated game with Scottish TV cameras coming along, he had to get on the road at six. Snow and horrendous gale-force winds caused the cancellation of the game, but en route Paul had had to deal with more pressing matters: helping the drivers of high-sided vehicles that had toppled over on the A75.

For all the anxiety, Paul is a matchday enthusiast. He genuinely wants to prepare the best pitch possible, to present a nice, neat ground for players and supporters alike. Today he is confident it will be game on at Gretna.

7.20 A.M.: HANDS-ON COOKING – THIS IS PERSONAL

Kidderminster not the most romantic of settings on a cold December morning. In fact, it's a slightly strange place. This may be Edward Elgar's Worcestershire, but the look and feel are more of a northern mill town. There are few vehicles around this morning – the odd one negotiates the ring road; lorries drop their loads at town-centre shops – and there is the unmistakable clatter of stainless steel as market traders set out their stalls (as many football managers will metaphorically do later in the day).

On the corner of Lion Street stands Murdoch's Wine Bar and Restaurant, next to the Lion Hotel. Both are owned by Brian Murdoch, an award-winning caterer at the town's ailing football club, Kidderminster Harriers. I push open the door and shout a loud 'hello'. Brian, a portly man in his mid-sixties, appears from the kitchen, which even at this Godforsaken hour is already steamed up. Just under eight hours ahead of kick-off, matchday is well and truly underway. On top of the two cooking hobs and huge oven sit six large cauldrons of soup and a single pot of veggie soup. They are bubbling gently. The vats are full of fresh ingredients. 'Timing is everything,' insists Brian, who understands the value of cooking soup so far ahead of the time when it will be eaten. 'They'll be perfect by half-time.'

He should know. For 43 years he's made the perfect soup for the food bars at Kidderminster Harriers. His concoction is a terrace cult classic –

even the club's fanzine was named after it. Supporters are known to make special trips for a slurp. 'That's when I decided to expand my repertoire,' he says with a laugh.

Work has also begun on making 120 cottage pies, mainly minced beef but some cheese and onion, topped with tomato too. These look so much more appetising than the usual lame, limp, pastry-crusted, mass-produced affairs, often microwaved to a temperature hotter than the sun, you get at most grounds. Brian's pies are topped with mash and are served in foil trays with a plastic fork, a hearty meal for £3.50. And this is just a small part of Brian Murdoch's repertoire. Later in the day, fans attending Kidderminster's League Two game against Rochdale will have the choice not only of soup and cottage pie, but curry, chow mein, chilli, roast pork baps, egg and tomato rolls, balti pies, pasta, hot dogs and burgers. I'm feeling hungry already. The smell is embracing. It is wonderful. There are no frozen chips, no pre-prepared packs or rehydrated rubbish. 'This is hands on,' says Brian. 'It's personal.'

The reason I'm here is to find out how a club that is bottom of the Football League with some of the smallest crowds can come top of football's catering division. We keep hearing mealy-mouthed platitudes about football being a business, but when it comes to food the primary practicalities seem to be at the whim of the providers, who concern themselves with the language of 'throughput' and 'economies of scale' rather than the palettes of fans. They, we are endlessly told, despite the obvious social changes elsewhere, prefer to eat only 'traditional' food, and by that is meant burgers, pies, fries, crisps, chips, chocolate and Coke, with prices rounded and ratcheted up past the price at which they are sold elsewhere and usually served without a hint of warmth or the faintest smile.

Brian Murdoch's story spins this inane logic on its head. His operation is as much about commercial nous as cooking. It is about providing quality food that fans enjoy rather than ripping them off, fattening them up and treating them like turnstile fodder. It is about healthy, wholesome, tasty food rather than expensive junk food. About giving rather than grabbing. It is the story of Brian Murdoch's unique contribution to English football and the thousands of fans who admire his cooking every season.

In truth, this isn't even a tale of matchday. Preparation of the soup started two days earlier when the meat was cooked off the bone. Most of the prep work – chopping up some 50lb of minced beef, 20lb of chicken breast and several hundredweight of potatoes, onions and carrots (all ordered from local suppliers) – is done on Friday. Same goes for the floury baps – large, local, quality. This is home-made cooking on a grand scale – and a family affair. Brian's son David and daughter Helen are part of his dozen-strong team today. It is all about a passion for food, for service and a desire to do right by the fans.

7.30 A.M.: BREAKFAST IN BED FOR THE REV Reverend John Boyers wakes in his south Manchester home. John is the club chaplain at Manchester United, who are at home to Portsmouth today.

Matchday can be a busy day for the Rev (John's moniker, not mine). It is very much a working day, but for his wife Anne, a full-time teacher, it is one of leisure. Considerately, John endeavours to share most of his spare time with her. Invariably, he hops downstairs, puts the kettle and toaster on, and returns upstairs with two trays of porridge, oatgrain toast and filter decaf coffee. Today may be matchday, and it will have its challenges, but that isn't to the exclusion of other facets of life.

Football club chaplaincy might, at first sight, be viewed as an anachronism, a Victorian hangover from the game's formative years when so many of Britain's major clubs were formed as church teams. It was an era when muscular Christianity was espoused with the same zeal as the temperance movement had in its mission to persuade wayward youngsters to sign the pledge, thereby banishing the demon of drink and other temptations for idle hands. But it is a relatively recent development. There were a few club chaplains around before John Boyers became chaplain at Watford in 1977 (he moved to Manchester United in 1992), but he has given the role meaning and definition.

These days John and his colleagues certainly face a challenge. Football clubs are often said to worship the god of greed; the top clubs in particular appear to have little time for their less affluent brethren, and in many ways the game appears to be, at best, morally ambivalent. Manchester United is, of course, the biggest beast in the jungle, and much more than a mere football club. It is viewed as a 'global brand', its players are perceived to be role models (but frequently fail to display the responsibility that comes with it), and its fans adore the club from near and far. The soap opera of Manchester United appears on the front, back and business pages of newspapers each and every day, whether it's about the latest gobbling up of shares, the behaviour of players, speculation about who may be coming or going, and sometimes – although I realise this is a bit far-fetched – the results of their matches.

John is well versed in the arguments about football needing a spiritual dimension, but delivery in the moral climate currently surrounding the game is something far different. Today I will find out exactly how significant his job is and how valuable a contribution John and his colleagues can make. Few roles in football, it seems to me, take us so close to the heart and soul of the game, or challenge our concepts about what the sport is truly all about, about how we can educate players and about how we should treat the wider football family with respect and compassion.

For the Rev, that starts by bringing Anne breakfast in bed and opening the morning post.

7.40 A.M.: THE CHAIRMAN ARISES Rob Bradley has had a good night's sleep and is looking forward to matchday. This isn't always so, however. Rob is the chairman of Lincoln City, a post to which he was democratically elected in 2000/01 as the supporters trust director on the board.

A month earlier, the perils of the job and 'too much living' (he points to a three-day 'bender' in Prague as a contributory factor) took their toll on his 54-year-old body. He went from his home in the Newport area of the city to Lincoln General Hospital complaining of chest pains after watching his beloved club at Wycombe and found himself lying on a bed in a corridor overnight awaiting treatment. He was diagnosed with angina and warned to give up smoking. His lifestyle has affected his home life too: Rob has split from his wife, Polly, claiming he could no longer do 'the couples thing'.

These seem heavy prices to pay for helping to save the city's football club from ruin. It had debts of £1.4 million and lapsed into administration in 2002 in the wake of the collapse of the ill-fated ITV Digital deal, which resulted in financial hard times for many Football League clubs. These clubs either had already spent their anticipated share of the revenue or had made decisions based upon the income they would receive. 'In the wee small hours you worry about it,' acknowledges Rob. 'There was an individual at the club who said to me, "You know if this club goes under it will be your name who finished it in the history books because it'll be your name over the door?"'

Today, though, he is chipper. He is feeling fitter and has given up smoking. Lincoln are doing well, pushing for the Coca-Cola League Two play-offs and about to announce record profits. It is a remarkable turnaround, and even though as chairman Rob was prepared to take the blame, he refuses to take the credit when things go well. Rob describes himself as a 'frontman'. The chairman, he insists, 'sets the tone' for the club; it is others who have done the actual work. 'I am just an architect and a football fan – that's it – who, by some freak of circumstance, has become the chairman.' He still wakes up in the middle of the night sometimes, thinking, 'Christ, we could do this and that', but reckons this is no different from any other director or supporter.

Smartly dressed in a modern grey suit, black shirt and red tie, this morning he has some of his own work (he is a self-employed architect) to deal with before moving on to club matters. He leaves the house, as always, without eating any breakfast – 'a habit of old which I know is bad for me'. Later he will 'show his face' at a youth-team game and then head down to Lincoln's ground, Sincil Bank, where he will put himself around far more than most chairmen would ever consider. 'It is a privilege to be involved,' he says, 'but I've had decades to think about what it must be like to be involved in a football club. I'm not in this because I put some money in and want to rest on my laurels. I am the elected supporters' representative on the board, and I always think this could end tomorrow. So I am determined to enjoy it while it lasts.'

Rob still has that optimistic fan in him. Today he will be as crochety as sin as Lincoln struggle during the game, but that is fine because that is how a true fan feels. And it's good to see one in the boardroom. Rob loves matchday. 'If you've lost twenty on the trot it doesn't matter,' he insists. 'If you win the twenty-first, the feeling is amazing because you've had to wait so long for it. There are always positives.'

7.50 A.M.: THE GAFFER GETS UP In Bristol Brian Tinnion wakes up. No group of people feel the strain of matchday more than managers. Tinnion, 37, is in his first season in charge at Bristol City. He spent twelve seasons as a player with the club, amassing nearly 500 appearances, before moving into management, initially as a player/manager until he found that too much. The responsibility has come earlier than expected for the former midfielder who was popular with the fans, not least because he had an unerring ability to score goals with his trusty left foot. He is having to cope with a drastically reduced budget and trimmed staff with fewer experienced players on board than in the recent past, but he has no complaints. 'I knew that when I took the job,' he says.

A tall man with a relaxed demeanour (he will spend most of the day with his right hand tucked inside his trouser pocket), he seems a naturally calm person. Bristol City means a lot to him, he cares passionately about the club, but he has already learned there is little to be gained from worrying. Unlike earlier in the season, when he had the obligatory gaffer's sleepless nights, he now makes key decisions, like who will play on Saturday, before going to bed so that uncertainties are cleared from his mind. The players are told, too.

Brian and Catherine, his second wife (each has two children from previous marriages, and another is on the way), are only just getting used to the busy, intrusive life of football management. 'It's a 24/7 thing,' says Brian, in his warm Geordie tones. 'The phone never stops ringing; the football club is never away from you. I never switch mine off just in case it is that one phone call I want. Your mind is always somewhere else.' Matchday, in particular, is tense. 'You feel nervous, obviously,' he continues. 'You want the win. In management it's the worst day really because all week you can enjoy working with the players but it's the Saturday that counts. It is all about getting the three points. Take the Saturday out of management and it is really enjoyable. But when you get that win at quarter to five you are delighted and look forward to the next one.'

This morning he is relatively happy. There is little for him to do early on. He will head for the training ground to watch the youth team play (he was an academy coach while playing and has a deep interest in youth development), then return home to drop off the kids with friends and bring Catherine down to the game.

Today, City need a win at home against Port Vale, who are struggling further down the table, in order to boost their hopes of reaching the play-offs. The club has been at League One (formerly Division Two) level for six seasons, and a city the size of Bristol demands a bigger, better football club than the one they currently have. That is the pressure heaped on Brian's shoulders. 'It wouldn't be the good job it is if it wasn't a challenge,' he says defiantly. That doesn't make matchdays any easier.

8 A.M.: FROM CHICKEN AND CHIPS TO TOAST AND GOAL It used to irritate my mum to death. When I heard the thud of the newspapers on the hall floor I would race to get my copy of *Goal* magazine (and later *Shoot*, or both). Although both my brother Phil and I were fairly decent risers, Saturday was different. My dad would work on Saturday mornings and Mum, who also had a full-time job, would head into Worcester to have her hair done and get the weekend shopping. Still in my pyjamas while munching endless rounds of toast and marmalade, I devoured Goal, cheerfully ignoring Mum's constant pleas to get dressed. Every facet of football fascinated me, even Bobby Hope's haircut – the real reason I supported West Brom (they also had a good kit and whacked eight past Burnley in the first season I really followed football). In the late sixties and early seventies there was little in the way of Saturday-morning television. We had *Junior Choice* on the radio in the background.

Eventually I would dress and head out with a football under my arm and go in search of mates. If I was a poor riser, Terry Owens was terrible. I spent countless hours kicking a ball against his parents' garage door waiting for him to wake up. Steve Mann was little better. We played for hours outside his house because the Manns had a brick wall that was about the width of a goal. Mainly, we played on school fields. Saturday was all football.

In truth, our sporting weekends started on Friday evenings when as a family we would get in Dad's car and head to the works sports ground built by him and his fellow colleagues at Archdales, an engineering factory. At Archdales Sports and Social Club, my parents, who were sporty people – they met through sport – would play tennis in the summer while Phil and I played cricket in the nets; in winter we played football while they played table tennis. Afterwards we would all go into the bar: Dad would have a pint, Mum a glass of wine, and Phil and I would drink Vimto and eat a bag of crisps. Sometimes we would indulge in the relative luxury of chicken and chips on the way home. It was idyllic. If only Mum could get me to put on some clothes on Saturday morning and put down the latest copy of *Goal*.

8.10 A.M.: AT HOME WITH THE WHISTLEBLOWER Referees don't have homes; they crawl out from under stones. That is a common conception many fans have about football officials, whose *raison d'être*, it is assumed, is largely to spoil everyone's fun before scurrying back from whence they came, satisfied with their squalid afternoon's work.

Football League referee Paul Taylor lives in a quiet middle-class corner of Hertfordshire. Cheshunt smacks of suburbia. It is a classic commuter town that sits to the north of London, just outside the M25. Paul is a local man who has a demanding job in BT's computer department in the city. It is New Year's Day, and the season of goodwill to all men (does that include referees?) is coming to a close. Hours-old resolutions are being fractured with alarming ease. And New Year's Day, perhaps even more than Boxing Day, is a traditional part of the football calendar. Many clubs can expect their biggest gates of the season today.

Paul Taylor's home is much like any other seasonal family home, a scene of domestic bliss. Christmas tree, decorations, opened presents, chocolates. Over an early-morning cuppa we discuss what it can be like to be a referee. His wife, Mel, doesn't go to Paul's matches. She isn't much of a football fan and doesn't like the abuse hurled her husband's way. 'It's unwarranted,' she says. And one thing's for sure: today, as at all matches, he's going to get some stick. Paul dismisses it 'as part of the job'. It's a passionate sport, he reasons, and people are entitled to their views, otherwise it wouldn't be the great game it is. He seems unperturbed by the fuss. However, refereeing affects their home life. They are ex-directory – 'you have to be, just in case'. They even have to make sure they are not listed on the 192.com website. Threats have been made, 'from cranks probably, but you never know'. What about their eleven-year-old son Joe? Do referee's sons get bullied or ribbed at school when their fathers hit the headlines? 'No,' Paul replies. 'I actually think he gets a bit of street cred from having a dad who is involved in football.

And I bring him mementos back from matches. I don't think he sees the negative side too much.'

Paul has a cold but is otherwise bright and alert, ready for the off. Mel is still in her nightdress, and Joe is still in bed. Bank holidays, Christmas, New Year, it's always the same – 'We don't have one,' says Mel. Unusually, this year Paul was at home on Boxing Day. He has had an ankle injury, but did squeeze in a midweek match at Hull between Christmas and New Year, so there have been early nights, and no drinking or excessive eating. 'We just accept it,' Mel continues. 'You hear a lot about the players and their sacrifices, but what about the referee?' Good point. I have often wondered why referees give up their time and offer themselves up for this sort of scrutiny, and I am hoping to find out what exactly it entails.

8.20 A.M.: THE AFAN LIDO BOOT ROOM I'm cheating here. All the people I have introduced so far have been at home. Not Phil Robinson. I've arranged to meet him at the Runtech Stadium, the home of Afan Lido FC, which play in the romantically named Vauxhall Masterfit Retailers Welsh Premier League.

I've met Phil before and know what he is like. He may be touching sixty years of age, but he is a livewire. Basically, he does everything here at Afan Lido, a club he set up in 1967 as a mates team, which has dramatically and incredibly worked its way up the Welsh football pyramid. They wouldn't have achieved this without the driving force that is Phil Robinson. He used to play and to manage; he has always been secretary (his job title now, which seems laughably weak) and director of football; and he runs the club bar, which is open six nights a week. There was no point arranging to meet Phil at home because although he told me his matchday hours are nine a.m. to one a.m. (yes, a.m. – the following morning), knowing Phil he would only head to Lido anyway. When I called to make the arrangements he was 50 feet up in the air fixing the floodlights. That's Phil!

At the ground I can hear a distant murmur. I shout hello, Phil responds, and I head towards the voice. Phil is in a small room adjacent to the dressing rooms, hands in a sink surrounded by footballs, scrubbing them clean, ready for use later in the day. He can't shake my hand and gestures to that effect, but he has a warm smile and is genuinely pleased to see me. He is sporting a blue Adidas tracksuit and looks remarkably fit for his age. He puts this down to 'good, simple clean living' and a life in sport. He also used to be a competitive bodybuilder, 'until the steroids came in', and a sports instructor at Afan Lido leisure centre, which is on the other side of the car park, tucked behind the seafront at Aberavon Bay in Port Talbot. The football club started as an offshoot of one of his classes.

Footballs washed, Phil heads for his office. Afan Lido is a community club, and aside from the senior team, which is at home today in a vital relegation fixture, there are 21 other teams from under-eights upwards with games this morning – and Phil has to organise the lot. 'I co-ordinate what goes on,' he explains. 'If there are any problems I am here at the club.' Well, sort of. He is also coaching the under-fives, 'to get them started', and the girls team. From midday he is even busier, preparing the food, opening the bar, and Lord knows what else.

They call him Mr Afan Lido, and this busy life is the way Phil likes it. He is nervy on matchdays. 'When I used to manage I wouldn't sleep,' he recalls in a rich South Wales accent. 'Now I'm better, but I still get that knot in my stomach that will never go. There is something special about matchday. You come to the ground. You start your work. You check to make sure all the teams are OK and all the referees are there, and make sure, if it's bad weather, that all the games are on. It's fantastic.'

8.30 A.M.: THE CHIEF EXECUTIVE ARRIVES FOR WORK Neil Doncaster breezes in through the main reception at Carrow Road at much the same time he does most mornings. But today is special. Norfolk may be snowbound – there was a thin white layer coating the flat fields either side of the A11 as I made my way here – but the Premier League's swanky leaders Chelsea are in town to cement (they hope) another brick in their championship-winnng wall. Chelsea, of course, are fuelled by the seemingly bottomless pit of cash provided by Roman Abramovic, a Russian oligarch who, along with his four personal bodyguards, will also be in town. Everyone is excited. Norwich face the more mundane task of trying to scramble together enough points to stave off relegation. They are failing at present. Only West Brom (aargh) lie beneath them in the Premier League table.

Neil, smartly dressed in a grey suit and dark overcoat, gets down to business. As chief executive of this most realistic, down-to-earth, you might even say financially hamstrung, club in the Premier League, Doncaster has a different agenda: to motivate and squeeze every last drop out of the club in their quest to preserve their status among English football's big boys.

It isn't easy. Norwich were one of the early victims of the Premier League. Like many smaller clubs they fell into debt trying to keep up with the top clubs when large amounts of money poured into football in the 1990s. In 1997, when Neil came here, they had £8 million of unsecured debts and were haemorrhaging £3 million a year. A few years earlier they had infamously toppled German giants Bayern Munich in the UEFA Cup, but were struggling near the foot of Division One. What has happened at Carrow Road since then is nigh on a miracle. The club has been turned around, not just because of the investment of supercook Delia Smith and her husband Michael Wynn-Jones, who helped to clear the club debts, but because Norwich have implemented a range of imaginative programmes to build a true community club, to make the maximum of their resources and put the club on a strong, long-term financial footing.

All the media talk has been about Delia's infamous outburst the previous Monday – the 'let's be havin' you' speech. The club is full of anticipation. Neil will be here until nine p.m. tonight, but this is just one of his usual six twelve-hour days a week – a commitment that has personally cost him a lot. I am about to discover the true price of being married to the football business.

MORNING GLORY

9 A.M.: THE LITTLE BOY WHO WENT DOWN THE LANE I believe you have to learn to love football to get the most out of it. As a boy, Saturday mornings were about playing, either with my mates or at school, and then thinking about the 'proper' games in the afternoon. When I was a teenager, it was all about following West Brom everywhere around the country and organising the supporters club we had started in Worcester. As a journalist, it has often involved endless preparation to make sure that I can get to where I need to on time and that I know enough about the protagonists. Or finding the time to follow the Albion. But I fell in love with football in a simple way – by watching my local club, Worcester City.

Before I met him, I feared Bob Marley might be one of those saddos who had changed his name by deed poll in memory of the late, great Jamaican reggae singer. As I've mentioned, Bob's real name is Kevin. But apparently there were two Kevins in the football team he played for, so he grew up with the nickname Bob. It stuck.

I must again declare an interest here. St George's Lane is the place where I watched my first ever football. I am still slightly in awe of the place whenever I walk through the ornate ironwork gates at the Lane. There may be several dozen other lanes in Worcester, but mention the Lane and people have only one place in mind. My grandfather, Arthur, and grandmother, Edith or Nanny (my dad's parents), would walk me down through the tangled web of terraced streets a mile or so from their home on Tunnel Hill, clad in my blue and white bobble hat and scarf, and clutching a rattle. Like West Bromwich Albion, the other team in my life, City wear blue and white stripes.

I owe so much of my interest in sport to my grandparents. It wasn't just St George's Lane they took me to from the age of, I guess, five or maybe six. At an even younger age I was introduced to New Road, the superb, scenic home of Worcestershire County Cricket Club. They looked after my older brother Phillip and me for the summer holidays, and on many of those long, hot summer days we'd head into Worcester on the bus armed with sandwiches, cakes, chipsticks ('chipples' as we called them), bottles of squash and mini-cricket bats and balls. When we reached New Road the scent of morning dew and freshly mown grass filled our nostrils. Smell is the basest of senses, and my mind is easily whisked back to those days. I hardly recall watching the cricket, though; I was just itching to clout a ball around a grass area next to the scoreboard at the Diglis End of the ground. During lunch and tea intervals, we eagerly hopped on to the pitch along with any other waifs and strays, and batted, bowled and fielded to our hearts' content, often to the irritation of spectators who would occasionally spill their cups of tea and drop sandwiches as edges sliced off our bats or errant deliveries flew into their laps. You watched a bit, learned a lot, then imitated what you'd seen. It sounds idyllic. It was. Maybe it's an age-old thing, but I delight in seeing kids carrying on that tradition at New Road and other county grounds today. Thank heavens I was lucky enough to have been introduced to such a wonderful professional sporting setting at such a young age.

One evening, when I was about five or six, I remember being dragged over to the pavilion at the end of play. There was lots of clapping. It was boring. I later found out this was because Worcestershire had won the county championship (it was 1965) for the second year running. They had a great team, though I didn't really understand things like that back then. Names like Don Kenyon, Ron Headley, Tom Graveney, Basil D'Oliveira, Norman Gifford and pacemen Jack Flavell and Len Coldwell were Worcestershire legends. Dolly is still my all-time sporting hero, a man who overcame hardship to arrive in our small city and play cricket with immense grace and a huge thumping heart. He kept a dignified silence during the infamous D'Oliveira affair when the despicable South African apartheid regime rejected his right to play cricket in the country of his birth with an England touring team. Why? Because he was 'Cape coloured'.

If the sun always shone on New Road, it always rained down the Lane. Worcester City's ground still resembles somewhere the Munsters might go on holiday. But watching Worcester City in the 1960s was far from the dismal experience it has been in recent years. Back then, the club enjoyed big crowds for non-League football. I've tried to piece together when I first went there from flicking through a wonderful time capsule called *The Official History of Worcester City*, which doubles as just about as good a pictorial social history of English football as you'll find, and from checking the shirts on various team photos I reckon it must have been 1964/65. Worcester's average gate back then in the old Southern League First Division was an impressive 3,049. I can't recall specific matches, but I do remember some of the players, such as former Aston Villa forward Roy McParland, ex-Wolves winger Norman Deeley, and a young striker who went to Peterborough, Johnnie Fairbrother. Not many players left Worcester City to go upwards – they still don't – so Fairbrother was a notable name. He never made it. Avergae gates increased the following season to 3,193, swelled by the 9,211 crowd for the local derby against Hereford United (City won 2–1), a traditional, blood-curdling Easter fixture of which I have many fond memories.

There was a frisson of excitement around St George's Lane in those days. We sat in the new wooden main stand built in the wake of Worcester's best ever day, the 1959 defeat of Liverpool in the FA Cup fourth round. In the previous round they had whacked Millwall 5–2 and went on to lose narrowly to Sheffield United in the fifth round. Some 17,042 fans were shoehorned into St George's Lane for that match, 15,000 for the historically significant Liverpool game. That defeat led to Liverpool sacking their manager Bill Taylor, and into Anfield swept a certain B. Shankly who transformed the club. The rest is history. You'd think Liverpool would be eternally grateful, but in 2001, when Worcester City asked them to play a special match to celebrate their centenary, the humourless Scousers, in the mean spirit so typical of the Premiership's elite, declined to send even their youth team. What a shame.

Sadly, all those shillings paid by the many thousands of fans who trooped through the gates of Worcester City year in, year out were never used to propel the club forward. Much of it, according to local legend, never even reached the club's coffers. Instead, it slipped into the pockets of greedy gatemen and corrupt officials who were supposed to be custodians of the club. Allegedly. Today, Worcester City's board have to live with that legacy and the frustration of being stewards of a non-League side in a city whose 100,000 population is far bigger than many League One and Two clubs' home towns.

The spirited cup runs are a thing of the past. Currently the club languishes in mid-table mediocrity in the newly formed Nationwide Conference North League. They haven't even played at the highest level of non-League football, the Conference, for twenty years, let alone mounted any sort of challenge for entry into the Football League.

9.10 A.M.: MY LIFE, MY HISTORY, MY IDENTITY Neil Williams and his partner's son Josh have stopped for breakfast and are progressing northwards along the M5 through Somerset and into Gloucestershire. You don't make these sorts of journeys unless you really love a football club. Where, I wonder, did Neil's passion for Wrexham start?

'I was born in Wrexham but I was raised on a farm in a small village called Cilcain,' he explains. 'There were only 32 children at the local school.' Other kids in rural Flintshire supported the usual big teams. Not Neil. 'I had the choice of supporting Liverpool or Man Utd, but I chose Wrexham. They were the nearest Football League team.'

His Uncle Gordon took him to his first game at the age of ten in May 1977 because no close family member actually enjoyed football. It was a big game against Crystal Palace in the old Division Three. 'If we had won that night we would have gone up,' he recalls. 'I was in awe of the people around me supporting this one team. It was excellent. With a couple of minutes to go we were winning 2–1 and we were going up. Then they scored twice, and that's when it hit home what it was all about – the highs and lows of being a football supporter in a couple of minutes.'

Such experiences put some children off the game for life; others grow fonder in times of failure, which is when the club needs us most. Quite often there is a triumph-in-adversity thing about it. As a boy I stuck by West Brom as my big team to support, not because they won things but because they were mine. They played some entertaining football in the late sixties and in the early seventies were paying the price, but they were my club, the nearest 'big' club, and the worse things got the tighter I clung to them. I cried when they were relegated from Division One in 1973, but I never gave up on them or football. I wanted them to win.

For Neil, Wrexham did the decent thing and went up the following season. 'We had the likes of Mel Sutton, Bobby Shinton and Brian Flynn playing for us. But we spent too much money and down we went again.' Neil says this with the kind of ironic smile that lower league fans tend to have. For the perennial winners – fans of the likes of Arsenal or Manchester United, or Celtic or Rangers, used to the grinding predictability of success – this is an alien concept. But for the rest of us, well, it's actually a bit more interesting. Some you win, some you lose. Football supporting isn't just about backing the winners, it's about a special bond with your club and the people who go to the game.

Neil's dad wasn't much of a football fan, but he took him to his first international match at Wrexham's ground, the Racecourse, against Turkey in November 1978. Neil was eleven years old. Wales won 1–0. 'My sister was upset,' he says. 'She didn't like it and wanted to go home at half-time, so we left. I was annoyed because my sister had spoilt my day out, so on the way home I threw her shoes out of the car and got a good walloping off my dad!'

Neil was hooked. 'After a couple of years my uncle stopped going so I found out that our local milkman in the village used to go, so I went with him. I then found other people from our small village were Wrexham fans so it was no problem getting a lift.' The alternative was the solitary bus that ran from Cilcain to Wrexham on Saturdays. 'I normally ended up missing it and had to walk home for five miles from where the nearest bus dropped off. That is tough on cold, wet, dark winter nights. If there were two or three of us it wasn't too bad, but I hated walking home alone.' Such martyrdom breeds devotion to a football club.

Neil's love of football was reluctantly put on the backburner for a while when his father died. Neil was fifteen and he had to take over the running of the farm, along with an uncle. The following year he went to agricultural college to learn how to manage a farm 'properly' and to deal with the paperwork. He returned from college but things didn't work out, so Neil moved to Cornwall to work for a tourist attraction called Dairyland. 'I was a shepherd in charge of 400 sheep.' One wet February morning he thought, 'Why the hell am I doing this?' and quit. After working in an off-licence and for a local health authority, he moved to his current job as a purchasing manager with scuba specialists Parker Diving Limited, a small, family-run firm in Helston with 62 employees.

Despite the distance, Wrexham FC remained a part of his life. 'I have always followed them. Not, maybe, as often as I could have done because of the distance, and it isn't a cheap day out. It costs me £80 in petrol, and the cost of getting food and tickets – you're talking maybe £150 just to go to a game of football.' Neil doesn't have a season ticket and has to pick his games, to be fair to both his partner and his wallet. He restricts away trips to those in the south, although he has been to Carlisle, which is close to a 1,000-mile round trip.

And it isn't just matchdays. He once travelled to queue for the rare few tickets – Wrexham were given just 1,500 of them – available for the FA Cup quarter-final at Chesterfield in 1997, and flew in from a work trip in America to the game, which they lost narrowly. 'The only time I have ever cried at a football game,' he muses. 'It was 0–0 at half-time, and we conceded a comical own-goal to lose. They closed the door and that was the end of our dreams.'

The FA Cup. In the week before I travelled with Neil, Exeter had earned an unlikely draw at Manchester United and got them back home for the televised replay. The Devonian club made £1.4 million out of their two games. How Wrexham, a club that have had so many memorable cup exploits – they've been venerable giant-killers of the likes of Arsenal down the years – could do with that now! 'That would secure the future of most smaller clubs,' notes Neil. 'It has paid off Exeter's debts. But then you need people at the helm who are football people who know how to run a club, not businessmen looking to get what they can out of the club.'

Wrexham's plight hasn't been the usual one of a club overspending to 'live the dream' or speculating to accumulate. They have been well managed. But two years ago a Cheshire property developer, Alex Hamilton, bought the club, gained control of the freehold of the ground and, perfectly legally, decided to sell this valuable strip of real estate on the edge of the town. Last summer, he gave the club twelve months' notice. This has since been extended for another year but for most of the season the immediate threat of eviction hung over the club. They have fallen into crippling debt. Without a ground, they face demotion from the Football League, which docked Wrexham ten points for falling into administration early in the 2004/05 season. This is a controversial measure designed by the League to prevent clubs that are deep in debt and practically insolvent from digging themselves into further trouble by continuing to invest in their playing staff and therefore enabling them to improve their League status and stepping over rival clubs that may have chosen to manage their finances more astutely.

With £4 million of debt, the likelihood of being thrown out of their ground and the possibility of relegation, Wrexham hardly looks an attractive proposition to prospective buyers. But unless someone buys Alex Hamilton out soon the future looks bleak. Still, fans like Neil are not prepared to let the club die without a fight. 'If we lose our ground and the club disappears, what about our children and our grandchildren? They won't have a professional team to support in North Wales, and that is why I feel so strongly about seeing these games. The club needs our support in their hour of need.'

Wrexham's ground, the Racecourse, is the oldest in Wales. It staged its first match in 1872, and the club was actually formed at the Turf Hotel, which still backs on to the ground. It has historical significance and that very week was staging a Wales U-21 international. It has also seen recent investment. 'It is a cracking ground,' Neil says. 'We have a new stand [the well-equipped Pryce Griffiths Stand] and things ought to be looking up, but with this points deduction we just feel everything is against us.' Wrexham is the only Football League club in North Wales and is certainly the only stadium capable of holding big rugby or football matches in the north of the principality. 'To lose it would be a disaster for Welsh sport.'

So today isn't just about going to a football match for Neil, it is more significant. 'It is like a pilgrimage. It is hard to explain to anyone who isn't a true football supporter what it means, but it is like a calling. And I feel that more now than ever at this moment in time.' Losing Wrexham, would be, he insists, 'like losing a part of your body, or a member of your family. It would hurt Josh because he has been coming with me for years and has been a mascot here.' These sound like extreme words, and they are. Neil vows to chain himself to the club gates if ever it is closed. 'If it meant the club surviving I would make this journey every week if I had to. It is all part of being a football supporter. I am not a glory seeker. I am just another Wrexham supporter who loves his team. And I will support them whatever.'

Unless you understand the strange passion of football, this nigh-on religious zeal must sound far-fetched. It has certainly been underestimated at Wrexham, and elsewhere. If the umbilical cord that exists between football clubs and their communities is broken, there can be trouble on the road ahead.

9.15 A.M.: EN ROUTE WITH THE REF Paul Taylor has packed a vast array of kit, equipment and paperwork, which I intend to ask him about en route to Ipswich. He kisses his wife Mel goodbye. 'Good luck,' she says, squeezing his hand. I'm sincerely hoping he doesn't need it.

Ipswich should be no more than an hour and a half's drive away. It may sound as if we are leaving ludicrously early, but referees are mandated to arrive a minimum of two hours before kick-off. Paul usually plans to get there at least three hours in advance, and the visiting fans of West Ham will travel along the same A12 route we are taking. It wouldn't do to be seen stuck in traffic. 'The one thing for certain at professional level is that you need a referee for a match to go ahead,' says Paul, negotiating the traffic near his home. He has broken down en route to a match before but still made it, so it's a good habit to leave in good time. Also, the bigwigs at the FA keep a close eye on the performance of referees. Unlike any of the players or anyone else connected with games today, it is only the officials whose performance is assessed, monitored and reported upon.

9.20 A.M.: 'MOSES, MOSES, STOP THE RAIN' Once I became a regular supporter, one of the reasons I stayed in love with West Bromwich Albion was the wit of the supporters. The Black Country is noted for its humour, and it continues to produce notable names, including Frank Skinner, Lenny Henry, Julie Walters, Josie Lawrence and Meera Syal, as well as older legendary performers such as Tommy Munden, Harry Harrison and Lizzie Wiggins, the 'Duchess of Dudley'. It is self-deprecating humour, the sort of wit lots of uppity fans of even uppitier clubs would not consider mildly funny. The Albion is full of it. 'Get up, y'owm killing the grass' is a common one if an opposition player goes down; 'I'm going home to watch Anne Frank, to cheer myself up,' said one fan after yet another defeat during Albion's ill-fated first season in the Premiership in 2002/03. But I heard my favourite witticism at a game against Bolton in March 1980, which incredibly ended 4–4. It absolutely hammered down all day. In less resilient times it would have been abandoned, but the referee gamely played on. Albion had Remi Moses playing his first season for them in midfield. You knew a song was coming along sooner or later. It did: 'Moses, Moses, Stop the Rain.' A classic.

I was thinking of this one night in Cumbria recently …

There are few worse matchday feelings than waking up and not knowing whether your game is going ahead. I used to ponder this constantly when I worked as a local radio reporter. Local derbies kicking off at eleven o'clock on Boxing Day or New Year's Day were the worst. Midwinter mornings are the most susceptible to frost, and the pitches have little time to thaw. Would the game be on or off? That question would circle your mind constantly. On Friday evening Michael Fish, John Kettley or some other TV weather person would point to blanket frosts, and the blue isobars inevitably seemed to cover the Midlands. Then you would wonder about it all night. In the pre-internet days, even with the help of actually working for local radio, you often couldn't get through to the club concerned. My wife Teresa is also a sports journalist; back then she was covering Bromsgrove Rovers, so we were both in the same boat. Are we working today or what? Why not stick to a tried-and-trusted three o'clock start time?

But this is worse. I'm in a hotel in Carlisle, stopping overnight on my way to Gretna to meet groundsman Paul Barnett. He has the onerous task of ensuring the biggest game in Gretna's history can go ahead. This is all about the romance of the cup: the tiny border town where young couples traditionally speed to get married, often against their parents' wishes, is hosting a magical Scottish FA Cup third-round tie against Dundee United. David v. Goliath stuff. Gretna, the minnows, with the smallest community (population 2,000) in Scottish League football, but top of Division Three, taking on Scottish Premier League giants Dundee United, who, crucially, are struggling for form. It has upset written all over it. Gretna's chairman, Brooks Mileson, is even letting fans in for free (how unusual is that – a chairman refusing to cash in on a windfall day?) and the game is being televised. The pressure is on Paul's shoulders.

And, sadistically maybe, though he has agreed, I want to see whether Paul can cope. The weather has been iffy all week. Paul and his team have worked prodigiously to prepare the best pitch they can, but it has rained heavily all night and lots more is predicted for matchday morning. On Friday I had to make the difficult decision whether it was worth trekking up from the Midlands for this tantalising match, but last night Paul was chipper about getting the game on. The rain should stop mid-morning, and the wind, he thought, would help dry out the pitch. It is a tough test for him, it will be nip and tuck – but, look, I want challenging conditions. I want to see Paul's mettle truly tested as a groundsman. He's worked so hard. Should he succeed, or, better still, should Gretna win, what a story! Imagine how I would feel if that happened and I hadn't gambled on the game going ahead? If it's called off, so what? There will be other days.

Only here I am, the wind hasn't stopped whistling all night, and Radio Cumbria has gone into emergency mode. Paul phones what might euphemistically be called 'early doors' to explain how his journey in from Dumfries was a nightmare, punctuated by stops to assist toppled-over lorries. The emergency services are advising people not to venture outdoors unless they really have to; staging a football match would be, at best, folly, at worst, crazy. It's off.

Damn, a wasted weekend. Maybe I can drop in on a game on my way back down the M6. The Baggies are at Preston, which is geographically handy.

First, a hearty breakfast. I cannot see out of my bedroom window. Correction: I cannot see *down* from my window. Had I been able to I wouldn't have been so shocked by the horror that awaits me in the reception area. I have selected the only evening since 1835 on which Carlisle's two rivers simultaneously burst their banks. Sodding typical. And I have, naturally, chosen a hotel in the worst flooded area of town. Outside, the roads are one vast lake. The water in the car park is past my car's wheel arches and rising. I can barely look at the unfolding horror. It will soon be submerged, an insurance write-off. The hotel staff, who haven't bothered to wake their guests and don't seem to know what to do, have optimistically pressed towels against the outside doors, but these will soon be breached. The hotel ground floor is inevitably going to flood. We are already cocooned and I am furious, apoplectic with rage that no one had told me earlier and annoyed with myself for being here at all. Did I need to gamble?

But my mind also very quickly turns to concern for surrounding householders. Some are submerged. The bungalows, which are usually occupied by elderly folk, look particularly susceptible. I am told they were evacuated during the night. Thank God for that. Losing a car is going to be a mere trifle compared to most.

There is no option but to sit tight and wait for the cavalry to arrive. As the floodwaters rise my thoughts turn to how I'm going to get out of here. When will I see my loved ones again? And how am I going to find out how the Baggies are getting on later?

9.25 A.M.: RUNNING AWAY TO GRETNA So you see I didn't get to Gretna that day, but I remained intrigued about the rapid rise of this small club on the England–Scotland border and I wanted to meet Paul Barnett, their amiable groundsman who was extremely helpful even when it was going pear-shaped a few weeks earlier. I also wanted to see what investment Brooks Mileson had made at this club that was doing so well at the top of the Scottish Third Division.

As I drove up the M6 past the Lake District, it felt like returning to the scene of a crime. A few weeks earlier, the devastation, not least because of high winds, led to dozens of lorries toppling over, which were then laid one after another on the shoulder of the M6. It was eerie at night-time. Yet in the early morning this is such a majestic landscape; the mist rolling in off the hills on a cold day is an awesome sight. This time, I skirted around Carlisle without stopping and drove straight on to the A74.

As you enter Scotland, Gretna, in case you don't know, is the first town you meet on the western side of the country. 'Welcome to Scotland' says the sign as you enter the town. You soon pass the Gretna Registry Office and the infamous Blacksmiths Shop – it's all a bit touristy these days. Gretna, as opposed to Gretna Green, where couples traditionally elope, is a small town with a few thousand residents. Gretna FC's home, the Raydale Stadium, is unobtrusive, tucked away behind a school and a row of shops. For a small club, it boasts a large car park and fancy gates. It is hemmed in on two sides, but there is space to move the ground northwards to create a bigger stadium, and those plans, as I will find out later, are currently being prepared.

When I reach the ground, Paul Barnett isn't hard to spot. He is the chunky one in a blue fleece looking anxiously at the penalty spot at the far end of the ground. His colleague, Selwyn Bryden, has a fork and is digging into the ground. By the look of the furrowed brows I am expecting a quagmire when I reach them. Instead, there is a small amount of surface water and a muddy patch in the six-yard box. The game will definitely go ahead. Paul needn't have worried or lost any sleep. If you compare it crowd-wise, Scottish Third Division football would be well down the English non-League football pyramid. But this is an outstanding surface.

As we head back to Paul's office for a brew, he tells me about the state of the pitch when he arrived in June 2003. Gretna had joined the Scottish League system the season before that, having previously been in the Unibond Northern League in England. The first-team manager Rowan Alexander, who is still Gretna's boss, was groundsman. 'A lot of improvement was needed,' recalls Paul. 'It had been run like a village club and they were in financial trouble. The equipment here was poor. The pitch had been verti-drained and had 60 tons of sand on it.' Verti-draining is, basically, a process where deep holes are dug into the ground to allow water to seep away from the surface. It promotes grass-root growth, and the holes are covered up with sand. 'It was OK, but it needed to be a lot better. I only had four weeks to prepare the pitch for the opening game of the season.'

Northern businessman Brooks Mileson was planning to invest some money in Gretna and made Paul his first signing. 'He made me an offer I couldn't refuse.' Mileson has transformed Gretna. He has funded a full-time playing squad and employed a number of commercial staff. Paul, along with two colleagues, manages the ground. Not just the pitch, but the terracing and general maintenance too. 'It is a lot more professional. It is a proper football club now. It's not a part-time concern. Everything here is building for the future.' Mileson plans to rebuild the ground, turning it into a 6,000 all-seater stadium, good enough for the Scottish Premier League. In the club office situated in a Portakabin along one side of the ground, there are plans posted on the wall. Paul's office is the old club office, basically a small shack in which lots of things are dumped – rain jackets, keys, toilet rolls, all manner of things. It is next to the clubhouse, which, like all bars at small sports clubs, is proudly festooned with the pennants of notable opposing teams who have played here. There is also, unusually for a small club, a players' lounge and boardroom.

Mileson brought 'Barney' in to develop a billiard-table-style pitch, and he has been given the tools to do the job. 'Basically, what I ask for I get,' Paul says, 'as long as I can justify it.' He doesn't have a budget, he just orders what he needs. 'I don't go to Brooks and say "I want this, I want that," I have to make a good case. But he does back you or says no. It is my department, I get on with it.'

To the casual observer – and that includes me, for I know absolutely nothing about groundsmanship or pitch maintenance, the language used or the skills needed – it seems a simple case of making sure you've got some decent grass and mowing it regularly. You need to keep the frost off it in winter and water it in summer. Job done. Simple. So why do you need someone to do this full-time? Paul chuckles. 'That's all there is to it, is there?' he asks, leaning back in his chair, then wiping his hands across his face and shaping a 'where to start' gesture. I sense he wants to lead me by the hand through the basics of what it is like to be a football club groundsman.

'That out there,' he begins, cocking his thumb over his shoulder towards the pitch, 'is mine.' He runs through what he has done and what he feels he needs to do to keep it looking in good nick. 'I have levelled it out, but feel it needs re-levelling again soon.' There haven't been any complaints, but Paul, who checks for this sort of thing intently, has spotted some undulations. He watches the bounce and roll of the ball during matches, barely bothering to keep track of the ebb and flow of the game. He has been told he can have a new pitch next year, which basically involves rolling up the top surface of the existing pitch and laying new grass. The existing surface is only nine months old but hasn't 'bedded in', according to Paul. 'It has done well but hasn't coped with the rainfall we've had this winter.' It looks fine to me, but Paul preferred his previous pitch, because its roots were a lot stronger. He also plans to install a drainage system, which they didn't do last time. Then there is the equipment. His first priority was to buy a decent triple mower, which cost £10,000. 'Grass is all about the quality of the cut,' he explains. 'The number of cuttings it can do per metre improves the quality of the pitch.' He also had an irrigation system put in last year, so at the push of a button he can water the pitch when he wants to, even an hour before a game if necessary.

Groundsmanship is now a highly skilled practice. Again, like so many other facets of British football, this most professional of sports had long been happy to lag behind in the dark ages. It would spend millions of pounds on players, yet the pitches they plied their trade on were often mud-heaps. In the last fifteen years, though, the game has undergone a revolution. Whole pitches can now be relaid in days, even in mid-season – unthinkable a few years back. Newcastle United apparently allocate £300,000 to have their pitch relaid twice a year. The technology has improved too, and so has the training and knowledge of groundsmen themselves. Paul recently took a course in machinery work. 'It is a professional job to produce a pitch,' he says. 'You have to know how to lay it, feed it, spike it. All these things are variable depending on the weather and season. There is a lot to learn. Summer is my busiest time. When the last ball is kicked I have to start re-seeding and working on drainage.'

Barney learned his trade 'hands on'. He was the youngest ever groundsman in the Football League when he joined Scarborough. He was born in 1972 in Whitby, but his family moved to the seaside town when he was six years old. When he left school he went to horticultural college to do a sports turf management course but never finished it. He got a placement at Scarborough FC and was soon offered sole responsibility for the entire ground. Scarborough had just been promoted to the Football League, so Paul travelled on the team bus to away games and learned from talking to the groundsmen at other clubs. 'If you don't ask, you don't learn' is his motto.

The club's fortunes fluctuated throughout the 1990s, and in 1999 they were relegated from the Football League and drifted into financial hardship. Which is when Brooks Mileson stepped in to help. Things briefly picked up again, but in 2002 Paul got out. He had never had any real financial backing there to create the sort of superior surface he is now preparing at Gretna. 'In April the pitches were awful because they dry out, and the players moan because they get blisters. You learned how to do things better, but you also need backing.' He moved on to Sunderland's academy ground, but was laid off eighteen months later when the Wearside club was relegated, fell into debt and needed to trim their costs. Paul then worked briefly for Morpeth Council before the offer he couldn't refuse from Gretna came along. 'I prefer to be involved at a small club,' he says. 'Premier League clubs are impersonal. You build up a relationship with players and management at this level. You're encouraged to do the job better when they come up and say, "The pitch is good and playing well." It doesn't happen higher up. It is taken for granted.'

We leave his office and walk in front of the small main stand at Gretna. He shows me the water tank he has installed. A few years ago not even the top clubs would have had anything like this. He usually marks the pitch on Fridays. For all the worry, he loves matchday. 'There is nothing quite like it,' he says. 'It is put up or shut up day. If the pitch looks good it makes you stick your chest out with pride. If someone says "Barney, the pitch looks brilliant" and you see the crowd filing in, the whole place looks fantastic.'

Conversely, he has heard of some clubs where they blame the groundsman if they lose. At Scarborough one of the managers used to moan even though he insisted on training on the pitch on Fridays. It made Paul despair, especially when it was glibly suggested he should just run a roller over it. As for asking players to replace divots as golfers do – well, it's best not to mention that to Barney if you want to avoid an ear-bashing. Today, despite putting up temporary goal frames in the corners for the warm-up, he still has to place cones around the penalty area to prevent players from running there and preserve the vital parts of the pitch for when it matters most – matchtime.

But the strain of matchday never goes away. Paul could spend every waking hour on his precious pitch, but football in Britain is played in all kinds of challenging climatic conditions. Gretna is in a seemingly perennially windswept part of the country. It's a tough, rugged area where protection from the elements is difficult. 'It is stressful at times,' he concedes. 'When you are pushing for promotion you cannot afford any games off. There are financial implications for clubs. You may get a bigger gate if a game is played when it is originally scheduled, usually a Saturday. Less people may come along for an evening game, so it's important.'

Barney, of course, has just endured a horrendous few weeks. The Dundee United cup tie was postponed twice before eventually taking place. He has turned up this morning to discover that the reserves are at home on Monday night. Nobody bothered to tell him, or even to ask his advice; wouldn't that have been a good idea after the battering we have had? This isn't unique to Gretna, it's an entrenched way of thinking. Groundsmen are just silent people who work away in the background, quietly making things happen. They are the engine room of the game. Without their labours, matches cannot go ahead. The reserves game means he will have to roll the pitch tonight and do some work tomorrow – his nominal day off. And then some journalist bloke turns up and asks how he justifies doing this on a full-time basis.

9.30 A.M.: COCO POPS IN BED In his new four-bedroom house on the northern edge of the city Bristol City defender Danny Coles wakes up. He yawns, stretches his arms out wide and heads downstairs for breakfast. He pours some milk on his Coco Pops, grabs a spoon and a huge bottle of mineral water, and heads back upstairs to bed to munch while watching morning television and sharing a cuddle with his fiancée.

Danny, who is 24, will 'chill out' for another hour or so. A talented six-foot tall defender who has already clocked up 150 appearances for Bristol City, he went on the transfer list earlier in the season at his own request. He is widely regarded as one of City's better players, and he hopes to play at a higher level – the Championship or, preferably, the Premiership. Although he is a Bristol lad and is playing for the team he supports, he isn't prepared to wait for the club to progress to meet his aspirations.

He insists he 'needs to rest', so his fiancée will do all the household chores today. His priority is to conserve his energy for this afternoon's match and get the right fluid and food on board. He has a cold and a sore Achilles that he will need to stretch before leaving for the ground, and he needs to drink plenty of water because he is prone to cramp attacks.

Professional footballers, eh? To many of the interviewees in this book, who are beavering around at the crack of dawn, this must seem like the life of Riley. It's the sort of thing children do to the despair of their parents, who routinely shout upstairs for them to get out of bed and get dressed. And Danny will be extremely well paid in comparison to most if not all of them.

It's a vital game today. City are in the top half of League One and have games in hand on their rivals, so are in a good position to push for a play-off spot. A win today at home to Port Vale will keep up the pressure. Should they earn promotion it would be a remarkable achievement for new manager Brian Tinnion, a former team-mate of Danny's, who has taken charge and had to slash the club's wage bill and work with a smaller and mainly younger squad. Danny is one of his lynch-pins and will be needed as a rock at the heart of their defence. When he gets out of bed.

9.40 A.M.: 'AT IT' Bob Marley is one of a dozen directors who later today will be described as 'bleedin' useless' by one particularly irate fan. They are not widely respected for their hard work or stewardship of the club, just wearily considered to be incompetent or 'at it', spiriting money into their pockets instead of crushing the club's half-a-million-pound debts.

It's a myth, of course. 'We'll have an AGM soon and we'll be reporting a £40,000 to £50,000 loss again,' notes Bob. There are no easy solutions, unless a sugar daddy dances over the horizon – and then, as so many other vulnerable clubs can testify, you have to keep a keen eye on anyone offering a myriad of promises and fool's gold. The board's main task, it seems, is to keep a constant vigil on the club's overdraft to prevent it from spilling over its top limit. 'Worcester City won the Southern League Cup a couple of years ago – the first trophy the club has lifted in twenty years,' says Bob. 'We have made small progress, but if we achieve anything more than mid-table mediocrity this season we'll have done well because we can't afford to do any better.'

This is not what the populus of the so-called 'faithful city' (the city was loyal to the King during the English Civil War) want to hear. Plans to sell St George's Lane for housing and relocate to a new out-of-town ground, which would clear the debts and give the club a fresh start, have been an on/off saga of epic proportions. It's so bad even the FA have been able to throw up a new national stadium in quicker time. 'We're in the entertainment business,' Bob reasons. 'Our entertainment is football. When we move to the new ground we'll be in the leisure business. That includes first-team football, after-school clubs, crèches, guided tours, IT clubs, testicular cancer centres for guys, breast-feeding clubs for mums – a whole different kettle of fish.'

Worcester City Council's lack of support for this community venture is staggering. Had they thrown themselves behind it with a smidgen of the gusto with which they have backed half-baked DIY store or supermarket planning applications, the ground would have been built years ago. Instead, the city's football club has been allowed to rot, shored up by the goodwill of directors who can't really afford it but put their hands in their pockets on a routine basis.

A tale of what might have been is exemplified by the rapid rise of Worcester Rugby Club, backed by the deep pockets of local multi-millionaire Cecil Duckworth, who has invested millions of pounds in a sport few local people really give a toss about but which regularly attracts 8,000 regulars in the Zurich Premiership. The club has risen from nothing in a decade, which just goes to show the thirst in the city for a popular, well-run, winning winter sports club. It could have been Worcester City Football Club.

No, the role of the non-League football director is not easy. 'If people think clubs of our ilk are going to survive purely on football, they are wrong,' Bob continues. 'It's not about a 6,000 Football League-standard capacity stadium, it's about providing facilities that will be there in 30 years' time. We need hotel and conference facilities. We need to be a focal point for 500 kids who will be wearing club colours and playing for Worcester City around this community. If we do not deliver this new ground and those facilities, we have failed.'

Had he lived in Worcester all his life, maybe Bob Marley wouldn't have got involved. Such fanciful notions are easily scoffed at. But on this cold, damp December morning, wearing only a club short-sleeved shirt and sipping yet another cup of coffee, Bob's intense football matchday begins. And it will be maintained at a pace that would make your average blue-arsed fly envious.

It starts with sifting through some early-Saturday-morning dilemmas. He checks his post – bills mainly (obviously). Then the club's 'kit man' (a boot cleaner, basically) needs paying. Bob whips a £20 note from his back pocket. He's struggling to keep him on side because the players have petulantly thrown their boots around the dressing-room floor again. 'Where else am I going to realistically find someone prepared to scrub twenty pairs of boots?' he asks. The ungrateful wretches could always, as I'd assumed non-League players did, clean their own boots. Bob then marches on to the pitch to check the surface is OK with the groundsman. Bob can talk the lingo – he is a former horticultural student and ran several garden centre/landscaping businesses in the 1980s before a lifestyle change was needed after he crashed his car into another vehicle having blacked out through tiredness, the result of working constant 100-hour weeks.

The major concern this morning is the Santa Fun Run Bob has organised tomorrow for Leukaemia Care. As hosts, Worcester City will split the profits with the charity and make £11,000. Over 1,000 people dressed as Father Christmas are taking part, but when the manager of the local Leukaemia Care office quit and was ordered to clear his desk immediately, guess who stepped into the breach? Bob. He wouldn't be the first director to deal in such a way with an unexpected crisis. Weeks later he calls me from the roof of the main stand where he is repairing tiles so the game can go ahead. 'At it,' obviously.

9.45 A.M.: THE FOOTBALL FAMILY ROBINSON Imagine the appetite you might have for matchday if you ran a club you had started 38 years ago and that still relied on you for its future. Imagine being Phil Robinson at Afan Lido.

Phil is still busy making sure all the arrangements are in place for the 22 teams playing in the club's red shirts today. For anyone who has ever tried to organise just one team, let alone so many – involving children as well, playing on several sites, needing lifts in cars, throwing up child protection issues, not to mention all the run-of-the-mill things like booking pitches and referees, and making sure all the coaches know what they're doing – this seems like a huge nightmare. Phil is also tired. 'Bit of a do last night,' he tells me. Phil manages the club bar, which is open six nights a week, and last night there was a function on. He didn't, and regularly doesn't, get to bed until gone one o'clock.

But he's handling this morning's work with unerring ease. Any problems are swiftly resolved. Phil is a nice guy who gets things done efficiently and with a smile. He doesn't row and he doesn't panic. He has been doing this for so long and has planned things meticulously all week, so it should go swimmingly. Later he will coach some very small children, five-year-olds and younger, who have been brought along by their parents because they recognise this is a good place to learn the rudiments of the game. Phil is great with them. He also coached some of their parents.

Phil Robinson takes great pride in Afan Lido, as well he might. What he has achieved since the club was established is a remarkable feat. What started out as a group of mates looking to field a side in the Port Talbot and District League is now a huge community club that, over the years, has developed some 200 players who have gone on to represent Wales; several names have also played top-flight club football, including John Hartson and Brian Flynn, who are both club presidents. Lido's senior side play in the highest rung of Welsh football, the Vauxhall Masterfit Retailers Welsh Premier League, and have competed in the UEFA Cup. For me, it is one of the most remarkable clubs in Britain, and it has been achieved without a fat wallet funding it.

It all began in 1967. Afan Lido's ground, the Runtech Stadium, is tucked behind Aberavon seafront in Port Talbot, which is a few miles west of Swansea. Port Talbot is a steel town – the huge former British Steel tower is one of the landmarks that greets visitors. The ground has gradually developed from the Lido Sports Field, opened in 1971, into a 4,000-capacity stadium. 'It was two football pitches and a cricket square,' recalls Phil. 'It was just an open space. No changing rooms or nothing. We changed in the hall in the sports centre.' It's next to the sports and leisure centre from which the club took its name. Phil, a championship-winning weightlifter and bodybuilder, worked there as an instructor and, with some teenage friends who played five-a-side at the centre, started the football team. 'I worked out what we had to do and we entered the local Port Talbot and District League in 1967.' Phil, who was born in 1945, was 21 at the time.

Their rise through the ranks was meteoric. Two years after formation they joined the South Wales Amateur League and moved from local parks pitches to a local school ground. They rose rapidly through the amateur league and made their way into the Welsh Football League, which was a semi-professional league. After two seasons they won promotion to the First Division, and then to the Premier Division. In 1984 the Welsh football pyramid was reorganised and a national league was formed. Afan Lido won promotion again in 1989/90, and after a further restructuring the League of Wales was formed in 1992. Afan Lido were founder members. In 1994/95 they finished second in the League and won a place in the UEFA Cup. They played RAF Riga of Latvia. Their home wasn't up to UEFA standard so they switched the home tie to Aberavon Rugby Club. A crowd of 2,200 saw Lido lose 2–1, but they earned a creditable 0–0 draw in the Baltic state. 'Afan Lido in the UEFA Cup – the ultimate,' says Phil, in a lovely Welsh burr. 'Imagine a club you had started playing in Europe. Marvellous.' They were relegated from the League of Wales but bounced straight back in 1998. When I visited in April 2005 the club was facing a fight against relegation.

Those are the bare bones; the detail is more fascinating. 'We're a community club,' Phil tells me. 'Most of the players in the senior side are local – they have come through the club system as juniors.' This was unheard-of language back in 1972 when Phil started the junior section with an U-12 team. Most of them ended up in Lido's first team. Community clubs are now all the rage with the Welsh and English FA, but Afan Lido saw the sense in developing their own players and coaching their coaches way back. 'I think they pinched that from me,' Phil comments. 'It just got bigger and bigger.' Lido now have 260 U-19 players. 'All Port Talbot lads,' Phil says proudly. Photographs of every Afan Lido player who has played for Wales adorn the clubhouse walls, resplendent in their caps. There is a story behind each one, including a father and son combination. 'We didn't expect to go as far as we have,' Phil adds. 'It was just a dream, but somehow we did it. We had breaks along the way, and the players who were good enough. You can coach them, but they've still got to be good enough to do it.'

The beating heart of Afan Lido, insists Phil, are the coaches. 'Every one of the 22 teams we field have qualified coaches and are up to date with first aid. I got myself qualified when we started taking it seriously [a few years after the club was formed] and I have instilled that through the club. If you are qualified, you know what to do. You're not just stood on the touchline bawling and shouting.' Most of Lido's coaches are ex-players who were encouraged to take their badges. It means they not only stay in touch with the club and create an ongoing legacy, they also naturally put something back into the system, back into football, back into the community. 'We make sure that everyone in the club is keen to get their qualifications and go as high as possible. If you have better educated players, they become better players.'

If all this sounds obvious, that's because it is. Phil understands these principles because he had to pave his own career as an amateur sportsman. Football, the most professional of sports, has often lagged behind. From the start he took players into the gym 'to get them bodily' fit. They stole a march on other clubs because Phil also made sure they ate the right food. He still advises the players on nutrition. And they take notice. 'They have to if they want to be successful.'

For Phil the ethos at Afan Lido is all about giving local kids something to do – 'a chance to build some self-esteem' as Phil puts it, in an area continually ravaged by unemployment and, twenty years on, still torn apart by the conflict of the miners' strike. 'In the simplest sense it keeps the kids off the streets. You aren't just teaching them football, you are educating them as well.' Phil can think of any number of youngsters the club has helped over the years. They even take young offenders referred to the club as part of their rehabilitation. 'We are successful more times than not. All the boys know if they misbehave they won't be part of the club, and that makes a difference. If they are bad at home they don't play. They develop into young men and they are thankful for what we have done for them.'

Phil has been secretary of the club throughout. He was team manager and coach at the outset, but sometimes he dropped out of managing, bringing others in. 'The ones who had played at the club did well, those who hadn't played for us didn't.' One of them was Phil's son, Mark, who played in Afan Lido's first team and is now manager. Phil's other son, Neil, also played for Lido. Mark's son James plays for the U-10s. It's like a family business. Phil's wife, Linda, helps run the bar and prepares and serves food on matchdays. Phil, whose other roles include director of football, is paid the princely sum of £89 a week for his multi-skilled labours.

Times are hard, you see. Lido's crowds, which range between 150 and 350, are not big enough to keep the club afloat, certainly not in the Welsh Premier League. Last summer, the club chairman, David Dale, who underwrote the club debts, moved to Spain. The club's youth academy has collapsed through lack of funds. It has caused Phil lots of sleepless nights. The club he has so lovingly created is struggling and, financially at least, there's not a lot he can do about it. 'We have a new chairman, Sean McReesh, who is a local businessman. He's great, but he hasn't got the financial clout David had, and we are struggling financially. I don't know how we have got through.'

However, Phil insists that the lack of income hasn't been the primary reason for Lido struggling on the pitch. 'We should be doing better,' he says. 'The players are good enough, but just not doing it.' There are no prima donnas among them: most are homegrown, and they are all paid the same. 'If we had an extra £300 or £400 to spend we wouldn't have gone out and bought any players because they aren't about, and we have what constitutes a very good side. But we've struggled to score.' He shrugs his shoulders. 'That happens.' Phil wouldn't want to see the club spend lots of money on players anyway – it goes against the club ethos. 'I get a big kick out of seeing a boy come up from the junior team into the first team, going through all the various levels.'

I mention the romantically named League leaders TNS (Total Network Solutions), a club run by computer systems businessman Mike Harris, who has renamed a mid-Wales village side after his company, spent lots of his spare cash and now looks like seeing some return on his investment. (Indeed, in 2004/05 TNS swept all before them, winning the Welsh Premier League and the Welsh Cup.) I wonder, if a Welsh Premier League version of Roman Abramovic came along to invest in Afan Lido, would things be the same here. 'No, they wouldn't,' says Phil tersely. 'Things change, and I accept the Welsh Premier League is getting more professional. It has to. Money is becoming the main thing now. We will have to attract outside income to compete. But I don't want to see us paying lots of money and different amounts. That definitely took us down last time, so we stopped and went back to doing what we do now. We don't pay a lot of money compared to the rest of the Welsh Premier League.' And Phil recognises his future could hang in the balance too. 'If someone did come in he might say this and that need to happen for the club to develop further. But if it is right for someone to push it further, then so be it.'

It is hard to imagine that happening. Despite being tense about today's game, Phil still derives 'enormous pleasure' from giving the kids a grounding in football and passing them on to the other club coaches to develop. Who knows who might be among the four- and five-year-olds Phil is coaching today? Another John Hartson or Brian Flynn maybe?

Soon, Phil will have to turn his attention to other matters – the senior side and opening the bar. A win today against Llanelli would go a long way to preserving their Welsh Premier League status.

9.50 A.M.: A MEETING WITH THE CHAPLAIN Having waded his way through the morning post, John Boyers is preparing for the day ahead. John balances his role as chaplain at the world's biggest football club, Manchester United, with being the national director of SCORE (Sports Chaplaincy Offering Resources and Encouragement), a charity John founded in 1991 with the help of the Baptist Union of Great Britain which works interdenominationally to serve the UK's sports chaplains. It trains and supports clerics across many UK sports, not just football but cricket, rugby, golf and horse racing, among others, and at major sports events such as the 2002 Commonwealth Games and 2004 Olympics in Athens.

Matchday is a busy one for John. 'It is the day it all comes together,' he says. 'At smaller clubs it may be the only day when everyone assembles. All the part-time staff are in, so it's a good time to meet everyone. But at a larger club it may not be. You don't want to get under their feet so you have to be wise, sensitive and understanding. You don't want to get in the way of players, managers and coaches, or the catering manager or gatemen. I usually just show my face and say, "Look, I'm around if you need me," but I don't take up their time.'

There is a myth John is keen to dispel from the start. 'It isn't about getting free tickets for games or the kudos of rubbing shoulders with famous players. It's a case of, when a crisis occurs, being on hand if you are needed. Suddenly you can be involved in the pastoral and spiritual care of people in a very real way that makes a valuable contribution beyond that which normal human resources personnel offer. What the chaplain can offer is care and a spiritual dimension. The quality delivery of the service is the most important thing.' It can be unpredictable. 'You never know what will happen, or in what capacity you will be needed. Gordon Wilson, the chaplain at Sheffield Wednesday when the Hillsborough disaster happened, was at the ground for 48 hours but hadn't gone to the game because it wasn't a Sheffield Wednesday fixture [it was an FA Cup semi-final between Liverpool and Nottingham Forest]. It is something he bitterly regrets, but you can't always assume when you'll be needed. You just have to be there when you can.'

John also recalls an infamous incident when the Coventry defender David Busst broke his leg in 98 places in a freak horrific injury at Old Trafford on Easter Monday in 1995. It finished his career. 'I immediately thought, "This is bad", and left my seat to go down to the touchline. I was with the medical team, paramedics and doctors when the ambulance arrived. I thought, "What would the club chaplain be expected to do?" I was advised not to go to the hospital that day as he would be rushed into emergency and highly sedated for the rest of the day. But they said, "Can you come back in the morning, Rev?" I went the next day, and three days a week for the next eight weeks. You hope nothing crops up, but you don't know what may crop up.'

John checks his pockets and muses with his wife Anne over the merits of wearing a full dark-blue overcoat. Today he plans to watch two matches: this morning United's much-vaunted U-18s are pitting their skills against local rivals Manchester City; this afternoon he will head to Old Trafford, the so-called Theatre of Dreams, where the biggest crowd in the Premiership's history will assemble to see if the home team can beat Portsmouth and nudge within six points of League leaders Chelsea.

9.55 A.M.: THE REF HITS THE ROAD This is a slightly uneasy interview for me. I feel a bit of a fraud. It's a bit like interviewing someone from a political party or campaign you virulently hate, but as a journalist you have to be fair and professionally polite. I mean, if there was an anti-referee party I would undoubtedly be a paid-up member. Crikey, you can imagine the political support they would have (ah, but would anyone listen?). Yep, like all fans I have shouted at them, sworn that they are blind, accused them of having dubious parentage and fascist tendencies, and suggested in frank terms where their assistants might want to shove their flags. Spending the entire day with one and actually being nice, seeing him out of his uniform and hearing his point of view, could be potentially awkward. I am even intrigued and pleasantly surprised that Paul and the other people who have approved of and helped to set up this interview have been so genuinely positive about getting involved. It wasn't what I was expecting. I thought referees would be the most secretive, fastidious bunch to deal with for the book. In fact, they are actually keen to show what a referee goes through and to allow every possible access. Paul is open, frank and – something else I wasn't necessarily expecting – good company.

So we set out on Paul Taylor's matchday. Although refereeing is a part-time occupation, it requires much more dedication than merely turning up on the day. As we hit the M25 (we are looping around clockwise to join the A12), Paul runs through his schedule for the past week. On Sunday (Boxing Day) he missed his scheduled match at Cardiff through injury; Monday, he had to see his physiotherapist (yes, refs have them) and did a light training session; on Tuesday, he was the fourth official at Tottenham v. Crystal Palace, which took up most of the day; Wednesday, he refereed Hull City v. Doncaster Rovers, which meant checking out stats on the internet, preparing paperwork for the game, leaving home at midday for a 230-mile drive to Hull for the evening kick-off and not returning home until three a.m. Luckily, Paul can work from home and does flexible hours, so he can start his normal day job at ten a.m., although if he has misconduct forms to file they have to be telephoned through before midday (and having issued seven yellow cards and three reds in the Hull game, that took up most of Thursday morning). Friday was a light training session and prep work for Saturday.

On matchdays Paul will usually arrange an overnight stop if he is travelling more than 100 miles, but never stops in the town where the game is taking place because there is a risk that he will book into the same hotel as the away team, which would leave him open to all sorts of allegations. 'You don't want to make it a potential problem,' he says.

On top of this, well-known referees are constantly asked to do talks at grass-roots level to chivvy up the troops who are just starting out in refereeing – all very understandable, but time-consuming. In summary, Paul concludes, 'I do something every day of the season relating to refereeing.'

There are no midwinter breaks in La Manga or Florida. How often do you hear about failing teams jetting off somewhere exotic so the players can 'bond'? If a referee is in a rut, he can't do this – he is dragged through the mud. They can't hide; in fact, they just have to get back on their bikes and pedal away furiously again. No one forces them to do it, but it's a fact of life that stands in stark contrast to the players' experience.

As we hit the A12, Paul explains how he started. It was when he was a student at Warwick University, where he studied English and Film – hardly what you might call classic referee-type subjects. I'm sure many fans would expect referees to have opted for science-based subjects involving lots of petty but provable statistics and minutiae. Paul had been to a non-football-playing grammar school, but at university he wanted to play the game. He wasn't very good at it, though, so was substitute for the university team most of the time. And as everyone who has played at that level knows, subs in recreational football end up running the line. 'I thought, "If I'm doing this, I'd better learn the rules of the game."'

He didn't need to use his Economics A level to calculate that as he was paying up to £5 a game effectively to be a linesman week after week, he might as well earn £15 by being a referee. By the age of nineteen he was earning a tidy side income refereeing on Saturday mornings and afternoons and Sunday mornings, and keeping himself extremely fit. 'It was a useful supplement to my grant,' he recalls. 'In the late 1970s earning £40 over a weekend was phenomenal money.'

Thus began Paul Taylor's route up the greasy pole of refereeing. Uniquely, referees are the one group of people in football who have to pass through each level of the game to reach the top. Paul was fast-tracked. 'If you are young and bright and seem to be able to cope, you are soon appointed to more challenging matches.' Within seven years of starting he became a Football League linesman – or referee's assistant to use the correct parlance. And at 29 he became one of the youngest referees to be appointed to the Football League list (this was before the Premier League breakaway). Some might consider this to be quite young, possibly even too young, but Paul's voracious appetite for officiating meant he had reffed several hundred games, more than most footballers would have played at the same age.

The abuse has never bothered him. His response to the media criticism of referees is that 'good news doesn't sell'. He knows referees are only newsworthy when they have, or people think they have, made mistakes. 'You know that when you go into the game. You just have to get on with it. If you were hurt by the abuse you would easily give up.' And most do, usually within the first few months after qualifying at grass-roots level. None of this is directly to do with the press, more the abuse from parents and players in junior and recreational football. Largely this is copycat behaviour learned from observing the antics of top-level players and managers who refuse to accept any onus or responsibility to act as role models unless you quiz them on the size of their salaries. It is sad and difficult to eradicate, and is a growing problem for grassroots football.

I remember making a radio feature a few years ago about a mentoring scheme where experienced referees went out with younger, newer officials to help and support them. We chose to cover a junior game in Coventry where a sixteen-year-old Mr Bean lookalike (unfortunately he ran a bit like him too) was bullied endlessly by parents who were blind to their children's inadequacies and even more myopic about their own actions and the view that it is just a game. Even though I was openly waving a microphone about – which often has a knack of making people check what they say – they just bawled and shouted at him. I don't recall anyone shaking his hand after the game.

But Paul is a strong-willed character. It is no surprise he overcame the pitfalls. He progressed from refereeing in the old Third and Fourth Divisions within two years and made his First Division debut at Coventry City in 1991. He didn't make the initial list of referees who formed the first Premier League panel when it was set up in 1992; instead, he stayed in the Football League. He joined the Premier League list in 2000, and a year later they were made full-time professionals, but at 42, Paul calculated that his well-paid 'day' job wasn't worth sacrificing just to be a full-time referee for a few years. So it was back to the Football League, where he tends to get many of the bigger games – like the clash today at Portman Road.

Paul is due to retire at 48, an age he will reach in June 2007. Although with European Union age discrimination laws due to come into force in 2006, if challenged, he might be able to stay on longer.

10 A.M.: RUNNING LATE Bob Marley runs to his car – I'm trying to keep up. Our first port of call is a small industrial estate across the city, to collect wheel braces for the lead vehicle for the Santa Fun Run (you can hire them apparently). We detour to collect some signs he's ordered – mile markers mainly. He checks them, cheekily nabbing a lollipop and dancing around questions about why the club hasn't used their services more often.

The fun run is a once-a-year event, but I wonder how much time Bob puts into being a football club director. 'Easily 25 hours a week,' he says, totting it up. 'Today is ten hours, tomorrow will be another eight to ten hours, then all the stuff you do during the week. My week ahead is: Monday night, chairing a meeting for two hours; Tuesday, taking the U-13s training for two hours; Wednesday, training the ladies team for two hours; Thursday, I have two Worcestershire FA council meetings; and on Friday there is a club function. So I am out every day or night of the week doing something.'

Each of Worcester City's twelve directors has an area of expertise which will take up similar time. They are routinely expected to dole out several thousand pounds for the privilege. There's a personal cost too. 'It has definitely been one of the material factors in my marriage breaking up,' Bob tells me. 'No doubt about that. And other directors will say when they have to put money into the club sometimes they can't tell their partners because they'd bloody kill them! It's like that for all of us.' Bob recites a spiel he recently gave to a prospective director. 'I told him he needs to go home and tell his wife that his life is going to be turned upside down. He needs to tell her he is going to be out for a minimum of two or three nights a week and at least one whole day at the weekend. He is going to invest at least £5,000 of their money each year into the football club, so he needs to tell her they are going to have lots of rows about it; he needs to tell her that he will get no thanks or support for it; he needs to tell her that maybe once a year there will be a function she can come to but that in the main she'll think he's living it up and that he's just out socialising. Then he'll need to tell his fellow directors at work that he is probably going to be spending something like one to two hours a day of his paid work time dealing with matters at the football club, that he will pick up the phone at least half a dozen times a day for the football club, and that they will have to pick up the bill. Once he's had those discussions he must ask himself, "Have I got their support, and do I still want to do it?" He shouldn't talk to us about being a board member until he's had those discussions.'

And there's more. 'Alongside all those are the legal commitments of being a director of a limited company. You still, theoretically, have a business to run which should bring in a profit to its shareholders. You have all the corporate governance and directors' meetings to attend. You have confidential manager and players' information. And you have to negotiate salaries and wages and legal bits and pieces. It's a different type of person who can take on board all the things you need to be a football club director and put your emotions to one side. Your emotions tell you to double the manager's wage budget, but you can't do it. You see what happens when clubs do that. They go bust.'

So many football club directors let their hearts rule their heads, but Bob Marley's focus is on the community side of the club, and that makes him a bit different from most.

10.10 A.M.: A NAVIGATIONAL DETOUR We depart. John Boyers sets his recently acquired satellite navigation system for Manchester City's training complex on Platt Lane in Moss Side. It's only a few miles away from John's home in Sale, across south Manchester. Who needs spiritual guidance when there is sat-nav?

Attending these youth-team games is an essential part of building relationships with United's players for John. His job doesn't focus on saving souls or thumping a Bible in front of trembling-hearted teenagers, but part of his matchday role and overall attempt to put some soul into Manchester United is gaining the trust of players at all levels. Some of today's younger players may be the first-teamers of tomorrow, and if he is to develop long-standing relationships he has to win their faith now, and sometimes that means standing in the wind and rain beside a muddy pitch in Moss Side.

En route we are chewing over standard Mancunian minutiae – today's arctic weather in a city where, by repute, it rarely refrains from raining – when John's mobile phone rings. 'Hi, Keith.' It's Keith McIntosh, Manchester United's health, safety and welfare officer. 'No,

I didn't ... Roy Unwin? He must have worked for the club for years ...
I'll give Mike a call to see what he says. Thanks for letting me know.'

Our plans are about to change. I'm about to discover that sports
chaplaincy has a bit more urgency about it than coffee mornings at the
vicarage. 'That was a call to let me know that Roy Unwin, who has
worked for the club for years, died last night,' John tells me. 'I'm going
to see if there is anything I can do.' He pulls over to make a call to
museum manager Mike Maxfield. 'Just had a call from Keith Mac to tell
me about Roy. Do you feel it would help if I dropped in? ... How are
people bearing up? ... What time will they start to arrive? ... What about
Roy's wife? ... Do you want me to drop in? ... Well, I was on my way to
Platt Lane to see the youths, but it's no problem ...'

John takes a detour to Old Trafford. We're not far away (on the A56,
the main road into Manchester from the southwest), and John is
ignoring the constant pleas of the polite young lady on the sat-nav
system to turn right. 'Take the next right.' She is efficient and polite, but
I wonder if she will eventually snap. 'I said right! Look, I said right!
Right now. What the hell is wrong with you? Are you deaf?' I wonder if
they do a 'partner style' version where you can orchestrate a row but
still somehow manage to find your way to your destination. John
switches her off, destination Old Trafford.

10.15 A.M.: ANGER WITH THE FA Neil Williams has reached
Worcestershire. Kidderminster, in fact. We actually pass the island close
to Brian Murdoch's wine bar, where he is carefully preparing the food
for this afternoon's match.

Neil's thoughts are with the FA. He is disappointed that football's
governing body has rules that allow someone to buy a club and evict
them from their ground. 'How many of these people are going to
continue to be allowed to get hold of football clubs for their own
means?' he asks. It's a good question. Wrexham are not the first and
probably won't be the last to be taken over by someone who doesn't
have the well-being of the club as their main interest. Begrudgingly, and
belatedly, a fit and proper person test has been introduced, but this
doesn't exclude most people, and certainly won't prevent them treating
football clubs as any other type of business if they are allowed to. Alex

Hamilton hasn't broken any rules, only some hearts, if his plans effectively drive Wrexham out of business. He has just made hard, cold decisions that suit his interests.

Supporters at the Clubs in Crisis rally at Wrexham later in the day will call for the governing body to act to save smaller clubs from being cherry-picked and for the game's riches to be more evenly divided. Their rally will be truly heart-warming.

Despite the geographical difficulties, Neil has been helping the Wrexham Supporters Trust, the fans' group which is trying to do all it can to preserve the club. He staged a balloon race to raise money and had 3,000 leaflets printed to promote the previous Clubs in Crisis day, held in November 2004. He also wants to arrive in good time to collect more of the shirts that have been sent to the club offices for a fund-raising auction he is organising; the signed replica shirts from all 92 Premiership and Football League clubs, he hopes, will provide some £15,000 for the WST. 'We will try everything and anything to raise money. I have been in touch with Christie's and Sotheby's, the big auction houses, to find out how much they might be worth. It should be several thousand pounds.'

Fans do their bit, but unless it is backed with gusto by the FA at Soho Square, how long will it be before clubs start to disappear?

10.20 A.M.: TRYING TO BE POSITIVE I'm sitting in an office just off the Soho Road, but in Handsworth, far away from the FA's HQ in Soho Square. The Soho Road is a main thoroughfare, properly titled the A41, running from Birmingham to the Black Country. The man sitting on the other side of the table, Phil Hamilton, is fighting back the tears during an emotional explanation of the meaning of matchday.

'I love football to the max,' he says. 'It's my adrenalin, my drug. If I don't have football at least three or four times a week I'm desperate. On my wedding day I was thinking about football. I wouldn't have had the many great experiences I have had if it had not been for football. In essence, it is a simple game to play, but it teaches you so much about life.'

You can forget your pine, glass and chrome panels here. Or six-figure salaries. This is the sharp end of soccer. Most shops here are boarded up or have corrugated-iron shutters. Handsworth is a notorious Birmingham district. On the one hand, it has a wonderfully eclectic multicultural mix, but it also has depressingly high rates of crime and unemployment. The four young men convicted of the so-called and well-publicised New Year's Day shootings – the murders of Letitia Shakespeare and Charlene Ellis – had been sentenced earlier in the week. It was a tragic episode in the ongoing turf war between gangs whose territory overlaps this broad sweep of northwest Birmingham, from Handsworth through to Aston. If you wanted to stake out the land in terms of landmarks, you would say it stretches roughly from West Brom's ground, the Hawthorns, over to Villa Park.

Phil has been a youth worker in the city for 25 years. He's a sports development officer for an environmental regeneration charity called Groundwork, which aims to reclaim green space for communities. Phil tells me about George's Park. Run down, under-used and under-funded, it had been a haven for all manner of anti-social activity but has latterly been transformed into a communal space with ball courts, a skate park, bandstand, bench seats and a children's play area. Crime has consequently dropped by 15 per cent in the area.

Groundwork's office is close to where the 1985 Handsworth riots started – the junction where Villa Road, Lozells Road and Hampstead Road meet, names stamped into most Brummies' minds as no-go areas. Trying to spread and sell the message that football is a national game for each and every person to participate in, or even that matchday is something special, is tough here. But according to Phil, 'football works on many different levels'. He uses the power of football to engage the young men who fall prey to the gangs. If he can get them playing sport, get them to appreciate the in-built ethos and discipline needed to prosper in the game and enforce the positive health benefits and the detrimental effects of an anti-social lifestyle, he stands a chance of steering them on to the straight and narrow. But he faces a race against time. 'We have to reach them before the gangs do, at about the age of fourteen,' he says. 'I have seen people's lives take a 180-degree turn because of football. In a nutshell, football keeps them out of trouble.'

That last statement isn't to be underestimated. In places like Aston and Handsworth, trouble doesn't meaning scrumping, it means drugs and gang warfare involving guns. The grim statistics show that 60 per cent of the youths in Handsworth will be offenders or victims at one stage or another. 'It breaks my heart,' says Phil, who coaches several teams throughout the week. 'Saturday is football, football, football, but it's all about playing rather than watching.' He runs two teams in Aston. One of them, Fentham, have reached a local league final, the Shapla League, to be held on the hallowed turf of Villa Park.

It is a rare connection that Villa, a large Premier League club that the same week announced that manager David O'Leary would have a £20 million transfer kitty for the summer, have with their local community. 'It is appreciated,' says Phil, who set the league up ten years ago, initially for young Asian men, although it has now expanded. He is pleased Villa provide their pitch for the final but is disappointed that no one from the professional arm of the club is likely to look at the players. 'There is a vast amount of talent right under their noses, but they don't look here.'

This is just one of a number of ways in which Phil feels professional clubs fail the communities on their doorsteps. He explains the problem. He grew up on Trinity Road, one of the roads surrounding Villa Park. Phil's family, like so many in the immediate environs around Villa Park, settled here from the Caribbean. Being black, the matchday rules were you did your shopping in the morning and stayed indoors between midday and six p.m. until the football crowds went home. To venture outside during the 1970s and 1980s often meant enduring a barrage of racism from the predominantly white fans who poured into areas largely populated by ethnic minorities. 'Villa was just a big football stadium where I lived. They did nothing for us. I used to be shit-scared on Saturdays, so I felt no allegiance towards them.' Phil supports Liverpool, alienated by his local club which failed to acknowledge the inconvenience their business caused local residents. It's easy to say 'Well, if you choose to live near a football ground …', but for economic reasons, wherever you go in the world immigrants settle in the poorest parts of town, and in post-war Britain that often meant the areas around inner-city football grounds.

Small wonder Phil's father hated football. He loathed it even more when his son, then 23, broke the matchday rule. He was innocently waiting outside a pub for his mates to turn up for a game of football when he was chased by a gang of visiting Manchester City supporters. With almost dreadful understatement, I had to tease from Phil what 'being chased' actually meant: having to hop over a fence and down an embankment, being effectively hunted down and cornered on wasteland and repeatedly stabbed. One of the wounds punctured a lung, which nearly killed him. He was hospitalised for a month. The perpetrator walked free after a legal technicality. Is it any wonder football has failed to attract black and Asian fans in significant numbers? 'There are some black and Asian fans who go to Villa,' Phil points out, 'but they could reach more people if only they were seen to be doing something for the community.'

This isn't just a race issue. In the economically deprived community surrounding Villa Park, and indeed in Handsworth where Phil now works, escalating admission prices have also been a barrier. I ask Phil how many of the boys he coaches, or rather their parents, could afford to watch a Premier League football match. 'No way, no way!' he shouts. He tells me about one (single) parent who couldn't even afford the one-off £25 for a passport so her daughter could go on a youth exchange trip to Ireland. 'Her son needs a pair of trainers [too]. It's difficult to find the money for long-term things like that, let alone blowing £20 or more on something that only lasts 90 minutes.'

Phil can only charge 50p per match to his players because to ask any more would be prohibitive. How much could he push it, I wonder, before he would lose players? 'Even at £1 we would lose some,' he replies. 'If I went to £2 that would be pushing it, and £3 would be the absolute tops.' The money raised is nowhere near enough to pay a referee a fee of £20 a game and £15 to hire a pitch. Phil just pays it out of his own earnings, as he does when it comes to washing the well-worn kits Fentham teams use. Their U-12s kit is ten years old. 'I don't think about it, I just do it automatically,' he says. 'I have been doing it for so long I don't think about it. I never get down about the money I have spent on football.' But what about top players' wages, agents' fees and TV money? 'Well, that gets me down, and it is unfair. There is too big a division between what is happening at that level and what we have to survive on, but it doesn't suppress my feelings. These young people need me. They need people like me.'

Matchday is all about getting up early, pumping up balls, sorting out kit and arranging to ferry kids to games. Hopefully the pitch and referees will have been booked well in advance. Phil describes his wife as a 'football tolerator'. 'It's too late to change,' he reckons. 'It will stay with me until I die.' This all sounds terribly familiar. My brother ran several junior sides, and my parents' house would, at weekends, be a nerve centre for arrangements. Phil has even signed himself out of hospital to attend matches. 'At weekends in the close season I go nuts.'

Given the lack of money around, the need for facilities and, arguably, the demand for his kind of work, Phil is scathing about Aston Villa's relationship with their local community. 'In my personal view, Villa don't do enough,' he says. He describes their efforts as 'piecemeal', intended, he suspects, to recruit new fans. He respects the people who work in the club's Football in the Community programme but wonders about the Villa's wider policies and outlook – like, for example, siting their training ground (as, to be fair, most major clubs now do) in the Staffordshire countryside some fifteen miles away from Aston. A few years ago, following a spate of thefts from cars parked in the vicinity of Villa Park on matchdays – perpetrated, allegedly, by local youths – Phil met representatives from the club to suggest they needed to build links with the community to help prevent this from happening. The response was to raffle off a signed football to raise some funds. It made Phil despair.

Although Villa have developed local black kids such as Tony Daley, Mark Walters and, more recently, Darius Vassell, they don't seem bothered about finding the role models who could be so socially significant to the community on their doorsteps. Phil would love to see a local Bangladeshi play for Villa. 'Sixty per cent of the local population is Asian, but how many Asian players are there in the game?'

In recent years Phil has worked for a government football coaching scheme called Positive Futures, which is specifically designed to tackle social exclusion using the unique power of football to change lives. Phil ran a league in Aston Park, literally overlooking Villa's ground. It has recently moved to bigger and better facilities in Handsworth, and later I will see the scheme in action. This may sound like utopian nonsense, but it works. I have seen other schemes across the country where young people learn so much from sport, not just the middle-class Victorian ethos of 'play up, play up and play the game' but the discipline, the enjoyment of winning, how to accept defeat, and simple things like getting out of bed early to train, staying fit, eating well, not abusing your body through drugs, alcohol or tobacco. It improves self-esteem. It works. So does the Football Foundation, which gives £60 million to football's good causes every year. Sadly, the professional clubs give very little directly. A small sum – £20 million, lowered recently to £15 million a year – has been siphoned off recent TV deals, but this is a tiny percentage of the £3.65 billion Premiership clubs have earned since the league formed in 1992.

Phil explains what football has done for the boys he has coached. He recalls one pair of tearaway brothers. 'They were people whose lives were on a knife edge. They could have slipped into that vast dark hole. Instead they have become upright citizens because of football, and we now coach their children.' So what is it about football? 'As a coach, it's about being competitive. But being a youth worker, I realise it is what they learn around the way they play the game.'

A few years ago he was part of a group of people who got support from Aston's Asian community so that a team could be sent to an annual youth competition called the Ian Rush Tournament in Aberystwyth. It is serious stuff; players like Michael Owen, Alan Shearer and Robbie Keane have all competed as youngsters. It cost Fentham FC £36,000 to send a team for a week, and many community initiatives such as sponsored car washes helped raise the money. Most of the players had never been away from home before and had to learn lots of skills before leaving Birmingham: how to deal with authority, and with decisions that sometimes go against you; how to deal with being trodden on when you feel the world is against you. 'We got hammered left, right and centre,' recalls Phil. 'But it wasn't about winning, it was about learning.' Three years later, Fentham FC won the tournament. When Phil meets some of those now grown-up players, they say, 'Those days in Wales shaped my life.' How do you put a price on that?

Phil describes Fentham and its offshoot club, Arden Albion, as 'a way of life', not a sports club. The conduct and attitude are important. 'It is keeping the community together. It is a great community thing.' People like Phil have an enormous appetite for grass-roots football. He has even sold his car to support trips away. His story deserves to be told as a part of matchday as much as any in the professional game. And do you know what? The results of Positive Futures don't matter. The taking part does.

10.25 A.M.: A SPIRE IN SALFORD John and I reach Old Trafford, home of the world's biggest football club. It dominates the south Salford skyline, at the tip of a broad sweep of land which was once a condensed community stretching westward via an array of industrial estates (including the World Freight Centre and a wonderful-smelling cornflake factory) on to the massive Trafford Centre shopping mall and the redeveloped Salford Quays, with its Lowry Centre and loft apartments – which says much about Manchester's past and Manchester's present.

Old Trafford is like no other British football ground. It is huge, enveloped by massive car parks, most of which, even several hours before kick-off, are manned by burly security staff whose physical presence is enough to ward off errant strangers. We have to pass through three levels of this security so that John can park near the Manchester United Museum, where Roy Unwin used to work. 'I'm the club chaplain,' explains John, who doesn't possess a doctor-on-call pass, which would enable automatic and immediate access to otherwise cordoned-off areas of Old Trafford.

John wastes no time – spiritual aid is needed – and he speeds through the museum entrance past the gaudy red Man United Experience zones: the Trophy Room, the Legends section, the Munich and Treble exhibitions and the Roll of Honour. I can't spot the 'spent shedloads but couldn't lift the championship for 26 years' zone, or the 'only two European Cups despite all this smug grandeur' alcove. Maybe we took a short cut. But this is not a time for levity.

We enter Mike Maxfield's office. The United museum manager is sporting a red jacket and a rather worrying early eighties coiffeured quiff – an appearance that inadvertently clashes with the sombre mood. Mike has been with United since 1986. John asks if a staff gathering for some prayers to remember Roy would be welcome. Mike explains that only a few museum staff will be in today – tours are suspended on matchdays; tomorrow may be more suitable. John suggests we say a short prayer now and asks Mike if any members of staff would like to join us. A few tearful females file in.

10.30 A.M.: LITTLE CHEF WELCOMES YOU ... OR MAYBE NOT Paul Taylor is making good progress. The A12 is relatively clear and there are no delays. But my bladder can't hold out. Coffee gets you going in more ways than one, and I need the loo. We stop at a Little Chef, motto 'Little Chef Welcomes You'. Though not referees, it seems. I ask Paul if he is coming in. Realistically we are going to be very early, and we could have a quick drink, a chance to chat without the concerns of driving. He declines. In his FA jacket, tie and blazer, he is something of a giveaway. A referee's habit of old: you don't go where the fans may recognise you. How sad. Instead, he chats to a fellow ref on his mobile while I nip inside.

When I return, he asks if there were many football fans in the café. Lots. A smattering of both Ipswich and West Ham supporters. Paul may not be a household name or face, but he is recognisable and things can be taken out of context. If he is seen chatting to a particular group of fans and it is reported, how does that look? If someone bears a grudge, who knows what might happen? These seem like over-the-top precautions, but they are all facets of being a referee. Given that Paul reckons he does about 10,000 miles a year getting to and from matches, this seems quite a restriction. It makes you wonder what major referees like Rob Styles and Graham Poll do. They are instantly recognisable faces who have caused controversy. A quiet cuppa on the way home from, say, Old Trafford – and let's face it, Man Utd's fans live everywhere – could be fraught with difficulties. 'It's one of the things you do to prepare,' Paul explains. 'You think, "Which way will the fans travel?" If you're going that way too, do you really want to stop?' In the second half of the season, he checks out the previous encounter. If there were problems, he'll phone the referee to ask what happened. What were the flashpoints? Who was involved? It will help him control the game.

As we restart our journey to Ipswich I ask, given these hassles, why he does the job. 'I like football,' Paul replies. 'I enjoy controlling the game. It is the nearest you can get to the action. If you are, basically, a fan like me, it is a privilege to be involved. If you are travelling back from a game a long way from home on a Tuesday night when it's lashing down with rain and you are wondering why you are doing it instead of being curled up on the sofa watching TV, then you probably need to ask yourself some serious questions. The moment you start to think those thoughts it will impact upon your performance.' Although he has a young son, a loving wife and a demanding day job, Paul insists he has never felt that way. '

I think the self-criticism comes after the game, but then you start thinking about the positives, and think, "Well, I could have handled that better," so next time you face that scenario you deal with it.'

Then there is the fitness. We keep hearing that football is getting faster. Goalkeepers, for instance, can no longer pick up back-passes and hoof the ball up the pitch. There is no longer one ball used at a time: ballboys swap them with speed so there are fewer breathers. And Paul faces a double whammy: he is getting older as the pace of the game quickens. He's in his mid-forties, so he'll be at least ten years older than most players on the pitch, and up to 25 years older than some. Yet he has to match their pace. This must frighten him? 'You shouldn't referee to keep fit, you should keep fit to referee,' he asserts. I can imagine some blazered sage passing on this snippet of advice in a hut somewhere. 'The levels of fitness required are going up and I am getting older, so it gets tougher,' he admits with a laugh. 'We're fitness-tested three times a year.' Christ, it's worse than I thought – a triple whammy. 'Referees are tested on endurance and anaerobic capacity. We are required to run harder as you become more tired.' Shuttle sprints are introduced along the way. 'You run to exhaustion, basically. The bleeps get faster as you become more tired.'

I can imagine some players baulking at this sort of testing. I remember Gary Megson, shortly after he became West Brom boss, saying he had asked the squad to do a five-mile run, and some had refused. 'You have to taper your training as you get older because you have to work harder to achieve the same target,' Paul continues. 'At 45, you can't do what you did when you were 25.' I know. Paul and I were born within a month of each other. When I go jogging I can still run the same times, but the effort required is greater and the recovery longer. Improvement is very difficult. Even five years ago I felt differently.

But there is another crucial factor in all this: referees have to make key decisions, and anyone who has done distance-running knows that fatigue affects your thinking. 'There is a direct correlation between physical exhaustion and mental judgement,' Paul confirms. 'If you are physically fit, you are mentally alert. If you are off the pace and worrying about keeping up you are not concentrating on making decisions.'

The Professional Match Officials Limited, the body that looks after referees, has a full-time fitness adviser who devises individual training programmes for referees. It is difficult to find the time to train in between matches, which themselves help improve your fitness. Unlike the players and the full-time professional referees in the Premiership, most officials have to fit in sessions around games and work commitments. This isn't a sob story, just a refereeing fact of life.

I am wondering whether Paul Taylor will prove to be up for the game today, especially after his recent ankle injury. Though he did try out a new pair of boots on Wednesday in Hull. 'The best I have felt after a game in years,' he says.

10.35 A.M.: EXECUTIVE STRESS At Carrow Road I'm feeling grateful that chief executive Neil Doncaster has spared me the time; most other clubs at this level wouldn't even have the courtesy to reply to such a request, let alone allow a journalist to stalk the corridors of power on a big 'working' day. Neil is tall, bespectacled and smartly dressed in what might be described as not untypical garb for an ex-lawyer: grey suit, waistcoat, dark Crombie. He is extremely friendly, open and honest. He answers each and every question I ask openly and thoroughly, and when he suspects he may need to substantiate things, he races off to produce documentary evidence. All things that I find gratifying.

His day is a busy one. He starts at 8.30 a.m. and will be here for twelve hours. I am intrigued by Norwich City's story, their comeback after crippling debts, and today's match with Chelsea in particular. It represents the comparative poles of the Premiership. There's the swanky, fashionable Londoners bankrolled by Roman Abramovic, who has spent some £200 million in the transfer market since he bought the club in the summer of 2003; and there's Norwich, who are cautiously trying to avoid overspending (at £3 million they had to break the bank to bring in striker Dean Ashton), who have successfully shored up support in their corner of the country, and who have developed a genuine community club in Norfolk.

The media are full of co-owner Delia Smith's amazing 'let's be havin' you' outburst during half-time the previous Monday in the match against Manchester City. In one way or another, every radio station I have tuned into en route – Five Live, Talk Sport, Radio 2 – has mentioned it. I could have understood Norwich being cagey. Not so. They have a story to tell. And Neil Doncaster, who has played a central part, is keen to tell it, and to show me exactly what he does on matchday.

In brief, having dealt with routine paperwork (and inquisitive journalists), Neil effectively 'audits the game'. This involves all the usual matchday issues, such as the safety and security of spectators (Norwich is snowbound today), and the extra security that might be needed for their high-flying visitors (Abramovic is believed to be bringing his own entourage of security staff). Then there's Chelsea boss Jose Mourinho, whose actions will come under closer scrutiny after the previous week's gesture: during the Carling Cup victory against Liverpool, when Chelsea scored he raised his index finger to his lips as if to silence the Liverpool fans, though he later insisted it was aimed at the press. And Neil has just been alerted to an extra concern today: the intention of Delia Smith to sit in the Barclay End in a section frequented by Norwich's vocal younger fans. The wisdom of this decision will ultimately be decided upon by the safety officer, Leon Blackburn, but the debate involves Neil, head of media Joe Ferrari and marketing manager Andrew Cullen. Prior to kick-off Neil will also stand outside Carrow Road and field any questions from fans, and during the game he will tour the ground repeatedly making sure everything is working well.

I like Carrow Road. I have been here many times. As a fan, I came here several times with West Brom in the 1970s. I recall one particularly rumbustious journey, the first time I ever travelled on a 'soccer special' train (which, I gather, are about to be reintroduced). Lots of Albion fans were spectacularly drunk from very early on. The tone was set before we left New Street Station when someone pulled the emergency cord. The long journey east was punctuated several more times by fans piling off to clash with just about anyone who dared to crane an inquisitive neck at the noise coming from the train (I recall a couple of youths who unwisely flicked V-signs in the train's direction causing one mass exodus). They jumped on seats, smashed things and caused stewards to shed tears.

It got little better when we reached Norwich. Anglers were upended en route to the ground. Once inside the Barclay End, which the more vocal home fans shared not particularly harmoniously with the away supporters (leaving, sensibly I thought, the other three-quarters of the ground to watch the match in peace), some ill-advised home fans, who thought it was safe to make gestures towards the Albion fans as there was a downsloping no-man's land in between them, were descended upon.

On the pitch, Albion's players did little to lighten the mood by losing. It was not, safe to say, the most glorious day in the club's history, and it made me wonder whether it had been worth plodding around the streets in the dark all week delivering Dolphin Showers leaflets at the rate of £2.50 a thousand to save up the cash for the trip.

In later, happier times I saw Cyrille Regis score here to take West Brom to the top of the First Division in 1979, and our West Brom supporters club in Worcester ran much better hearted, though little less drunken, trips to Carrow Road. What else do you expect of a group of mainly teenagers on their way to the footy? More recently, Teresa and I have usually seen at least one game a season here as we have family in Norfolk. It's a club I have a lot of time for.

When I lived in London in the early 1990s I used to join a Norwich City-supporting friend, Gary Buck, for Canaries games in the capital and enjoyed the slick passing movement of a team schooled in the right way and containing the likes of Tim Sherwood, Ruel Fox, Chris Sutton, Robert Fleck and Jeremy Goss. Norwich were contenders for the first ever FA Premier League title in 1992/93 – a season in which, I note, they beat Chelsea home and away and, wouldn't you know it, Manchester United, who got their mitts on their first League title in 26 years. Norwich finished third, just two points behind Aston Villa.

They subsequently became one of the first of the relatively smaller clubs to fall into financial trouble in an effort to keep up with the big boys who benefited most from the inequities that emerged with the creation of the Premier League: those who appeared most on TV and who finished highest in the League took the lion's share of the takings and therefore generated bigger financial and commercial clout. Look at some of the clubs that participated in that first Premier League season, alongside Norwich: QPR (finished fifth, above Liverpool, Arsenal and Chelsea), Oldham, Sheffield Wednesday, Sheffield United, Nottingham Forest, Coventry City, Ipswich Town, Crystal Palace, Leeds United – they've all gone through hard times. Wimbledon, of course, have been franchised to another town as Milton Keynes Dons. Manchester City, too, have yo-yoed around and are also deep in debt at the time of writing.

And not a penny of the £300 million deal brokered by Sky and the BBC for the first five years of the FA Premier League was shared with the other 70 Football League clubs. The short-sightedness of these smaller clubs almost beggars belief. Couldn't they see where it was heading? The FA, too, must take their share of the blame as guardians of the game: their role in supporting a venture that could only accentuate the inequalities between football's haves and have nots is staggering.

Norwich was one of the first post-Premier League clubs to nearly go belly up. After their memorable UEFA Cup run in 1993/94 they overspent, sold their best players, were relegated and slipped into financial disarray. Their chairman in the good days, Robert Chase, left in 1996 with Norwich owing £8 million of unsecured debts and the club losing £3 million a year. And they weren't the only ones. 'That level of debt wasn't untypical in the First Division at that time,' recalls Neil. 'Particularly among clubs that had been relegated from the Premier League and had to survive on lower TV money and without parachute payments.'

The club's youth development officer, Gordon Bennett (aptly named, given the crisis), stepped in as temporary chief executive. Michael Wynn-Jones, his wife Delia Smith, Michael Foulger and Barry Skipper joined as directors and gave loans to cover the immediate losses. But a longer term strategy, identified by accountants Deloitte & Touche, was needed to turn the club around, in particular two key objectives: the appointment of a new company secretary (Doncaster) to provide a long-term business strategy for the club and a new marketing manager (Andrew Cullen). Both were appointed in November 1997 and are still in position at the time of writing, although Neil is now chief executive.

Neil insists he joined Norwich because he was inspired by the story of 'where Norwich City had come from, where it was going, and the role he could be expected to play'. He presented a five-year plan to the board, which was principally aimed at doubling the club's income within that timespan, whether they had returned to the Premier League or not. Key objectives included filling the stadium for home matches; regaining Premier League status; increasing income and capping expenditure;

creating a highly motivated staff to work together as a team to produce a quality customer focus; and, on the playing side, to develop a football academy. That Norwich achieved all these things, without being in the Premier League between 1997 and 2004, is remarkable, but it is the way they have done them that is impressive and to be applauded. It's all a million miles away from the resources their visitors have, who are expected to swan into town and leave with three points in the bag.

10.40 A.M.: TO THE MEMORY OF ROY UNWIN Roy Unwin was born in Salford in 1927 and had, by all accounts, and certainly not untypically for the age, a tough upbringing. The Salford he knew as a young man was different from the area surrounding Old Trafford today. It was a close-knit community of small terraced houses hunched around local industries. The football club, Newton Heath as they were known before becoming Manchester United in 1902 (having shunned the name Manchester Central because it sounded too much like a train station), was a part of that community – a focal point, yes, but not the dominating dome it is today.

The back-to-backs were knocked down as part of a massive post-war regeneration exercise during the same years when Manchester United were rising inexorably. For 40 years, from Busby to Ferguson, Roy played a minor role in their success story. He worked on the gate, in the ticket office, in the museum, as a tour guide and as a matchday steward in the players' corridor. He led the players on to the pitch at the start of games. Few people knew more about Manchester United than Roy Unwin. He'd seen it all happen. 'The things he didn't know, he made up,' someone cheekily suggested later in the day, not through malice but because, well, if Roy didn't know, who did? And frankly, who cared? A bit of a devil rather than a menacing Red Devil, our Roy.

He was taken to his first game at Old Trafford by his dad at the age of ten. The Manchester United of the 1930s was far from the giant it is today. They bounced between Divisions One and Two without conspicuous success. In 1930/31, when Roy was just four years old, they were relegated and managed only one five-figure gate all season and that was for the visit of Manchester City, whose fans, one assumes, swelled the gate. Only 3,900 trooped into Old Trafford for their last game of the season. Not so 'glory, glory Man Utd' in those days.

I don't suppose the Manchester United Experience dwells on this for long. The modern club is all about myth-making. All fans think, or are encouraged to believe, that their club is bigger than it really is. Some United supporters would doubtless baulk at suggestions that their club was once a failing provincial club. They have been fed the line that United's march to the top was inevitable. They were always a giant club, always will be. There is a nauseating arrogance about this, which rival fans find irritating.

Roy Unwin witnessed the creation of the club into a powerful force: Matt Busby's Babes fermenting; the tragic loss at Munich (which, while depleting the United team, ironically, via an unprecedented wave of public sympathy, simultaneously hoisted the club to emphatic heights); the rebirth with Charlton, Best, Law and co.; Sir Matt pouring his wounded soul into building a new team that would achieve what had been so cruelly denied those young men lost on the Munich airfield in 1958; winning the European Cup, that holiest of grails, in 1968. Roy will also have witnessed the decline. I can imagine him shaking his head at the anguish of relegation in 1973, and at the antics of the long-haired legions who gave United a fearsome reputation off the pitch as hooliganism took a vice-like hold on English football.

Yet those very fans kept the faith and kept coming from all corners of the country, even when United's League form was flaky, to say the least. Right through that 26-year gap without a League title – it's hard to imagine Europe's top clubs like Real Madrid, Bayern Munich, AC Milan, Barcelona and Ajax suffering such a domestic drought – coaches from Cwmbran, Cambridge and elsewhere continued to arrive, in a display of manic dedication that built the base for much of United's popularity today.

And so on to the era of Alex Ferguson, the only Manchester United manager worthy of mention alongside Matt Busby, and the hard-faced Premier League fuelled by Sky TV. A cash-rich era in which United have soared clear of every club in Britain, Europe, and maybe even the world in terms of brand loyalty, identity and money-making. They have even won a few trophies along the way.

Roy Unwin witnessed all this. Who knows what he really thought of some of the crass commercialism of modern-day football or of the multinational entrepreneurs, financiers and chancers who have tried to gain control of a club where he once took pennies at the gates? Certainly a remarkably changed game from the one he grew up with. He was part of it, for sure. The good times and the bad. A small cog in the wheel, but important, for people like Roy Unwin are the lifeblood of football. They make it all happen. We should cherish the memory of people like him.

These are the thoughts that flood through my mind as we stand, heads bowed, in Mike's office with Roy's laminated pass lying on the desk as John summons up a few words to reflect his loss. It is short and sweet, and the right thing to do. But it is difficult; at times like these Manchester United should thank God they have John Boyers on board. This was hardly where I was expecting to be within an hour of meeting him. It just goes to show, though I wish it hadn't happened, the value of his work.

10.45 A.M.: BOB MARLEY – DAD Bob Marley switches into a different guise – Dad. He's late. Whatever the reason, this isn't going to look good. We've got to get to an U-10s club Bob started with some like-minded parents a few years ago. The club, Hadley Rangers, is based a few miles north of Worcester.

We park down a remote country lane at the back of a line of other cars. Bob located this small strip of land, ideal for two small-sized pitches, but frankly, you'd never find the place unless you knew it was here. We hop through a gate, down a grass track to another gate, and duck under some rope to reach the field. It is very wet. Through a gap in the fence the faint, familiar sounds of junior football waft through the air – whistles, shouts, kicks. 'A super little setting,' Bob remarks with the pride of someone who set it up. The pair of Portakabins to our right cost £100 each. Straight ahead is the pitch, with parents and substitutes huddled either side of the lines. The home team – ours – is directly in front of us.

This is a tricky moment. As we make our way over to the game, Bob explains that his nine-year-old son Sam is playing and that his estranged wife, Mandy, who is in the process of divorcing him, and eldest son, Sebastian, are also here.

'Bit difficult this, isn't it?' I venture.

'Oh, it breaks your heart, mate,' says Bob, pausing for a rare moment of contemplation. 'It's really difficult.'

You bet. He sidles up to Mandy, says hello gently, and asks the score. We are late. Not by much, and not through malice or laziness, but by enough. It looks and feels what it is: Bob is the dad who wasn't here when his son's game kicked off.

Mini-soccer is brilliant. Bob is a huge fan. The kids here have to work to score goals because the small-sided game with miniature goalposts encourages skill. It's a far cry from so much of the football I grew up with, playing on full-sized pitches where brawn too often won the day. Lung-bursting runs just to reach the other end of the pitch overrode any skills required to manoeuvre the ball, while tiny goalkeepers were dwarfed by the huge frames they were supposed to defend. Any half-decent plodder could have poked one past them. What was the use of that? Sadly, mini-soccer hasn't necessarily fostered a better spirit among parents. Bob is no longer involved here. 'Both lads play various levels of competitive football,' he says quietly beneath the plaintive cries of a parent who is shouting himself hoarse. 'I take comfort from that. I was social secretary up to last year but I can't condone the way it's being done because I don't agree with it.'

'Squeeze, squeeze! Push up, push up!' urges the loud parent, bending down on his haunches. The confused back line of nine-year-olds fails to heed the warning. Danny Coles may be bawled at by Brian Tinnion for not responding to such a warning later in the day, but he is a mature 24-year-old professional footballer. When an adult shouts at a child as he might if they needed to hurl themselves out of a first-storey burning building, kids tend to get fazed. A goal is conceded. 'That was a joke!' he bawls. 'You've got to move in line!' He shakes his head in utter disbelief at their ill-discipline. He also looks around the parents for support, which isn't forthcoming.

'What does "squeeze" mean to an eight-year-old?' Bob asks me. 'It's something you do to a tube of toothpaste.'

Junior football is Bob's passion, spurred by his own sons' involvement but also by a sense of social duty, yet the attitude of some parents sickens him. 'It hurts to see dads having a go at their sons because theoretically they've made a mistake. It hurts to see adults shouting and screaming at kids.' We do what all parents should: watch the match, have a chat, applaud the players when they do something well, shout 'hard luck' when it doesn't quite work, offer words of encouragement when they take a knock and gee up the substitutes who are itching to take part.

We both note a player in the opposing team. You can read so much in the way children play sport. Any half-decent psychologist could map out the lives ahead of them. The boy is slight, quiet but not shy, has superb control and is precise with his thought-out passes. Not as boisterous as most, he commands respect because his actions speak louder than words. Bob habitually praises both sides, and when the boy goes on a mazy dribble and shoots narrowly wide, he claps and says, 'Well done.' One of 'our' parents cranes his neck with incredulity.

The bawling parent has now turned puce. A penalty has been missed. 'It's ridiculous!' he says, turning his head away in disgust, screwing his face up as if a noxious smell has wafted up his nose.

Walking behind the goal, out of the earshot of such parents, we ponder these reactions. 'Don't get me wrong, this isn't a bad club,' says Bob. 'I've seen much worse behaviour than this from other teams.'

Hadley bring on a diminutive blond-haired boy who is noticeably smaller than the rest. Bob tells me about the boy's awful health problems – a kidney complaint that has required dialysis treatment. He is eight but looks no bigger than most four-year-olds. He bounces off the other boys, eagerly flying into tackles he can't hope to win, and tries in vain to influence the game. He shows wonderful spirit. It is a touching sight and I want to cry. Bob does later, when we recall our day together.

Out here in the countryside, watching seven- to nine-year-olds sampling their first taste of football, hopefully beginning a lifelong learning path in sport and health – this is the true power of football in action. Children learning the rudiments of sport and pitting their skills against opponents: challenging, jumping, running, shooting, passing, helping your mates, celebrating goals, sharing your sorrows, saying three cheers at the end of the game, hopefully ignoring the excesses of their parents. Hopefully. These are things that make football a true national sport. It is easy to play, requires relatively little equipment, and all shapes and sizes have attributes needed in a team. Its rules are straightforward, and everyone is now encouraged to get involved. What happens later in the day at professional matches – the players, the eager fans, the commercialism, the social context – has no real meaning unless it is bred in children at this age. Unless they understand the sport.

So what does matchday mean to Bob Marley? 'It's everything,' he explains. 'It's judgement day. I was brought up in the era when football was only played on Saturdays. Everybody kicked off at three o'clock, and at twenty to five you saw the scores, so Saturday is *the* football day for me. Non-League football still revolves around that. You don't go shopping, you don't mend the car, you don't mow the lawns; Saturday at three o'clock is all about football. Whether I play, watch, coach, manage or support, Saturday is football.'

Bob grew up in a mining community in Staffordshire. 'Life was bloody hard. We lived in a council house and Dad was a miner. They fought for everything we had, and when you fight hard for something you tend not to let it go, so you don't piss it up the wall.' They had second-hand Christmas presents, scraped together tiny lumps of coke from slag heaps for fuel and welded together old bits of soap. A teenager in the economically depressed late 1970s and early 1980s, an era when the West Midlands industrial landscape was reduced largely to rubble and jobs (and therefore respect) peeled away, Bob saw many of his mates fall by the wayside. 'A lot of kids I grew up with were into drugs and you saw them go downhill. Some ended up in prison. You have life choices. I was lucky I had someone to guide me.' He thanks the headmaster and PE teacher at Kingsmead Comprehensive School in Hednesford for steering him along the right path. Bob has never drunk, doesn't eat fatty foods and works out regularly. But his parents were key. 'The attitude was, if you've got something to give, then give it. We were community people.' Bob's father was a Labour parish councillor, a Geordie brought up on socialist traditions. 'He gave a lot.' Bob's mum was a Cannock girl who always washed the kit and did what she could. 'That rubbed off on me, and hopefully my lads will pick up on that from me. Life is about giving, and that starts with seven-year-olds like these lads.'

To Bob, this is the most important part of his work as a local football club director – fostering a love of the game in the community, which will hopefully result in a spin-off for Worcester City FC. There is practical and financial sense to this abstract theory. 'We can't keep buying players or hoping our ageing fans will stay with us,' he points out. 'It doesn't work like that.'

Bob failed to make it as a professional footballer despite trials and training sessions with Wolves, Bournemouth and Colchester. 'I wasn't good enough, was I? No excuses. It was telling me something.' Instead he went to agricultural college, then set up a garden centre business and worked himself silly doing 100-hour weeks until he blacked out and drove his car into another vehicle. A lifestyle adjustment was needed, and he moved into a different line of work.

He moved to Worcester in 1993 and in 2000 was invited to join the board at Worcester City by his accountant. After being asked to shape a five-year plan to develop the business, Bob soon realised that commercialism was only part of the picture; what the club really needed to do was something it had conspicuously failed to do: reach into the community to find the players and fans of the future. 'Being a director wasn't about getting my name in the club programme,' he says. 'Building a big football development policy so in five years from now half the team is made up of local lads was. Building a policy that gives girls equal opportunity to play football as boys in this city is. Building a development policy, which means we have disability players and all sexes, shapes, creeds and colours playing football in our community, is. That is what it is all about.' Non-League football isn't noted for such breadth of thinking. Creating a winning team and putting bums on seat are the pressing priorities. But, says Bob in reply, sweeping his arm across the field in front of him and the eager youngsters on it, 'without it there is no football'.

The final whistle blows and the angry parent storms past us in dismay. 'Absolute madness – we battered them but lost,' he says, pointing over his shoulder towards the pitch. Bob doesn't take issue. Instead he heads for Sam, who came off early but has enjoyed his footy game. He excitedly talks over a couple of incidents with his dad and wants a quick cuddle – affirmation that all is well. It is a touching moment. Sam will stay with Mandy, older brother Sebastian will spend the rest of the day with Bob. Despite their marital difficulties, this potentially awkward handover is handled with admirable dignity by both parents. On top of everything else, Saturday is the day Bob has one of his kids.

Football helped to break up his marriage. It's not the only reason – Bob and Mandy, like so many couples, simply drifted apart – but he acknowledges it as a contributory factor. It is something he shares with many of the interviewees for this book. Married to the job, married to the club. Glib remarks that just aren't funny any more.

As we make our way under the rope (Bob stopping to thank the farmer who maintains the field for them), through the gates and back on to the road, Seb is full of what the day will hold. Bob Marley, football club development director, businessman, fun run organiser and parent, is about to adopt another guise – coach.

10.50 A.M.: BEING POSITIVE Back in Handsworth I have left Phil Hamilton to prepare for Fentham FC's matches. I have driven along the Soho Road and pulled into Holyhead School, which is, I guess, no more than half a mile or so from the Hawthorns, the home of West Bromwich Albion, whose ground I know so well. I'm looking for PC Alison Geddes, who runs the Handsworth Youth and Community Project here on Saturday mornings. It isn't strictly a football scheme: it was set up by Alison and a colleague, Dan Jones, from the police station around the corner as a 'diversionary tactic'. It is where the Positive Futures League, which Phil used to run in Aston, has now moved. There are no results to these games, but no matches anywhere will be as important as the ones played on these pitches today.

I find Alison in a playground organising a five-a-side game for a group of twelve-year-old boys. She is warm, friendly and dressed in a tracksuit rather than a police uniform. 'We just noticed there were a lot of kids hanging around being moved on by residents and who seemed to be mainly kicking a ball against the wall with nothing to do,' says Alison. Initially based at Holyhead Leisure Centre, they called the scheme a football project (there was no mention of police involvement) to get some youngsters along.

'A lot of them didn't trust the police for different reasons,' she explains. Sixty-five kids turned up to the first night. 'They recognised us as police officers even though we weren't in uniform. "You're Babylon,

you're the Feds, we're not having anything to do with you," they said.'
The level of mistrust between the youth of Handsworth and the police is
notorious. 'But we kept them together and said, "It's free. We don't have
to do it. This is a way for you to get good facilities, have somewhere to go,
have something to do. It's up to you. It might reduce the chance of you
being a victim or offender. Give us two weeks. If you don't like it, we
won't carry on."'

That was four years ago. It has since expanded into a youth club on
Saturday mornings and a Thursday-night football scheme primarily
aimed at giving local eight- to eighteen-year-olds the chance to
participate on a regular basis. It received initial funding of £28,000 from a
regeneration budget, which they used to hire staff from the local area. At
the project, Alison charges 50p; none of the food or drink costs more than
10p. The rooms they hire can cost up to £50 an hour, but they get them free
and rely on donations.

Alison showed me around. The project normally takes place in two
huge halls, but a wedding reception is being held in one of them today, so
while some are inside using a DJ mixing desk, playing table tennis and
using the computer and indoor gym equipment, another group is playing
five-a-side football outside with, literally, jumpers for goalposts. 'The kids
around here are lovely,' insists Alison, 'but there are always negative
images of Handsworth. It is always associated with crime rather than
other positive aspects of the community.' So much so that when a group
of outreach workers brought some boys from another Birmingham
district here to play football they refused to get off the bus. 'They were
absolutely petrified about coming to Handsworth because they thought
they would get stabbed or shot,' says Alison, who eventually persuaded
them to get out and play. They have now formed good links, but the
impression is still negative. 'Every time you see Handsworth on the news
it is usually a murder or something serious. We want to get positive press
for the area. The kids of Handsworth are good kids. There are some bad
lads, but we need to break down the barriers, build the friendships, and
work as a community to succeed.'

Not that Alison has a long-lasting loyalty to the area. She was born in
Bolton, and moved here for love. Her husband is from West Bromwich,
and when she moved down from Lancashire she gave up her job as a

printer to become a policewoman. 'You'll be good at it,' she was told. She is excellent. A couple of girls, no older than eight or nine years I'd guess, come up to us while we're talking. They are indeed lovely girls, polite, charming, willing and enthusiastic … but a bit bored. Alison suggests some things they can do. She has a rare ability to get on with people. Even though she is a policewoman in an area where there is deep suspicion of law and order, the kids cuddle up and talk to her like she was their mum or an aunt. 'I feel like they are mine,' she confides. 'If I had to give it up or move on, or I decided to start a family and had to leave, I would miss them so much.'

The brutal reality is she has to steer them on to the right path before the gangs look to recruit, which, as Phil Hamilton pointed out earlier, starts around the age of fourteen. Some of the kids have shocking role models. Their dads have either never been around or show their faces only when they please. To easily impressed teenagers, the gang leaders, who swagger around with the trappings of life, fill the void. They are the ones who are seen to be doing well. But, Alison reminds me, 'Football has a powerful sway in Handsworth. Most of the male population and some of the females are football daft. Football keeps them happy for hours. It is a simple game to play. It just needs a bit of organising and controlling to keep it focused.'

West Brom defender Darren Moore, who was born in Handsworth and went to Holyhead School, helps out. He is a rare player, a giant of a man – nicknamed Big Dave by Baggies fans because he resembles the outsized imaginary character in a Pot Noodle advert a few years back – and a committed Christian with the heart and tenacity to do this challenging work. He runs a burgeoning project called Faith in Football and coaches here on Thursday evenings. 'The kids love it because he is one of them,' says Alison. 'He made it. They can see that if you want it bad enough then you can achieve things in life. Darren is walking, talking proof. He is fantastic with the kids; nothing is too much trouble. He's a godsend.' Faith in Football is limited to a maximum of 100 children who play six-a-side games every Thursday evening. 'Everyone who works on the scheme is a volunteer and works for free. At the project we will push them to do something to the best of their abilities, whether it is football, dance, music, whatever.'

It isn't about talent-spotting, but one of the players who attended the Thursday-night scheme was Francino Francis, who was signed by Tamworth FC and has since moved to Stoke City. 'It is good to see them go on and do something constructive,' Alison continues. 'We cannot claim credit for his development, but hopefully he got something from coming to this group.'

Support from West Brom just up the road – again, like Villa in Aston – is piecemeal. The club's Football in the Community programme has a good reputation though, and they are prepared to put their faces around the community, including Handsworth, which is appreciated. 'They run free soccer schools for Handsworth kids,' notes Alison. 'And they give the scheme free tickets for matches, so it gives them the chance to watch a Premier League match, which is something they may not do again.' And that, as Phil Hamilton also noted, is a problem. Football is too expensive. Could most people around here afford to watch the Premier League football on their doorstep? 'No, I would say not. This is a recognised deprived area. Spending £30 on a football match just isn't done.' Albion used to do 'kids for a quid', but that was only if you bought a season ticket and were accompanied by an adult, and it stopped when the club regained their Premier League status. Now that they can put bums on seats they don't need the poor from Handsworth.

We walk over to the Positive Futures League, which is taking place on the school's astroturf pitch. It isn't an offenders scheme as such. But children who come here are often referrals from schools that think they need some extracurricular stimulation. It's open to anyone from Handsworth or any child visiting the area. The scheme moved here in March 2005 because there were too many players for the one Phil Hamilton ran at Aston Park. Some 100 youths aged between twelve and fourteen are taking part in six-a-side games which are rotated so everyone gets a game over a three-hour period. Kevin Brookes, a tall, muscular local man, is in charge. He has two assistants and a few fifteen- to sixteen-year-olds who are refereeing, providing other support and working towards getting coaching qualifications. None of the players is wearing a local team shirt. Not West Brom, Villa or even Birmingham City. Arsenal, Chelsea and Manchester United, yes, but there is little evidence of bonding with local clubs.

Positive Futures is a joint partnership between Sport England, the Youth Justice Board and the United Kingdom Anti-Drugs Co-ordination Unit. The aim of the initiative is to use sport to reduce anti-social behaviour, as well as crime and drug use, among ten- to sixteen-year-olds within local neighbourhoods. Since it was launched in 2000 some 70,000 young people have been involved in Positive Futures, half of them on a regular basis. The social agencies it works with – youth offending services, police, Connexions, drug action teams, community premiership and local authorities – indicate that it has helped three-quarters of the participants by raising their aspirations and self-esteem. In the areas where it has operated it is believed to have contributed to bringing down levels of crime and anti-social behaviour, lowered levels of drug use and truancy, improved behaviour in schools and increased sports activity.

In Handsworth the games are played with a lot of rough and tumble. There's certainly more commitment than at other levels of youth football played on matchdays. 'It's good,' says Kevin. 'The boys we are working with are improving.' I can sense a 'but' coming on. 'But a lot of kids lack parental role models. Getting here for ten o'clock is something for them to aim for.' Even getting the youths here into formal sports structures is difficult. Many Handsworth youths won't even go to Aston, Newtown or Lozells, or vice versa, for what Alison calls 'territorial issues'. And we're not talking about football rivalry here, but gang culture and the fear of shootings and stabbings. Alison believes organised football matches might be a 'tool' to break this down, but that looks some way down the road.

The boys here are not all charmers. It's mostly tracksuits and cheap bling. It feels like a rough, tough environment. As the session comes to a close, Alison asks Kevin to make sure that the field is cleared before he leaves. Last week a Bangladeshi boy got 'a right kicking' here. It wasn't linked to the scheme, but it did happen on space they had used. But they aren't all bad. When one of the boys accidentally thunders a ball into the back of my head he cheekily inches towards me with his hands in the air. I go to chase him for a laugh, and everyone smiles.

Both schemes, the Handsworth Youth and Community Project and the Handsworth Positive Futures League, are starved of cash. Alison is hoping a bid for a BBC Children in Need grant will be successful. I wonder what, say, a week's wages of one of Albion's players might do for this scheme – £10,000, maybe £20,000? Kevin's eyes light up at the possibilities. 'All my prayers would be answered,' he says. 'What could we do? Lots and lots, and it would all go to benefit these kids.' Kevin is also disappointed that West Brom, whose ground is so close to this league, won't send scouts along to look at players he has identified.

As I walk back to my car I think about the language Alison used – the police known as the Feds or Babylon. Such terms would be alien down the road outside the Hawthorns. How many West Brom supporters, who are mainly white and travel into the area from the Black Country and beyond, would understand either? As I get into my car and drive along the A41 heading away from Birmingham, past the corrugated-iron shop fronts – even a Lloyds pharmacy, usually one of the bright high-street shops, is boarded up – out along the Birmingham Road past the Hawthorns and its pink T-Mobile hoardings, I feel I have passed through an invisible barrier. This is now Sandwell, the Black Country. Around the ground everyone is white. The club shop looks like it is doing brisk business. Lots of T-Mobile sponsored bags full of club gear.

It's a case of chickens coming home to roost. In my late teens I started a supporters club for West Brom in Worcester. We did things correctly: put out adverts, got lots of members, had a committee, organised coach travel and attended meetings with other supporters clubs. It was 1977, the summer of punk. In football a chaotic bunch came together at Albion – the Three Degrees: initially Laurie Cunningham and Cyrille Regis, and later, when Ron Atkinson became manager, Brendon Batson. They were the footballing equivalent of a punk band, fast-flowing with unpredictable patterns of play. They were the first trio of top black British players making waves and playing great football at one club.

Tim Lewis (whose name will feature later in this book) and I were the only teenagers at the meetings, and the only ones with enough gumption to ask awkward questions to invited guests. I recall the club's then chairman Bert Millichip coming along and us quizzing him on what steps the club was taking to attract the burgeoning multi-ethnic communities on the club's doorstep, given that we had three successful black players at the club. He fumbled for words. 'Well, isn't it about time there was a strategy?' During the break I was rounded upon for being so disrespectful. I don't recall going to any other meetings afterwards. What was the point?

West Brom fans are not, by and large, racist – certainly not openly so. But nearly three decades on from the days of the Three Degrees, here I am driving towards the M5 wondering how much the good work of Phil Hamilton, Alison Geddes, Kevin Brookes and their socially useful schemes could do with, say, one week's worth of Nwankwo Kanu's wages. The irony is that, unwittingly, for little reward because it is not their main focus, they are doing football's bidding: stimulating an interest in the game, the way I and millions of other British men learned to love football, albeit in less socially challenging circumstances. The clubs don't court the fans in communities in their immediate environs because they don't see them as 'their' type of people. They aren't the ones who can buy the season tickets, the expensive merchandise or the Sky Sports subscriptions, and they are a world away from the cosy images the game wants to portray of energetic teenagers drinking Coke and chomping burgers while watching football matches with their dads. It makes you wonder what game we are playing.

10.55 A.M.: BOYERS, BOYERS, WHAT'S THE SCORE? John Boyers's next priority is to visit Roy Unwin's widow, Joan. Her daughter, Liz, is travelling up from Reading, so John wants to make sure she's not alone this morning and that he is at hand to offer whatever help he can and to deliver a few words of comfort.

We speed off in search of Manor Road, Salford. Praise be to sat-nav – the polite lady guides us there in minutes. I don't follow John into the house. That would be intrusive, maybe even (unintentionally) voyeuristic. Instead, I sit in the car and muse about John's work and sports chaplaincy. Indeed, how John came to do this valuable work in the first place.

John was born on 28 March 1949 in Grimsby. He grew up as a madly keen Grimsby Town fan (I had clocked the GTFC sticker in his study at home) and was a Blundell Park regular from a young age, remembering future England stars like Kevin Keegan and Ray Clemence playing against the Mariners for Scunthorpe United in their youth and, further back, a promising young full-back called Graham Taylor. He went to a teacher training college in Nottingham (where he met his wife Anne at a Christian Union meeting) and returned to Lincolnshire to teach geography at Cleethorpes Boys Grammar School and Wintringham School in Grimsby.

In 1976, at the age of 27, John changed tack. He had felt himself drawn towards the Christian ministry. 'There was no "Road to Damascus" experience,' he recalls. 'It was a gradual process.' He went to theological college in Northwood in London. Anne found a teaching job in Watford, where they lived. A year later John became a student minister at St James Road Baptist Church close to Watford FC.

Another Lincolnshire lad had also moved to Watford. Graham Taylor, the once-promising ex-Grimsby Town player, had made a name for himself as manager of Lincoln City and had been snapped up by Watford, who, although languishing in the Fourth Division at the time, were being backed by Elton John's wealth. They were also in pursuit of bigger gates and were set to implement some progressive thinking to help them achieve this goal. They were particularly keen to build bridges with their local community.

Coincidentally, both Mike Pusey, club chaplain at Aldershot FC at the time, and professional footballer Alan West, who was a practising Christian, came to do talks at St James Road Church around the same time. They planted the seed in John's mind to approach Watford about becoming their club chaplain. 'I thought, "Wow, is God trying to say something?"' There were a few clergymen at other clubs, other than Pusey – John Jackson at Leeds United, Jack Bingham at Stockport County – but these tended to be friends the club called upon to do weddings and funerals and generally to be around if needed. Graham Taylor was open to wider ideas. 'He saw the opportunity to build care and support into the club. Watford pioneered the idea of a really involved chaplain who wasn't just available but was actively involved in meeting players and other staff on the training ground and at matches. I would be on hand if needed rather than available for hire. I didn't have a manual to follow. No one came to me and said, "This is how you do it." I had to figure out a way forward. I saw football as a secular congregation and was encouraged by Graham Taylor, who wanted to foster this sense of camaraderie and of family and friendship within the club.'

Taylor is a much-maligned character, largely because of his ill-fated spell as England manager between 1990 and 1993 – although, interestingly, his statistical record is better than many other England bosses – but he has an enviable reputation for being a rare free-thinker in football. He is lucid and capable of seeing a bigger picture. At Lincoln he took players to meet fans in factory canteens. 'They come to our workplace, why don't we go to theirs?' was Taylor's logic.

At Watford the church and the football club came together under him. 'We were doing community stuff – youth groups, mum and toddler playgroups, all sorts of contact with the community – so it was logical to include the football club,' John says. Watford did things most clubs now consider to be the norm. They had a family enclosure, a crèche and a community programme. Everything and anything that could build bridges between the club and the community was tried at a time when most football clubs scoffed at such fanciful notions. They thought it was weak. John describes the club, without hesitation, as 'groundbreakers'.

11 A.M.: BUBBLING ALONG In Kidderminster Brian Murdoch's soup and cottage pies are bubbling along nicely. Steve, a giant of a man who has worked for Brian for 28 years, wraps his burly arms around a tray of pies and lowers them for my inspection. They look gorgeous. I want to dig in immediately. In two hours' time they will be ready for transfer to the ground.

This sort of catering is dismissed by the large chains who own the contracts for most of our major football clubs as quaint, not based in the real world. People like Brian, they argue, just don't have their problems. He just doesn't know their business. In fact, Brian knows their trade rather well.

Over a deserved mid-morning cuppa, Brian tells me his story. Born and bred in Wolverhampton, he did his National Service in the army, enjoyed it ('the best years of my life') and signed up with the Staffordshire Regiment for a further nine years when they doubled his salary. In 1962, at the age of 23, he bought himself out early. He moved to Kidderminster, which was then a quiet market town with a policeman on a pulpit controlling the town-centre traffic, to start up a food-vending business. He had worked for a friend of a friend once when he came home on leave, selling hot dogs in the streets. It was an unsocial job, mainly late-night, pub-kicking-out-time work, and hot street food was fairly new. 'It was taking off, though,' Brian says. 'I could see the potential.' Brian established kiosks in Kidderminster and Worcester, one he still owns on the quayside at the Brummies' day out town of Stourport, and others in Bromsgrove, Redditch and Malvern. He sold Westlers hot dogs – remember them? – which were boiled in small vats with stewed onions and pre-packed burgers from small push trolleys. His promise to those who worked for him was 'I'll pay your mortgage'. At today's prices, he was taking £20,000 a weekend.

As for football, well, it's hard to explain how Spartan catering at football matches was when Brian started at Kidderminster Harriers in 1962. At Worcester City I can recall kiosks in each corner of the ground, but they only really sold tea, coffee and maybe Bovril. If you were lucky you might be able to buy a bar of chocolate or a packet of crisps. Nothing else. Burgers were barely heard of. 'Before people like me came along they used to slice up luncheon meat in a bap and sell them as burgers,' says Brian. My first memory of the word 'burger' was when I bought a packet of crisps (ah, now I remember – I used to bring my own food in) at a small shop opposite Worcester City's St George's Lane ground, now long gone. They sold hamburger flavour crisps – whatever that meant. I vaguely recall them tasting of onion. I was none the wiser as to what a hamburger was after chomping them. Something to do with the German city, I guessed.

At Kidderminster's ground, Aggborough, which in those days was something of an inferior club to Worcester – they even had a cycling track encircling the pitch and virtually no terracing behind either goal – Brian was charged £30 a season rent, which he clawed back by charging 6d for a cup of tea. Ever adventurous, Brian's early claim to fame was as the first man to bring the polystyrene cup to England. He'd been to a catering exhibition in Glasgow which showed off this simple invention. Before polystyrene there were plastic cups, which were hopeless at holding in the heat. Basically, unless you were impervious to pain, wore wicket-keeping gloves to the footy or didn't mind the skin peeling away from your fingertips, you couldn't hold on to a hot drink long enough either to drink the contents or get back to your seat.

Having brought quality cups to Kiddy, Brian set about the food. He had opened a café in the town on the same corner where his wine bar sits today. He'd acquired the building for the princely sum of £750 during a period of slum clearance. Always a man to spot an opportunity, with the town centre being rebuilt, he realised the potential of a greasy spoon café catering for the men doing the work. 'Kidderminster is built on my bacon sandwiches,' he observes with a laugh. He made his own soup too, which sold well, and one day he decided to take some along to the football. It sold like, well, hot soup. Word spread, and he built up a devoted clientele. The café lasted twelve years. Brian then opened a wine bar, (they were rather fashionable in the early 1980s), and bought another chunk of the street to build a 24-bedroom hotel.

Miraculously, around the same time Kidderminster Harriers took off. They became a big non-League club, progressing from the Southern League into the Alliance Premier (now known as the Conference), and started to attract decent-sized gates of 1,500 to 2,000, more for bigger matches. Aggborough was expanded and reshaped. The cycling track disappeared and covered stands were built at both ends. Brian increased the number of kiosks in the ground to four. He gained an enviable reputation whenever Kidderminster went on a remarkable cup run. In 1994, when they reached the FA Cup fifth round, beating Birmingham City and Preston North End along the way before losing narrowly to West Ham at Aggborough. 'It should have been our best ever day but everyone was too engrossed watching the football and didn't want to lose their place to bother eating or drinking. We did no better with a 7,500 crowd than we did with 4,000.' His facilities weren't up to it either. Brian recalls the electrics tripping during the West Ham game. 'West Ham scored when I was trying to find the trip switch – I will always remember that.'

His best takings came a couple of seasons later when the big Boxing Day derby against local rivals Bromsgrove Rovers was delayed by an hour to allow a section of the frozen pitch to thaw. To fill in the time, fans inside, and those who smartly hadn't paid their money outside, ate and drank. Big bucks for Brian, who cleverly served those outside through a fence.

In 1997 he won a *Total Football* magazine award for his soup, but his repertoire has now expanded. The cottage pies were introduced when the club entered the Football League, and the replacement of a terraced area along the railway side of the ground with the new, seated East Stand gave him a chance to install better facilities and make curries, chillies, pasta and chow mein dishes. He now has £40,000 worth of catering equipment in the two kiosks on that side of the ground, and his own signage: Brian Murdoch's Quality Fayre. For a short time he also did the club's corporate catering, but lost the contract, which still smarts to this day.

As Brian and his team load the trays and cauldrons into a van and a car for the short trip to Aggborough, he runs through the logistics of his efforts. In order to make money from the concession he pays to Kidderminster he has just 23 League games, three pre-season friendlies, hopefully a few cup ties and some West Brom reserve fixtures which are sometimes played at Aggborough. That's 30 to 35 games on average gates of 2,400 during a three-hour opening period. In other words, roughly 90 hours of selling time per season. 'It's not much when you consider the time that goes into preparing the food,' says Brian. He has to work hard to make it pay.

As Brian double-checks to ensure all his staff will be in today, my mind wanders back to a football catering conference (yep, they exist) I covered a few years ago for a football magazine. Brian, I found out during our discussion, had been there too. It was a Mad Hatters' Tea Party, a nether world of mindless corporatism. A man from Mars held a chocolate bar aloft and triumphantly declared it to be 'perfect football food': edible on the move (he showed us how), hand-sized (he slipped it into his pocket) and tasty (he screwed his face up in a 'yummy' expression). Overall, 'a superb piece of technology'. The delegates marvelled; I started to laugh. Rangers' catering manager bubbled about 'brand identity'. His Blue Nose burgers, he said, had gone through the roof. Why? Because people identified with them. The cartons had little club logos on them. They also help to bolster sectarianism and are just about the only food fans can buy inside the ground, which may explain their sales figures. But it wasn't the time or place for such conjecture. Another caterer, who'd devised a spring roll on a stick, boasted as if he had split the atom. The audience simpered.

I can't wait to see how Brian Murdoch sells his wares. One thing's for sure, it won't be because of branding. It will all be down to the quality of his food.

11.10 A.M.: GAFFER TALK Bristol City manager Brian Tinnion's working day starts at the training ground in Leigh Woods, a semi-rural location southwest of Bristol and a five-minute drive from the club's home at Ashton Gate. He isn't coaching this morning but watching City's U-18s academy team take on Southampton, who are the FA Youth Cup finalists.

It is a pleasant early-April morning, and this is a wonderful setting for a competitive FA Premier League Academy game and a relaxed way for the gaffer to start the day. Brian chats to other members of his managerial team: assistant Keith Millen, who is a Vinnie Jones soundalike (thankfully without the devilish demeanour) and was youth coach here last season, and development coach Shaun Taylor. Brian cut his managerial teeth at this level, coaching the youth team while coming to the end of his playing days. Many managers wouldn't dream of watching their academy teams on matchdays, but Brian is keen to monitor their progress. He has already thrown a few into his first team. Dave Cotterill, Scott Golbourne and Cole Skuse have all been taken out of the academy side and added to Tinnion's first-team squad in recent weeks. Another homegrown player, twenty-year-old striker Leroy Lita, is City's top scorer and a much-prized asset. Nodding towards the pitch, Brian, who is dressed in a suit, smart shirt but no tie, says he has known all these boys for a long time. 'I coached Cole Skuse when he was fourteen,' he tells me.

A familiar off-the-record gripe from academy staff (I know, I've interviewed enough of them) is that the people who manage the senior teams neither understand nor appreciate the work they do. Too many, it is argued, have never coached at their level. Jobs are given to big-name ex-players who go straight into top-line management without earning their stripes with the youth teams. Therefore they have little or no interest in developing the club's own talent, preferring to dip into the transfer market and blaming their board for lack of funds or ambition or both if they fail to give them what they perceive to be enough money. Brian Tinnion is a bit of both. A big name in Bristol for sure, but he earned his managerial stripes when he was playing. He used to come down here on matchday mornings when he was a player. 'I understand what the academy is all about and what they are trying to do. It has been important this season. The youth-team manager

[Tony Fawthrop] moans that they lose players, but you want that to happen. You want players to progress – that's the idea of an academy. It proves it is working.'

He keeps his distance, he doesn't stand with the coaches, but this is the wholesome side of the job: working with young players, coaching them, seeing them progress. 'They know me and I know them,' says Brian. 'They know I care and have worked with them, and that I am fair. They might not always like the decisions I make – that's the job – but they know I will always do the best for the club.'

His big test, of course, will come later in the day, when City take on Port Vale. A win will nudge them near to the play-off places, which would be an achievement in his first season in charge. The atmosphere at Ashton Gate promises to be tense. City supporters, more than most, expect their club to be doing better. City have spent all but one of the past ten years at League One level, and there is simmering anger. The club has accrued large debts too, and Brian, who took charge in the summer of 2004, is working on a reduced budget. 'The expectation is massive, and they expect us to win promotion,' he acknowledges. '[The fans] think we are bigger than anyone else in this league, but the fact is we're not. We have financial problems like every other club in this league, so we can't bring big players in.'

Brian hails from Durham and was a Newcastle United supporter. He played 32 games for them before being transferred to Bradford City for £150,000 in 1989. Four years later, after 145 games for them and 22 goals, City splashed out £180,000 for him. Brian was a popular player here, making 495 appearances in 12 seasons. He scored a spectacular goal in one of Bristol City's more memorable victories of recent times, in 1994, when they dumped Liverpool out of the FA Cup at Anfield. He doesn't feel he has been given any leeway by the supporters. 'Every manager I have played under here has had to deal with that, and if you can't accept that responsibility you shouldn't take the job because it can put you under. If the pressure and intensity wasn't there, the job wouldn't have the same appeal.' Blooding younger players has helped, though. 'They see the academy players as their own and give them time. It has been important this season.'

Football management is a precarious occupation. It's not for someone who values job security, and it's not for the faint-hearted. The average British manager lasts eighteen months, and proof of its tenuous nature is standing in the Southampton technical area this morning in the shape of Steve Wigley. He replaced Paul Sturrock as Saints manager early in the 2004/05 season, but his position was the subject of weekly speculation, and in December 2004 he was replaced by Harry Redknapp. Wigley has now returned to his job at youth level, although it has been mooted that England rugby coach Sir Clive Woodward is favourite to get it after the 2005 summer British Lions tour, which Woodward is managing. Wigley goes about his task with utter enthusiasm and dedication, and his side will ultimately beat Bristol City with two late goals this morning.

Although watching the youth team is a normal part of Brian's home matchday routine, away games are different. Although there have been fewer overnight stays this season due to cutbacks. If the trip is more than two and a half to three hours away, the players will usually stop over. Brian prefers this. 'It gives the players a chance to get the journey out of their legs,' he says. 'It's good for the players to get away, to be able to get a good night's sleep. They like going away on the Friday and getting prepared. But there are restrictions and you have to deal with it.'

I wonder whether it is harder to prepare the players for home or away games. There have been loads of lurid tales down the years of bored, cooped-up footballers escaping to go on the lash the evening before games. 'No, it's fine,' Brian replies. 'You can eat with them, make sure they go to bed and have a meeting the next morning to explain what you expect from them, and to go through [the opposition's] strengths and weaknesses. They have all conducted themselves well this season. They're no trouble. They've knuckled down and our away form has been good.'

Management has come earlier than expected for Brian at a club which is dear to his heart. He also played earlier in the season but decided to focus solely on management after eighteen games, has tried to introduce a new way of thinking. Players used to drink and eat what they liked; now they are breathalysed and focus more on nutrition. 'There are fines in place if they are found with alcohol on their breath. We've tested them a lot this season, but not one of them has failed yet.' None of them has been reported for a night out on the tiles either. 'They know what we expect,' says Brian. He admits there was a drinking culture at the club, not to mention within the wider game. 'We are trying to change the culture. Trying to get the youth-team players to look up to the first-team players so they don't abuse themselves with alcohol or anything else. If players don't want to change then they have to go. They leave, and you bring people in who do want to be part of the culture. You aren't going to change it overnight, but I am determined to change things. I want them to be able to give 120 per cent and be physically and mentally able to do that every time you ask.'

This is a modern approach to football management. Brian has taken his coaching badges up to UEFA A level. The next tier, in fact the highest level, is the Pro Licence, a qualification designed primarily for would-be Premiership and international managers that in England is available only to existing managers, which means they have to do it by distance training. 'It's very difficult to find the time to take it,' says Brian, who is nonetheless keen to take his pro-licence badge.

Budgetwise he is having to work with what he has got rather than buy expensive players. 'The squad has been trimmed,' he tells me. 'We have had to use our academy. The manager here last season [Danny Wilson] spent £800,000 on players. We missed out in the play-off finals so the finances simply aren't there this year.' He has just eighteen outfield players in his squad; last year it was 28. 'It is a massively reduced budget. But this club means a heck of a lot to me. I've been here for twelve years and I'm going to make sure I'm successful.'

Such talk is cheap in football. Brian knows he will be judged on results, and it's something he prepared for in his late twenties. He lodged next to the then club scout Tony Fawthrop, the current youth-team coach, and went on scouting trips with him. 'I enjoyed watching the way teams played and the different systems they used. I have always watched games.' He is on the managerial learning curve and is still getting used to the torturous hours consumed by scouting trips, watching players and opposition teams, and the hidden stuff, such as talking to agents and players you are looking to buy and sell. But managing footballers, he insists, isn't that difficult. 'Players aren't stupid – they know when they aren't doing it. Managers don't drop players, players drop players, because if they play to the standards we set they get picked. If they don't, they get left out. It's simple.'

Today he has asked all his players to eat a low-fat carbohydrate meal before midday. They must be at the ground by 1.15 p.m., and he will do a brief team talk at 1.30. They then do warm-ups on the pitch and have any medical treatment they need before being briefed once again at a quarter to three. All the detailed tactical talk and work for the Port Vale game has been done in the past couple of days. 'Nothing is left to matchday other than going out and getting the three points,' says Brian, before leaving for a private chat with his managerial team. He will head back home soon to pick up Catherine and return to Ashton Gate.

A few weeks ago he did a question-and-answer session with supporters in a club bar. He is determined to run a tight ship and be open with the fans who have backed him so far. But matchday is all about getting those precious three points.

11.15 A.M.: 'GOOD MORNING, MR CHAIRMAN' Lincoln City chairman Rob Bradley rushes out to meet me before I have had a chance to get out of the car. In haste, I grab my things, and in Rob's car we head off to a college where Lincoln City's youth team are playing.

Rob is dressed to kill. He looks younger than when we previously met some four years ago, not long after he had taken the helm at Lincoln. He's had a bit of an image makeover – clothes can take years off people – but I also guess he has grown into the job too, and is finding circumstances a lot easier. Back then, Lincoln looked doomed. They were deep in debt (£1.4 million worth) and fighting for their lives near the foot of the Third Division. They survived, finishing eighteenth, but a year later they descended to 22nd and their debts had grown (£1.8 million), and with the collapse of ITV Digital they had no option but to go into administration. Rob told fans at the final home game of the 2001/02 season against Rochdale that it could be their last ever match. Twice that summer they went to the High Court to prevent the club from being wound up. Swingeing cuts were made, including sacking manager Alan Buckley and quashing the contracts of several players, and they agreed a CVA (Creditors Voluntary Agreement) with those they owed money to, which squashed the debts and allowed the club to leave administration five days before the start of the 2002/03 season. Incredibly, Lincoln made the play-offs in each of the next two seasons, losing to Bournemouth 5–2 in the

2003 final and 4–3 on aggregate in the semi-finals to Huddersfield in 2004. Even more remarkably, they made a profit of £250,000 for the 2002/03 season. Rob confides he is about to announce record profits of £735,000 for 2003/04.

Throughout our day together we will discuss how this was achieved and what a chairman voted in as the supporters' representative on the board does that is different from most football club chairmen. First, though, we have a youth team game to go to, and judging by Rob's urgency I gather we are behind schedule.

Not many chairmen would bother doing this – in the course of writing this book I went to four youth games, and other than Bob Marley at Worcester City, who coaches anyway, there were no directors present at any of them – but Rob believes it is essential to show his face occasionally, to demonstrate support and to chivvy up the troops. When we reach the college where the game – a Football League Youth Alliance North East Conference League encounter against Hartlepool – is being played and saunter round to the technical area, youth coach John Schofield seems genuinely pleased to see the chairman. 'Good morning, Mr Chairman,' he says in a manner vaguely reminiscent of the way cap-doffing blue-collar workers used to address factory bosses.

Hartlepool's youths are quicker, neater and smarter in their play. Their senior club plays in League One, and only a string of fine saves from Lincoln's keeper prevent a first-half mauling. He is one of a number of younger boys pushed into this age bracket to compensate for missing players. A few have been added to first-team manager Keith Alexander's squad, including Jack Hobbs, a sixteen-year-old full-back who later in the day will become the youngest player ever to represent the club at senior level. On this cold and misty Saturday morning, with only a few friends and family watching, it is a question of the players getting down to character-building graft, the sort of solid experience that will doubtless come in handy for these boys when they have to dig in at senior level, should they prove good enough to become professional players.

While watching a scoreless first half full of honest endeavour, Rob explains how he became chairman of the club. In November 2000 former chairman John Reames, who had been Lincoln's main benefactor for fifteen years, was looking to sell the debt-ridden club. He offered his shareholding for a knockdown price to a fans group called IMPetus, a supporters trust chaired by Rob at the time, which bought a 30 per cent stake in the club. As the largest single shareholder IMPetus effectively had a controlling interest in the club, and in February 2001 Rob was voted as their representative on the board and therefore became chairman. He was the first head of a supporters trust to be elected as the chairman of a British football club. On his appointment he announced: 'Lincoln City is now a community club owned and run by its supporters. This is a historic day for the club and for football in general.'

The ramifications were significant. Bradley wasn't just a token 'fan on the board', there simply to appease the fans, who could easily be ignored if the main board members felt like it. He had been elected by members of the trust. Their votes counted. If they didn't like the job he was doing they could vote him out. He was also honour-bound to implement policies that they had decided were in the interests of supporters and the wider community .

Some 125 British clubs had fans' trusts at the time of writing this book, backed by a government initiative called Supporters Direct, funded by public money. Its central aim is 'to help people who wish to play a responsible part in the life of the football club they support' and to offer advice and information. The ambition is to promote the concept of democratic supporter ownership and representation through mutual, not-for-profit structures – a vision that recognises football clubs as civic and community institutions – and to preserve the competitive values of League football and the health of the game as a whole. Trusts are set up as Industrial and Provident Societies, non-profit entities designed to ensure they are democratic, transparent, representative bodies for supporters to join. Some seek merely to act as a lobbying group at clubs, others to buy a stake; some have bought their clubs outright. Again at the time of writing – the growth and influence of supporters trusts is growing at a rapid rate – 60 trusts hold equity in their clubs, 39 have supporter representation on club boards, and nine clubs (two Football League – Chesterfield and Brentford – and seven non-League, including York City, AFC Wimbledon and AFC Telford) are owned by trusts. It is estimated that thirteen clubs have been saved from liquidation by supporters trusts, which have brought an estimated £10 million of investment into football with 85,000 fans joining them across the country. If you consider the financial ill-health of the game in recent years, the major reason there hasn't been a domino effect of clubs dissolving one after another into liquidation has to be the efforts of supporters trusts and Supporters Direct.

Beneath those broad-brush headline figures lies the human cost of involvement – supporters like Rob, a father of three, self-employed architect and madly keen Lincoln City fan, who gives his time not for personal gain and self-aggrandisement, nor to promote or protect his own financial interests, but because he cares about Lincoln City. Being chairman is time consuming and has involved lots of headaches and heartache. He had to sack manager Phil Stant, who had been a popular player, in his first week. The financial collapse of the club in April 2002 took its toll that summer: he was constantly away from his work, though luckily he is self-employed and can make up the hours. But the strain was enormous. You only do this if you love a football club down to the soles of the soggy boots we have acquired while wandering back to the car.

Rob recalls his early visits to Lincoln's ground, Sincil Bank, as a boy in the early 1960s. His dad, Gordon, used to take him to matches from the farm where they lived near the small village of Spilsby, along the A158 between Lincoln and Skegness. He remembers the magic of floodlit matches, and they bring back powerful personal memories for me too. Night matches at Worcester City were always special (City play their evening games, unusually, on Mondays and always attract bigger gates than at weekends). Slipping off down the Lane after stew for tea on Monday evenings was alluring – something, I'm sure, to do with the way the pitch was lit up. For Rob, it was seeing Lincoln Cathedral. This truly majestic building that dominates the skyline was symbolic of how he saw Lincoln, as a 'throbbing metropolis'. At Sincil Bank he stood on a metal milking stool to watch the games. 'Everyone used to laugh at me,' he recalls with a smile.

He had a 'soft spot' for Arsenal – he liked the gun on their badge – and still looks for their results, but watching football was all about Lincoln City. As a teenager, Rob used to bike to Spilsby, which was two-and-three-quarter miles away from home, and travel on the 'road car' to Lincoln with his older brother Phil and his dad (if he could get someone to do the milking). Later he did it with some mates. 'It was a bloody long journey an' all – about an hour and a half, and it would only go twenty mile an hour – but we'd have the day in Lincoln and it was fantastic.' There were record shops, music shops – any shops, I guess, if you are brought up on a farm – and there was also, of course, what Rob calls 'the soap opera' of football: the colour, the excitement, the noise of a match at Sincil Bank, with Lincoln, the Red Imps, playing in their red-and-white-striped shirts and black shorts. 'We'd get a *Sports Echo* at the station and read it on the way home. They were fantastic days out.'

He worked for the Lincolnshire Water Board in Skegness before moving to the 'throbbing metropolis' itself to work as a building surveyor. By that stage he was a home-and-away fan, but when kids came along he restricted himself to home games only. These days he is truly back in the fold. 'For the past ten years I have hardly missed a game. It's not an anorak thing, it is simply enjoyable. You've got friends you meet all over the country and it's a great crack. If you sneak a late winner you stay behind and have some drinks, and I'd get here are at eleven, maybe twelve o'clock. That's eight hours of bloody good enjoyment if you ask me. If somebody else wants to play golf or something like that, that is up to them, but this is my equivalent and it's wonderful.'

We're now back in the car, and Rob loses concentration briefly. He has nudged a little over 30mph on a long, straight road and the punishing flash of a speed camera zaps us back to reality. It will take Rob back to twelve points and a probable ban. I feel guilty because we have been chatting.

Is football like a drug, I ask? 'Yes, I think it is,' Rob replies. A lot of people wouldn't admit to this next statement, but I'm sure it has been felt many times: 'When you're on the top floor of the maternity wing watching your wife give birth and you can see the floodlights and you're missing Lincoln v. Hereford ... It sounds wrong because you're so chuffed to be there, but you're looking across at the floodlights and thinking, "I wonder how they're doing?" There is nothing sad about that. I'm proud of it and I love it.' Nod or tut – your choice. But I know which camp I fall into. Teresa and I listened to Manchester United v. WBA just hours after Nicholas was born. Why not?

11.20 A.M.: OUR SPIRE, THEIR FLOODLIGHTS John Boyers gets back in the car. Roy Unwin's wife, Joan, was understandably distraught. She had gone to bed the previous evening, as ever, leaving Roy reading his newspaper. When he hadn't come upstairs she thought, as so many times before, he'd fallen asleep. She came down to wake him but found he had died peacefully in his chair. Can you imagine her trauma? Neighbours had rallied around, and some words of comfort from John had helped. 'I knew you would come,' she had told him. 'I just didn't realise it would be so soon.' (Liz, Roy's daughter, later wrote to thank John, and said, 'I don't know how we would have coped without your support.')

This is John's job. Rather than having a traditional community or congregation to serve, his 'flock' are each and every one of Manchester United's 550 full-time and 3,000 part-time staff. Supporters too, sometimes. He is also involved in aspects of the club's community programme. He assumes a duty of care to all of them, grafting pastoral care on to the corporate responsibility the club, like all employers, has towards its staff. With the best will in the world – for example in times of bereavement – human resources staff are not best equipped to do this work. John's role is more personal.

As we drive on to our original destination – Manchester City's training ground at Platt Lane, Moss Side (again, the polite sat-nav lady is is guiding us there) – we discuss how John developed sports chaplaincy. A bit like a floating midfielder, a football club chaplain has pretty much a free role. He is a confidant. The things discussed with John don't go any further. He certainly doesn't report back to whoever is in charge. John recognised this 'early doors'. In particular, football clubs have lots of young men, many living away from home, who are trying to find their way in a high-profile sport. It can be a lonely existence. Some earn fame and fortune beyond their experience, and they don't know how to handle it. Others find it an oppressive environment, full of 'barrack-room lawyers'. The potential to fall by the wayside is massive, and footballers are not always well guided. Agents and managers may look after their welfare, but quite often it's a secondary concern to their own interests. Players lack people they can truly trust, and clubs are villages. Gossip spreads. A casual comment said in jest can be blown out of all proportion. It can even make tomorrow's headlines. Everyone has their own agenda. So who can these vulnerable young men turn to? Often it is someone like John Boyers.

But football clubs have other communities – staff, fans, maybe even the wider society. If church doors are to be flung open then logically that has to include football as much as, if not more than, many other activities. I tread delicately here. Football and religion. Oh, so many parallels and comparisons have been pored over so often. Referring to St James Road Baptist Church and Watford FC (on Vicarage Road, after all!), John remarks, 'They saw our spire, we saw their floodlights.'

Football stadiums are massive modern structures reaching into the sky. They dwarf surrounding buildings, including centuries-old churches. I hear people all the time, albeit jokingly, refer to them as shrines – places to make regular pilgrimages to. Clubs often draw their congregation from far and wide. It is the only true mass gathering in many communities that takes place on a regular basis. Football clubs even have community departments, which, to some extent, is pastoral work of sorts.

As an assistant minister John was allocated a day and a half a week to work with Watford FC. When he became senior minister in 1984 the role continued. When Graham Taylor left in 1987, his replacement, Dave Bassett, was keen to carry on with a chaplain, but somehow things seemed different. 'A lot of key background people had gone,' recalls John. 'Watford lost stability. Elton John sold the club to Jack Petchey. Players like John Barnes and Tony Coton were sold. The club settled down to life in the old Second Division.'

By this time John was busy helping other clergymen establish links with their local sporting clubs. He felt they needed specific preparation and training. 'You've got to find the right person to work in this worldly setting. Someone who isn't put off by the rough-and-tumble language and secularism. Someone who can fit into that environment and cope. But also, they have to belong to the right sort of church that says "we're happy for you to give a day a week to this", and that isn't always easy because there are other demands.' That's why, along with fellow sports chaplains, John set up SCORE. 'We train them, introduce them to the concept, induct them into the club and get them into the networks; we offer resources and hold regional and national meetings. We try to maintain and develop a quality of service that chaplains can give to the clubs.' But turning SCORE into a business wasn't easy. It was set up as a charity, which means it constantly has to look for funding and secure means from wherever it can.

In 1992 John left Watford for Manchester United. On the face of it, United did with him what they do with the playing side of the club: they spot talent and procure it. United secretary Ken Merrett and his assistant Ken Ramsden, both committed Christians, had first tried to tease John away from Watford in 1987. 'It was a tempting offer but it wasn't the right time,' recalls John. 'I had certain commitments and they wanted to employ me on a full-time basis. We had an assistant minister who was leaving our church so the timing wouldn't have been right.' He rejected their offer. 'Me and Alan Shearer – the only people to turn Manchester United down!'

But Merrett and Ramsden were persistent, and five years later they got their man. By this time John was working as the national director of SCORE and had been chaplain at the 1990 Commonwealth Games. His sports ministry work was taking over, and he had decided to leave St James Road Church. 'I needed a new house because a new senior minister was coming to take my job,' John explains. Manchester United heard about this and made contact. 'Their guy was leaving the country so they had a vacancy. This time they said, "We want you to do what you did at Watford, part time. Will you come to us?" After much thought and prayer we decided this is what God wanted us to do.'

In comparison to Watford, Manchester United is a massive club. Like going from a small village church to a cathedral. But John went about his job the same way. 'I did here what I did at Watford,' he says. 'I gave time to build relationships with people and going where they are working, whether it is staff or players, full-time internationals or part-time cleaners. You try to help everyone.'

At its most raw, John's work is dealing with death and the welfare of loved ones of cherished employees who make up the fabric of the club. Roy Unwin was one such person. Without being too melodramatic, he gave his life to helping Manchester United become great, though sadly it seems his contribution was worth no more than a few lines in the

Manchester Evening News and a short quote from Sir Alex Ferguson, who described Roy as 'a wonderful gentleman ... everyone in the club had a great affection for him. He had a nice manner. He was never a man who would put himself forward too much, but he was always there for you.'

The same might be said of John Boyers. He works quietly behind the scenes, not thumping the Bible or preaching about relative evils (Malcolm Glazer's filthy lucre, anyone?) or berating the players' poor behaviour, just helping, providing spiritual support.

11.30 A.M.: GEARING UP AT GRETNA During the summer Paul Barnett only has eight weeks to get Gretna's ground ready. When he first came here he had to cancel all their revenue-raising pre-season fixtures because the pitch wasn't up to scratch. These are not easy decisions to make – impossible, in fact, unless you have someone with deep pockets behind you like Brooks Mileson. This morning the priority is to present a nice, neat, flat pitch. It doesn't look lush but it is short and tidy and there is plenty of grass on it. 'Grass needs light to grow, and there isn't a lot of that around at some stadiums,' Paul points out. 'The grass grows thinner so it wears out quicker.' This, however, is not a problem at tiny Gretna, which has one small seated area and a temporary seated stand at one end, a covered terrace behind the end where the spectators pour in and a small terraced ground-level section for away fans on the far touchline. Although gates have increased fourfold in the past three years they rarely break into four figures.

At one time a well-grassed pitch would have been the only requirement of a groundsman, but football is progressing. Managers now select a surface to suit their style of play. They can decide what grass length they want or if they want it fast or slow. 'We can give them, within reason, the exact pitch they want,' Paul says. 'Some want the ball to zip off the pitch quickly. Alex Ferguson does this all the time. He likes the pitch to be well watered before the game to take the bounce out of the ball and to make it skid. It gives the players more cushion.' The quality of Gretna's pitch has helped attract better players. 'We are looking to bring in Scottish Premier League-quality players,' notes Paul, 'so we have to offer the same standards of facilities, and that means a good-quality pitch.'

As we talk, someone pops in for toilet roll for the ladies' loo. Replacing toilet rolls and light bulbs, general maintenance, sweeping the stands – Paul and Selwyn, a tall man who has been a fan for 30 years, have to do all this, as well as put up temporary goal frames for players to use during warm-up so they don't wear out the goal areas. Paul's other assistant, Phil Smith, is off work with an injured ankle. Glancing across the pitch, Paul says, 'You should see it in the summer when the grass has been freshly cut, the lines have been marked last thing, and it has been watered. That is when it's at its best.'

Selwyn polishes the seats on the subs bench. Everything is now geared up for this afternoon's game against Elgin.

11.40 A.M.: A LEGAL EAGLE At Norwich Neil Doncaster is finishing off his morning chores. How did he get this gig as chief executive at Norwich City?

He was born in Honiton in Devon in March 1970, but his family moved to Croydon when he was three years old. He went to a rugby-playing grammar school, Trinity School, and after taking A levels took a year out before studying for a law degree at Bristol University. After taking his finals he joined Bristol solicitors Burgess-Salmon as a trainee. He qualified in 1995. At Burgess-Salmon he carried out company, commercial and corporate work, and one of his tasks was to handle the takeover of Bristol City by John Laycock and Scott Davidson and work on legal matters at the club. He was also involved in the flotation of Bolton Wanderers.

It was a labour of love. As a child, Neil went with his grandfather to watch Crystal Palace. 'I was a Holmesdale Ender,' he recalls with pride. This was the Terry Venables team, full of bright young stars including Vince Hilaire, Kenny Sansom, Clive Allen and Peter Nicholas, which swept from the old Third to First Division playing a snappy brand of football. 'Those memories stay with you,' he says. The tag 'Team of the Eighties', alas, eventually became a millstone around Palace's neck. They didn't become a significant force again until the late 1980s under Steve Coppell, when there was the effective partnership of Ian Wright and Mark Bright up front.

Neil didn't develop a great appetite for playing football because he attended a rugby-playing grammar school, but working within football was interesting. He spent six months in London working for the Transport Development Group (TDG plc) as an in-house solicitor, and then the opportunity to join Norwich came along. Neil mapped out his five-year plan to turn the club around, but the devil was in the detail. Anyone can draw a graph with an upward curve; achieving results is something else. Football fans have been educated to believe that the only results that matter are those on matchday, though Neil believes this is a myth. 'I totally disagree that it is a results-driven business,' he says. Old-school thinkers may look away now. I did a talk recently in Moscow called "Winning isn't Everything". That is the club's philosophy – ambition with prudence. Success helps, but it's not a prerequisite in driving up income.'

He hands me a raft of performance indicators showing how Norwich have been able to increase income without conspicuous success on the pitch. A key objective from the start was to fill the stadium on matchdays; today will be the 76th time the home crowd section has sold out in their last 80 games played here. 'We had a vast amount of spare capacity,' Neil explains. 'It was no good espousing values relating to the community if we weren't marketing tickets cheaply enough to attract young supporters and families. We sold season tickets to under-twelves for £35 just to get people in. We didn't make it difficult by saying, as some clubs do, you have to bring two adults to get a cheap child's ticket, we had a flat rate to get the kids in, get the grandparents and parents in, and get the families in. That is what we did. We made it dirt cheap.' You may as well have a stadium full of people paying less than a half-full stadium of people paying more. 'You say it as if it's logical and everyone accepts it,' Neil continues. 'It's beginning to be accepted within the game, but it has taken a long while. Getting children in makes it a family atmosphere.' Fumbling for more evidence, Neil adds, 'Research shows they want it to be a safe, secure atmosphere, and that is one of the things we've concentrated on. And it is borne out by a customer-tracking study asking fans how secure they feel in their own stadium. Above all, they do feel that at Carrow Road.'

It's so simple. I have sat across the table and listened to the views of people within the football industry – sometimes, frankly, in higher and more influential positions than Neil's – and heard them express all kinds of opinions without ever being able to substantiate their views. They just spout forth. They have never asked their fans what they think, or perhaps more poignantly, those who might become regular fans if things were different. Drawing the community closer to their club helped Norwich in lots of other ways. 'We had a culture here in 1997 where in the city centre all you saw were Man Utd, Arsenal, Chelsea and Liverpool shirts. Now, hopefully, you see a lot more yellow and green shirts.'

Those £35 junior season-ticket holders from the late 1990s, when Norwich were struggling at the wrong end of the First Division, are still supporters. Again, it's a provable fact. The data Norwich 'captured' about their fans, Neil says, have enabled them to market directly and carry out surveys. Again, there are people in the football business who consider this to be a waste of time, possibly even believing that it somehow panders to supporters, but at Norwich Neil Doncaster can prove it works. 'It is often said that if you get them young you have fans for life, and that is true. Our unique selling point was, yes, you can support the larger clubs, but will you get the chance to see them live? We can offer them that in an excitable, lively, affordable, safe family environment.'

Neil's research revealed something else. 'Supporters are far more concerned with their clubs being around in the long term than with short-term success. They want long-term viability more than them being as ambitious as possible.'

Oh, how this all ties in with disenfranchised communities in north-west Birmingham who have little connection with West Brom or Aston Villa, and the many other voices littered throughout this book (including mine) that say, actually, the things you feel proud about, the things that can reduce you to tears, are the passion that comes from understanding a club, from taking part, from playing the game, not solely the joyless pursuit of winning (and we'll come on to that later in the book). It's the fans who, despite some of the disgraceful things that have happened to their clubs, for example at Wrexham, are still the ones who do most; the ones who fell in love with their club not during moments of success but on long walks home in the rain at night. Many of the harder edged commercial achievements at Norwich – catering, conferencing, corporate sales, property rentals – have come as a result of their presence in the community, as well as the more obvious generators of increased revenue

– merchandising, publications, the lottery, etc. Catering profits, for example, are up sevenfold from £100,000 to £700,000, and that isn't just because Delia's name is stamped on things.

Norwich are also making the most of their location. They are the only professional club in Norfolk. Their community is spread far and wide in this rural county. But unlike many clubs that simply allow a Football in the Community scheme to operate from their premises (most fans probably don't know that FitCom is actually run and part-funded by the PFA; many clubs provide very little support other than office space, despite the obvious financial benefits they receive from this community work), Norwich run theirs as a charity: they are third owners in it, along with Football in the Community and supporters. Norwich uses what Neil calls the 'club brand' to run initiatives that may not necessarily result in more finance or supporters for Norwich City but that have wider social benefits. 'Football has an incredible power to address social issues and make a difference to lives, and I believe it is the responsibility of people within football clubs to use the power of their club brands as a force for good rather than in the cynical sense of turning people into supporters. We are an integral part of the community of Norwich and Norfolk, and it is our responsibility to give back when we can.'

Norwich aren't the only club to support this work, but the goodwill they have engendered has helped their revitalisation. So too has setting up an academy – another of the five-year-plan aims. 'The youth development system had been dismantled with the financial crisis of 1996,' says Neil, 'so many of the schoolboys went to other clubs and were successful there. We had to rebuild from scratch. We're now seeing the first harvest of that academy.' Neil points to the progress of young players like Ryan Jarvis, Ian Henderson, Jason Shackell and Danny Crow. This, he insists, is a vital part of building a community club. 'We're not separate from our community, we're part of it. We've seen UEFA's recommendations with academies developing their own players [in 2006 European football's governing body want clubs to field a minimum of four homegrown players per game], and we are supportive of those proposals because I think it is important to reinforce the link between the club and the region they come from.'

I ask what he thinks of the scorn poured upon these seemingly sensible proposals by England's top clubs. Refusing to criticise specific clubs, Neil replies, 'It depends how you see it: is it a chance to do something for the good of the game and the development of football generally, or the interests of your football club?' Maybe those who back self-interest, who would prefer to buy in expensive foreign players simply because they have the financial clout to do so, should have a word with the players, parents and coaches and anyone else involved in all the junior matches featured in this book and beyond.

I wonder how all this work filters into matchday, and what Neil, as the chief executive, actually does on matchdays. 'Eighty per cent of what happens in football is unplanned,' he admits. 'It doesn't flow seamlessly.' He points to the lively media coverage after Monday night's 3–2 home defeat to Manchester City and the reaction to Delia Smith's impassioned half-time pleas. And the sudden collapse of the ITV Digital deal in 2002, which he says 'destroyed the finances of 72 Football League clubs', taking £4 million out of Norwich's budget. 'We weren't geared up for it, and neither was any other club.' That huge gap in their accounts was eased by reaching the First Division play-off finals that year. Although they lost to Birmingham, they had come to a pre-match agreement that the losing club at the Millennium Stadium would keep the gate receipts. The goodwill of their community work then allowed Norwich to launch a share issue, which raised £3.9 million. Another £2.4 million was raised from a further share issue in 2003. Last year they made an appeal to fans not to redeem share dividends so the money could go into the manager's budget. Some £1.2 million was made available this way, which the club topped up in January 2005 by borrowing against future season-ticket sales, enabling them to buy forward Dean Ashton from Crewe. (Ashton went on to score seven goals in sixteen games for Norwich, and as an England U-21 international forward he is a good long-term asset, the sort of player the very top clubs used to clamour to buy but no longer need to now that they can scour the world for top foreign stars who can often be signed on free transfers.)

As we wander outside into the bitter cold, with orange-coated stewards beginning to turn up and the PA announcer doing some testing, testing, one-two, Neil points across to the new 8,000-seater Jarrold Stand, which opened last year and will soon have a community alcove added. I wonder if the concerns of overspending now are more worrying than the situation in the late 1990s. 'No,' Neil replies, 'we were lurching from crisis to crisis to keep the club afloat then. If you look at the TV money, we were earning just over half a million pounds a year against the approximate £20 million we will earn this year [2004/05].'

There is an admirable determination at Norwich not to 'live the dream'. Their fans have been educated by the leaders at the club: the board, staff like Neil and successive managers (Nigel Worthington being the latest, who is fully on side with the cautious approach the club is taking). 'The supporters aren't naive,' says Neil. 'They understand the financial wreckages of clubs and I hope they realise this club is run for the long term as well as the short term.'

These, of course, are not problems Chelsea need to ponder at present. They have a seemingly bottomless well from which to draw money in order to achieve quick success. I recall speaking to some fans outside Stamford Bridge in the summer of 2004. How did they feel about the club being bankrolled by a largely mysterious foreign owner who, unlike them, has hardly got Chelsea flowing through his veins? 'I don't fackin' care, mate,' said one burly forty-something fan. 'As long as we win the fackin' League once, I'll be happy. He can fack off back to Russia then.' With love, presumably. A different world …

11.45 A.M.: THE PLAYERS' PRE-MATCH MEAL At eleven a.m. Bristol City defender Danny Coles finally rose from his slumbers, showered, stretched out his painful Achilles heel, drank a lot more water ('Two litres already – I'm a bit paranoid') and done some more 'chilling out'. The way this boy is going he'll be frozen come kick-off. He has checked and packed his kit and is now sporting a blue club polo shirt, tracksuit bottoms and white trainers. He is dressed casually smart, and with some highlights flecked through his hair he looks every inch a modern athlete rather than a battered and bruised centre-half from the old days.

Now he has to cook his pre-match meal. If City were playing away this would be eaten at a hotel, all the players together at exactly the same time. For home games, manager Brian Tinnion has to hope his players heed the dietary advice they have been given to eat the right food at the right time – i.e. between 11.30 and midday, no later. The basic rule is a light, low-fat, carbohydrate meal. Pasta is the buzzword these days, and it's the ideal choice, preferably with tuna or an easily digestible tomato sauce.

Danny loves pasta, but not in the morning. I'm tempted to point out it will only, technically, be 'morning' for another fifteen minutes and that most of my interviewees have been up and about for several hours, but I resist. I also know what he means. Pasta isn't everyone's ideal daytime food. He could always have the next best option – a jacket potato with a low-fat filling. Danny opts for scrambled eggs on toast. 'Comfort food,' he says, which he liked as a kid. A bit like Coco Pops, maybe? The eggs on toast is duly cooked and scoffed by midday – 'A little late,' admits Danny, 'but not by much.'

Eating pasta and other high-carb foods is still seen as rocket science by the British football industry. Maybe as recently as a decade ago players still chomped steak and chips before matches in the belief that 'bully beef' would make them strong and help them perform better, even though any basic nutritional knowledge would have made it obvious that dragging dense meals around in your stomach will have a detrimental effect. I recall hearing a TV pundit, who should have known better, dismiss modern pre-match meals as 'hogwash dreamed up by non-football people'. How sad. How ignorant. Howard Wilkinson, the FA's former technical director, told me that when he played for Sheffield Wednesday in the 1960s you could follow your pre-match meal with bread and butter pudding two hours before kick-off if you wanted to. How is a footballer supposed to perform with that swilling around inside him?

To amateurs in other sports – people to whom footballers like to lecture about professionalism, dedication and sacrifice, such as Phil Robinson, who was a weightlifter and bodybuilder – this is barely believable. When I started running marathons in the early 1980s the merits of consuming low-fat, high-carb meals before a race were well known, a scientifically proved fact. But until continental and more enlightened British managers put their collective foot down, footballers continued to go on their merry way. I recall pulling in for a cuppa at a lay-by café en route to an interview at a club training ground and chatting to the guy who ran it. He told me how a particular player always popped in for a bacon sandwich on his way to training. I'm not rubbishing greasy spoon cafés here, but does a so-called professional sportsman really need to pile into such places on his way to work mere minutes before training everyday?

Danny Coles is of the generation who just accept sensible eating as the norm. It is no big deal. No sacrifice. No supposed slap in the face from people who don't know about football. He knows what he is expected to eat all week, and he understands the benefit of the food. He knows he should not eat any later than three hours before kick-off. He knows if he really needs something fruity maybe Jaffa Cakes will be available in the dressing room, and although he goes on about it a bit, he knows he should drink plenty of water. Players of yore, again amazingly, were actually discouraged from doing this, they were told that it would give them stomach cramps. It's simply staggering. On what will be a hot afternoon, Danny will easily use up the two or three litres he has gulped down this morning.

11.48 A.M.: A MANCHESTER DERBY The sat-nav lady has got us close to Platt Lane. Well, halfway along an adjacent road, Yew Tree Road, to be precise; left to our own devices, it's our choice from here. I've been here before, twice, but I make the wrong choice. I tell John to bear right. Wrong. We double back and eventually pull into Manchester City's academy ground as the players troop off at half-time.

Platt Lane is just a few hundred yards from City's former home Maine Road, which nestled deep in the heart of the infamous Moss Side district in south Manchester, home to some of the city's most deprived communities and known locally as 'the shooting range' because of the high number of drive-by shootings that have taken place down the years. Last season City went all lah-di-dah and moved into the City of Manchester Stadium, which was built for the 2002 Commonwealth Games, in the east of the city. Man City and Moss Side went well together. Plenty of potential, but hard, run down, failing, often depressing. At the City of Manchester Stadium, Man City are dwarfed. They look like a small man wearing a large suit. It may be stylish, but it just doesn't fit. They aren't United. They have stadium envy.

I like Platt Lane. At a time when so many other academies are tucked away in the countryside, often miles outside the city where their clubs are based, this is defiantly right in the thick of the things. It must be an uncomfortable experience for the trainees of other clubs who practise and play most of their football in rural settings. Here, only a trellis fence stands between the young prodigies and Joe Public: scallies on bikes, one hand gripping the fence, the other on the handlebar; lads in tracky bottoms kicking footballs against the wall; blokes sauntering up the road for a constitutional, maybe to put on a bet or to get some chips for lunch. Others are just watching. It is rare – free football.

There are two City v. United Manchester academy derbies being played here today. John Boyers wants to watch the U-18s. In search of a cuppa at the adjoining complex, he meets some familiar faces. 'Have you heard about Roy Unwin?' Everyone at United, it seems, knew Roy.

United's U-18s coach is Joaquim Francisco Filho, a Brazilian who worked at the acclaimed L'Institute National de Football (INF) in France, otherwise known as Clairefontaine, for 29 years, helping to produce the likes of Thierry Henry, Nicolas Anelka and William Gallas. He moved to Manchester United in August 2002. He says hello to John, as do the passing substitutes, nodding as they limber up along the side of the pitch. 'Hi, Rev,' says one of them. John offers lots of encouragement. 'Well played, Danny.' 'John, everything all right?' A thumbs up. John also chats to the club journalists who are here videoing the game for MUTV and are poised to do some on-the-spot interviews afterwards. The parents over the other side of the field, unlike the mini-soccer parents and surely with so much more at stake for their sons, behave in exemplary fashion.

This is all about building relationships. To John, it is vital. These youths may not be superstars now, but in a year or two they may be thrust into the limelight or leave the club disappointed or distraught, wondering what football can offer them. In future both roads may meet, making John's availability particularly helpful. I wonder which of these red-shirted youths will follow the path of recent United stars like Darren Fletcher, John O'Shea and Kieran Richardson into the senior team, then John explains his desire to build a relationship with players, and sometimes with parents too. It is all about trust. He isn't wanting to be confrontational or to push his very real faith on to people who don't want to know. 'Obviously I want to see Christian players involved in the game,' he says, 'but I think the role of the chaplain and the evangelist are quite different. I am very happy to respond to questions about God, faith and spiritual things, but I do want people to trust me as well. I'm a chaplain, not some insensitive preacher! A lot of the people I work with are not regular churchgoers. I meet those who are regular Christians for Bible study or whatever, but I go with a broader reference point.'

He is keen to get players to think about the very real moral dilemmas they may face, and he does educational work with the MUFC academy scholars, looking at areas such as friendship, bullying, coping with success, coping with failure, sexual ethics, bereavement, privilege and responsibility, decision-making, etc. 'These are things that help them cope with the issues of life as they grow up.' And it's where his credibility is crucial. That's why these players see John at matches on wet and cold days like today, taking an interest. 'They know me. I've been to their matches and chatted with them in the canteen. They are happy talking with me.' He reels off the list of household names he has known since they were youths: Gary Neville, Phil Neville, John O'Shea, Darren Fletcher, Paul Scholes, Nicky Butt, Wes Brown and a certain midfielder now at Real Madrid with a Posh wife. 'They can confide in me because they knew me as fourteen- to sixteen-year-olds. So can other players who have been here a long time because they have got to know and trust the Rev too.'

John's advice to would-be chaplains is 'to be a giver, not a taker'. Roy Keane once told a BBC website that if he had 200 conversations a week, 199 would maybe end up asking him to do something. A chaplain has to be different. He is there to contribute, to offer expertise, experience and specialist input. 'What we should not be doing is asking for autographs or to open the church fête.'

The game ends 1–1. A fair result, on what we've seen of the second half. A competitive game, for sure, but played in a good spirit, with some wonderful skills from relative free spirits whose coaches don't try desperately to drive results out of them, but encourage expression. This is what youth development is all about, developing individual players, and it's something senior coaches and managers all too often fail to understand.

We carry on our conversation on our way back to the car. 'One of the lads here was involved in a car crash,' John tells me. 'He was in intensive care in Wythenshawe hospital. The club had no access to him. They didn't know how he was getting on so they phoned me, and I put my clerical collar on and went to see him. The nurse said she was happy for me to go in if the family were happy. They were delighted that the club chaplain had come at this crucial time.' Serving in this way is important. It is this sort of commitment and involvement that establishes a bond and a friendship that lasts. The same goes for the senior players. 'I have seen Wes Brown twice when he's had major cruciate surgery, and he knows I'm not just doing what I'm doing to get alongside well-known players, because when the chips were down and when the crunch came I went to see him and help support him. He knows what I'm about.'

Top-level football can be an enclosed, cosseted world. I recall some years ago being told about a 24- year-old Premier League player who asked someone to go along with him to open a bank account. He had no idea how to handle his own affairs. They get used to having things done for them and can easily lose a sense of perspective when they pick up a weekly wage far beyond most people's annual income. John speaks of the importance of ways to keep their feet on the ground. He has been with groups of sixteen- to eighteen-year-olds to visit the Salvation Army in Manchester city centre at Christmas. 'They need to see things like that. When everyone has told them they are brilliant and they are going to be the next Pele, you need something that puts your life in reasonable perspective.' Last year some of the club's fourteen- to fifteen-year-old academy players went to Kenya for a pre-season tour and training camp. 'It opened their eyes to poverty and deprivation. It made them realise we are a wealthy nation and privileged people. That it doesn't matter if you are paid five, ten, fifteen thousand pounds a week or year, both are hugely different to what two-thirds of the world lives on. That perspective is invaluable.'

This is food for thought. It takes us back to Handsworth and the Positive Futures campaign and to the junior league Bob Marley has started across the Midlands. But now we're going back to John's house for soup, sandwiches and more philosophical discussion.

11.50 A.M.: INTO THE LAND OF MY FATHERS 'That is when I know I am home,' says Neil Williams, pointing at a mountain in the distance (the Ruabon Mountain) as we make our way along the A5 north of Oswestry.

You don't have to be a wistful romantic to hold such views about the local landscape. When I am nearing home after a long trip I always look for a hill off the M5 called Whittington Tump, which always reminds me of the hymn 'There is a green hill far away'; I think about singing it as a child during assembly at Stanley Road Junior School. There is something vaguely comforting about childhood when you have had a horrendous journey.

Neil is eager to see what sort of national support will materialise. A similar event held earlier in the season saw Wrexham's average gate of around 4,000 rise to almost 8,000. A bumper gate today would help again. 'I only became aware of how good other supporters could be when Brighton fans in the away end last season sang songs against our chairman and the man who brought him in,' says Neil. Brighton, too, are homeless, having been through similar circumstances. Although they have survived and are in the Coca-Cola Championship, Brighton are playing in a rented athletics stadium. Their supporters have built links with other clubs, including Wrexham and today's visiting club Doncaster Rovers, whose former chairman was convicted for burning their main stand down in an insurance fiddle.

People like Neil and Lincoln City's supporters' representative Rob Bradley are talented individuals who describe themselves as 'ordinary supporters'. But they have a range of skills to offer. So often businessmen and the wider media have been keen to portray all football supporters as nigh-on Neanderthals, Andy Capp types or caricatures like Dick Emery's skinhead father and son, or even the fans who descend upon Holby City's casualty unit wearing bobble hats (with proper bobbles: where do the props department get them, because clubs don't actually sell them any more?), or fans wearing 'bovver boots' and scarves around their wrists. This misconception falls apart when supporters rally round and pool together. Wrexham fans, like Neil, are doing what they can to save the club, find an alternative backer, raise cash in whatever way they can, anything to keep their football club afloat in murky financial waters.

The situation, of course, has been exacerbated by the growing disparity between the rich Premier League clubs and 'the rest', who have limited means on which to survive. It is an ignominious fact that Wrexham are the 37th Football League club to have slipped into either administration or liquidation in the years since the Premier League has been formed – which means that more than half of them have at one stage or another been insolvent.

Today, of course, is a poignant day, and Neil is angry. 'I'm not a violent man,' he says, 'but I can see far worse happening to some of these people than just a few threatening phone calls that they moan about [Alex Hamilton, the property developer who has cherry-picked this previously well-run club and its ground, has complained about threats]. They don't realise how much the football clubs mean to communities. So I can understand the anger when they say the things they do.'

We stop for petrol, and Neil pops to the loo. I ask his son Josh if he is teased by his schoolmates in Helston for supporting Wrexham. 'I am, a lot,' he replies. He has followed them since he was three. 'It is a cross to bear, but it's good being an individual. I probably go to five or six games a season. Normally I play on Saturdays.'

Neil is keen to get to the ground, park up and see what is happening. Wrexham's plight has been well publicised. He is one of many fans who have gone on Radio Five Live's *606* programme to let people know what is happening. He is exasperated. Everyone knows what happened to Brighton, that they lost their ground and had to play in Gillingham, and now at a temporary athletics track, while nothing is being done to help them find a new home. Alex Hamilton has always stated he will build Wrexham a new ground, but only once he has sold the Racecourse Ground and moved the club out – which effectively means they will be demoted from the Football League because they won't have anywhere to play. Which makes them an unrealistic business with no chance of clearing their debts. 'The decision has won us a lot of friends because we have been deducted ten points,' Neil says. 'Because it was his fault, not the fans' fault.' In militant mood, Neil runs through some of the ideas that have been mooted, including persuading fans of Football League clubs to cancel their Sky Sports subscriptions to show their anger to those involved in setting up and funding the Premier League. 'We want to put pressure on those in charge to let them know how we feel.'

All this is affecting his home life, and Neil has a sympathetic partner. He has been away on a business trip to Germany all week. Getting back and heading off for an entire day with Josh isn't likely to get him in anyone's good books. 'I know this sounds awful,' Neil explained to his partner, 'but I hope I will be with you for as long as possible. The support I get from you is appreciated and I'm not taking you for granted. But my football club might only be around for another three months and it also needs me now.' Sometimes Neil comes up for the weekend, or at least overnight, to break the journey, but that's hard to swing if you have been away all week. 'It is difficult. There are obviously things that need doing around the house and there are other demands. This takes up £150, and I will spend more than twelve hours sat on my backside on the road just for the cause of a football club.'

Because we have been chatting all the time the journey has flown by. We are now heading into Wrexham. Despite the problems, Neil is feeling buoyed up. 'That is the beauty of the game – you don't know what is going to happen.' He recalls a pre-Christmas game against Hartlepool, who hadn't won away all season. 'We thought, "We'll win this no trouble." They walloped us 5–1. That is why football is beguiling. You just don't know what is going to happen.'

COUNTDOWN
TO KICK-OFF

12.00 P.M.: GROUNDHOP DAY I I've driven to the picture-postcard Cotswold village of Broadway in south Worcestershire, much beloved by American tourists and coach operators. It is just about as removed from football's traditional urban heartlands as you can imagine. Not the sort of place you'd expect to find a diehard football fan. But Bill Berry is a fan like few others.

Bill is a groundhopper, a strange breed of football supporter that has emerged in recent years. Their hobby is to visit as many grounds as possible. Any venue with a roped-off pitch will count. And I'm not talking of minor achievements like visiting the 92 Premier/Football League grounds here ('did it in my sleep,' sniffed one hopper I interviewed a few years back), but leagues well down football's food chain, places that will never appear on the pools coupon or even in local newspapers.

These people are an anthropologist's dream because there are some bizarre self-imposed rules to groundhopping. Some won't count a ground unless they've seen a goal scored there; some feel the need to touch each crossbar before kick-off; some even try to get their hands on the match ball. A standard question is 'Do you issue?' By this, they mean a matchday programme – in the loosest sense of the word. We're not talking about a glossy publication here; a folded team sheet from the ref will suffice. One groundhopper who travelled from London to Yorkshire refused to watch the match because the club couldn't photocopy the team sheet for him. He stayed in his car and sulked while his mates watched the match. Strange.

Bill Berry is at the normal end of the weirdometer. For starters, unlike many groundhoppers (or trainspotters, or other manic aficionados), he's married to Ann, a lovely Scottish woman with a wicked sense of humour, who, though she fails to understand her husband's hobby (she has very little interest in football at all), is tolerant of his passion. In fact she quite likes the fact that he is out all day because it means she can do whatever she wants, guilt-free.

Bill also makes a living out of groundhopping. He edits a weekly magazine called the *Football Traveller*, which provides an up-to-date list of all weekly fixtures across Britain at all levels from Premier League down to small local leagues, some with wonderful names. There's the Frank Armitt Liverpool County Combination (how I wish it was Armpit!), or the Air Miles Manchester League, the Costcutter Ceredigion League and the Gordon Braasted Trophy (again, I'm sure this has been mispronounced or misspelled and is the stuff of local legend). The *Football Traveller* also carries programme reviews from the tiniest clubs in the football pyramid and photos of equally diminutive grounds. Bill has several hundred subscribers, and even though numbers have fallen in recent years, at £1.25 an issue, even when you take off printing and postage, it's a tidy enough income.

It's essential reading for groundhoppers. In theory, Bill's publication ought to have been crushed by the rise of the internet, but websites can't always be relied upon. And printing the fixtures off won't necessarily fit neatly into your pocket like the compact *Football Traveller*. Its unique selling point is that it is reliably up-to-date with kick-off times and rearranged fixtures, and when you are stuck in deepest Montgomeryshire on a rainy day and the game you were heading to is cancelled and you need an alternative, a compendium offering you a full list is exactly what you want. You have to understand the psychology of groundhoppers. They hate missing matches. I don't mean, 'Oh, that was disappointing, never mind, let's go home'; I mean, just one game at a weekend is usually viewed as a waste. Most will make long-weekend trips to certain parts of Britain or Europe – oh yes, this hobby knows no boundaries – and see as many as they can.

Bill, an angular man in his late fifties, restricts himself to one game on Saturdays. He isn't the sort of chap to leave anything to chance. His car has already been loaded with the essentials: hat, coat, boots, brolly, a vast array of books and maps, notebook (groundhoppers, as you can imagine, are fastidious note-takers) and much-needed mobile phone. We only have time for a quick coffee, during which Ann quizzes me why I want to spend a day traipsing around after her husband. 'Because it's a bit different,' I begin weakly, 'and maybe because groundhopping is saying more than we might imagine. It seems to me to be a rejection of the idea that football supporting is all about watching one team predominantly in one place. It is essentially about viewing games in all their many and varied locations, and I find that interesting.' Ann doesn't look convinced.

We move on to discuss the cost of top-flight matches. I explain that you have to shell out £40 or more to watch some Premier League games.

'How much?' Ann replies. 'That's for one game? What about if you want to take children, is that extra?'

I smile sweetly – of course it is. 'It's a lot of money for families,' I concede. Amazingly, I find myself in the unusual and uncomfortable position of vaguely justifying the rationale behind the price hikes of recent years (me?). 'I guess it's the price to pay for top stars. And enough people think it's worth it because the grounds are full.'

Ann is disgusted and confused. 'Well, I wouldn't,' she huffs.

Time to leave. Ann packs us off out the door with a little more empathy than when I arrived.

12.05 P.M.: IS THIS THE WAY TO AFAN LIDO? At Afan Lido Phil Robinson, club secretary, has dealt with administrative matters. Phil Robinson, director of football, has coached the little lads in baggy shorts, Afan Lido's under-fives, and made sure all the teams have kicked off this morning. Now it's the turn of Phil Robinson, bar steward, to get busy.

As you enter the ground, behind one goal, the layout is simple. The bar is to the right, refreshments are to the left, next to the changing rooms. The programme seller is straight in front of you. On matchdays the bar is well stocked for the couple of hundred or so fans who'll turn up. Most will enjoy a chat and a drink before the game; some will slip in at half-time to check out the scores; and, depending on the result, it could be busy after the game. Lots will have a beer to celebrate a win, a few will drown their sorrows if Lido lose, and there'll be a bit of both if it's a draw. Either way, Phil Robinson will be busy.

Phil runs the bar six nights a week and all day on matchdays. It's a friendly atmosphere with locals joking about why I want to speak to Phil. It seems slightly ironic that a fit-as-a-flea 60-year-old is racing around a smoky bar catering for drinkers. Grabbing a word is difficult. One minute Phil is beside you, the next he has scurried off to deal with some minor matter. Earlier, he nipped out to buy bread rolls for the hot dogs and burgers, which are being cooked, served and sold by the other half of this remarkable double act, his wife Linda, who has been with Lido all the way. She helps manage the bar, but on matchdays she concentrates on the food. And she doesn't just cater for the players and officials – right now she is preparing a huge oval dish of sandwiches and salad for them – but, along with another willing pair of hands, she will look after the refreshment bar too. It is vital work: Afan Lido need every penny they can get, and every drink or item of food sold is money for the club. Speedy service with a smile is what it is all about. The players can help too: not only would a precious win go a long way to preserve Afan Lido's precarious status in the Welsh Premier League, it would also mean that some folks will stay behind longer. And they'll help to fill the till.

I wonder how Linda feels about this obsession – not just Phil's constant involvement but her sons', Mark and Neil. 'She's been with it since the beginning,' says Phil. 'She has always watched our sons play and she is fully involved on matchdays.' They were supposed to take a break together to celebrate their 40th wedding anniversary in the middle of my research. I even postponed one proposed date because Phil had promised they would go away. When I eventually visited I asked Phil if they had gone away. Of course not. Do they ever get away from Afan Lido? 'We both enjoy our Sunday evenings together. That's when we put our feet up.'

You might reasonably expect anyone who has steered a club through the various levels and who does so many jobs to be a hyperactive, loud, bolshie, pushy character. Phil is the opposite. He is a quiet, diligent man – nobody's fool for sure, but not an irritant or an agitator. You get a glimpse of the real Phil Robinson whenever someone familiar turns up. 'How's it going, Steve, everything all right?' This is followed by something said so fast and in so strong a South Wales dialect that all I can do is smile at both parties.

It is clear he loves matchdays. 'To me, Saturday is special. When summer comes and there is no football you just don't know what to do with yourself. The world changes.' He says this with a laugh, with deliberate over-emphasis. What do you do? 'Er, I don't know. I still come down the ground – we have the clubhouse, there are always things to do. We get out and about – never sit in. I'm the sort of person who has got to keep training otherwise I feel I will wilt away. I still do weights and keep in condition. My life has always been about eating healthily, drinking correctly, looking after yourself and keeping busy.' He has been much more than a facilitator over the years, more a mentor for generations of Afan Lido players. 'Lots of players here have followed my lifestyle, they look after themselves. It was something I passed on so players could perform well, which is beneficial to them as well.'

It has just turned midday, and this is what Phil does every week if there is a home fixture or reserve-team game. 'I have to be busy,' he says again. 'I would be bad company if I had to sit in the house waiting for the game to start. I couldn't cope. I've never sat in the house on Saturdays unless everything is snowed or rained off.' Phil is even hoping he can fit in a few spare minutes to watch a junior game on a nearby field. He cares about each and every Afan Lido team at all levels. For all his efforts, he doesn't always get the chance to watch the home games. The club cannot afford to pay someone to run the bar; Phil just hopes that everyone will leave the bar during the game so he can watch. '"Please, please," I'm thinking, "go out, go out, so I can see the game."'

12.10 P.M.: A ROUND WITH THE DOCTOR In Birmingham Dr Ralph Rogers has finished his morning surgery. He rarely finishes early. There is always an extra client to squeeze in, and the very nature of sports medicine means that people often need to see you at a moment's notice. Ralph runs a private clinic, and hey, they are paying so they want their money's worth. In addition, sportsmen and women are often hypochondriacs. They usually have another niggle to mention, or at least need convincing that there's nothing wrong with them.

The reception area of this huge house – the sort of building in which you'd expect to visit a doctor or dentist – is grand but without the antiseptic smell that, when mixed with polish, usually makes me feel nauseous. I've been chatting to Liz, Ralph's partner, who is doubling up as receptionist today (she runs her own medical supplies business upstairs). It is her seat I will be occupying at Walsall alongside Ralph today. We've been chatting about sports medicine and how it seems to be underestimated in football. She shares my scepticism about the professionalism in football as a whole, not just in terms of medics, but coaches and administrators too. She was a fan of my previous book *The Sack Race*, about football management, in particular the revelations of how shockingly under-qualified many managers are in terms of coaching. 'I don't understand it,' says Liz. 'Why do chairmen keep employing unqualified managers? Why is anyone surprised they change their minds so quickly?' 'People keep saying that's just the way it is,' adds Ralph, folding his white medical coat away. 'I say that ain't the way it should be.'

This is why I like Ralph. I have met him before on several occasions. He is prepared to speak his mind. Being an American who has lived on the continent and in England since 1996, he also has experience of other sports and wider cultures than British football. We will discuss the ethics in depth over supper, but first Ralph and I have a football match to attend. Ralph slips on a dark overcoat over his suit. A tall man, he looks not only smart but professional. I wonder if he is required to wear club gear. 'I'm a doctor,' he replies, 'I'm not a coach or the kit-man. Come on, let's go.' Ralph's a man of style. We're off to the Bescot Stadium in an ice-blue Rolls Royce.

I know what you're thinking. Why should we listen to what Walsall's doctor has to say? If he was any good he'd be working for a top club. All fair points. What Ralph Rogers offers is a different perspective. The way he works is different from most doctors, indeed most medical men. He's not a quack, he's a sports physician, and what he has to say is important. Moreover, he takes his work seriously. His role as club doctor is more intense, literally more hands on than most of his ilk. And his route to the Bescot was much further than a trip down the A34 from Brum.

Doc Rogers, as he calls himself (it suits Ralph when he reels it off with his American accent), is highly trained. He has been to several medical schools in the USA and Europe. If you want to be boring, the letters after his name run MD PhD FECSS FACSM FFSEM, and he calls himself a sports and musculoskeletal physician. He has a BA, a BSc, an MA and a PhD in sports medicine. His PhD from the University of

Maryland's Department of Exercise Physiology was with 'Greatest Distinction with Congratulations from the Jury'. He is a fellow of the American College of Sports Medicine, the European College of Sports Science, the Royal College of Physicians and the Royal College of Surgeons in Ireland; he is a member of the British Medical Association, the Society of Orthopaedic Medicine, the American Medical Society for Sports Medicine, the International Federation of Sports Medicine, the UK Association of Doctors in Sport and the British Institute of Musculoskeletal Medicine. Aside from the Saddlers and running his own clinic, he is doctor to Warwickshire County Cricket Club and was with the Pertemps Birmingham Bullets basketball team and Birmingham City FC's academy. He has also been regional doctor for UK Athletics and doctor of medicine with the Eddy Merckx 2002 cycling team in Belgium. Outside sport, he is involved in corporate wellness and occupational medicine training and in musculoskeletal and orthopaedic care.

Sports medicine is something Ralph chose to specialise in. He is easily irritated when people leap from other disciplines into his field of medical expertise and shows me a BMA advert asking jobbing GPs to offer their services for free for the 2002 Commonwealth Games held in Manchester. In terms of getting a job in British football, he knew he'd be lucky if his education and experience nudged him ahead of an ex-pro who had done a three-month physiotherapy course somewhere. He certainly seems ludicrously over-qualified for a relatively small football club like Walsall, who are wedged between traditionally larger West Midlands clubs such as Wolves, West Brom, Aston Villa and Birmingham City. Although they have had recent spells in the old Division One, they are more at home in the new Coca-Cola League One.

Football, of course, cannot be in every fibre of his being (as Tony Blair might dramatically put it). He hasn't experienced the agonising sting of a wet football on his thigh on a freezing cold day, neither does he know what it is like to stand on an open terrace in the wind and rain. Football is a sport he watched on TV, even if more intensely than his compatriots, especially the onward march of Liverpool in the 1970s and 1980s – something to do with Kevin Keegan's hair and flair and their dominance of European club football. He grew up in New York where he played and appreciated many sports, not just those commonly associated with the USA but lacrosse (which he has played internationally) and martial arts (he is a second dan black belt in ju-jitsu). But does that exclude him from football, this most beguiling of sports?

What, then, is his view on sports medicine in football? 'It has got better since I've lived here,' Ralph replies. 'I have seen a change in the way we are educating our doctors in sports medicine. A lot of progress has been made, but it was so low. Maybe not among the Chelseas or Manchester Uniteds, but medical care is still treated as a minor aspect – and for that you have to look at the owners of clubs and their priorities. You can't expect doctors to work for nothing or very little, but they do.'

Ralph doesn't do only what many club doctors do: fulfil a matchday function by being on hand in case of injury or illness to player or spectator. His role is to be there for Walsall's players as well. 'Yes, as matchday doctor I'm here for the home and away players, but a team physician role is not just about treating injuries. I do pre-match injections and deal with other issues like psychology. Some guys want to talk, some want to bitch about things, which people in all walks of life do. Sometimes you've got to give 'em a swift kick up the ass – you know, they *think* something is wrong, but there isn't anything. Sometimes you have to ask, "What's your *real* problem?" You sit down and talk to them. You don't yell because you'd just lose respect, but you talk it through. What I don't want to do is take away that nervous energy. These guys are professionals, they have their own way of preparing for games. I don't say anything like, "Why are you putting Vicks on your chest or snorting up your nose?"'

Most of Ralph's work with the players is done during the week. As we drive along the A34 from Birmingham to Walsall's ground, Ralph describes how his approach differs from most. Too often the first port of call for injured footballers in the UK is the physiotherapist. 'The phys, the phys, man, it's all about the phys,' Ralph says with a laugh. 'And what is the magic sponge nonsense all about? Rub it over some guy's face and suddenly the blind can see and the lame can walk? I don't buy that. It's stupid.' Ralph respects the role of physiotherapists in football and acknowledges the sterling service they provide. Indeed, in many ways they are the only medical staff most players see unless they sustain a serious injury. 'But physiotherapy is only one area of medical expertise,' he says. 'You wouldn't let an optician treat you for a foot problem, would you? So why is the physio all-seeing and all-knowing? His or her role is important, but it isn't the only one. If you go to any other country in the world it is the team physician who looks after the players. It's tradition here that the physio is the man in charge. You see it with foreign players. They say, "Where is the doc?"'

He explains how it works in the States, and in many other sports. At a set of traffic lights, he draws a big circle on the steering wheel with his finger. 'The doctor is here,' he says, pointing at the centre of the sphere he has drawn. 'The physio is here' – referring to a smaller bubble he is now drawing on the margins – 'here is the masseur' – a similar-sized bubble – 'the osteopath here, the psychologist here, the dietician here and the podiatrist here. When a player is injured, a qualified doctor should diagnose the problem and the course of treatment, and that is when he should bring in these other guys. If a physio wants to prescribe injuries he should go to medical school.'

A club doctor, Ralph adds, should be doing all sorts of things, such as 'regular blood tests to see if players are eating right and how they are reacting to training regimes or any other problems. It's just not done here to that kind of level. These sorts of tests are actually mandatory in countries like Spain and Italy to participate in professional sport, so it is important. There are a lot of things we're not doing here that I think we should be. You can look around at a lot of big clubs and see they are not sports medicine trained. A lot of these guys are GPs who have an interest in sports medicine. I'm not jealous because I love Walsall and I'm very happy here, but for me that's an insult because this is what I do. They are not sports physicians. They have an interest, that's all.'

12.15 P.M.: THE REFEREE ARRIVES As we approach Portman Road, Paul Taylor's coach, the former Premier League ref Paul Durkin (who is also now a Football League referee), calls. He has his own game today but is just checking to make sure everything is OK.

This is something I'm surprised to discover – that a refereeing camaraderie exists. The jokes are ribald and the crack is evident. He's the fourth to call, and Paul has also made a couple of calls himself to fellow referees. Durkin is not Paul's assessor, he advises rather than reports back on Paul's performance – a subtle difference.

Paul parks as close as possible to the ground, 'just in case'. This, as I later find out, is a wise decision. At Ipswich he can park right next to the main reception, which is opposite a training pitch. He lifts a huge kit bag with unfolding wheels out of the boot of his car. The bag contains his own kit plus flags, electronic beepers and all the paperwork that will be needed today.

In the tunnel his first priority is to find each team's kit men and check the exact colours of the team strips. This used to be so the colours didn't clash, but now it is also to decide which colour shirt the ref will wear. Like Ford cars, referees used to be able to choose any colour as long as it was black; now it might be green or yellow. In Scotland the refs are cheekily sponsored by Specsavers, which is daubed across their shirts.

Paul drops his gear in the official changing room and heads for a lounge reserved for family and friends. There he meets his assistants for the day, Tim Howes and Trevor Pollard, fourth official Steve Artis and assessor John Elwin. They wish each other a happy new year, share a coffee, watch a bit of Sky Sports News and then get down to business.

12.20 P.M.: CORNISH RED ARRIVES Neil Williams pulls into the car park at a college opposite the Racecourse Ground in Wrexham. It is filling up already – mainly fans turning up for the pre-match meeting at the college. Neil is keen to show me around the ground. I haven't been here since 1979 when, on a warm May day, I saw England crash to a 4–1 defeat against Wales having taken an early lead. England's fans behaved appallingly. There was random violence and mayhem everywhere. Neil recalls stones being thrown into the home end, The Kop, some hitting children and ruining this proud day for the home nation who for once were masters of England on the pitch. Fans streamed home early, many at half-time. Sadly, it was days like those that finished the home internationals.

The Racecourse is a neat stadium. The new Pryce Griffiths Stand is a bright, modern structure, and you don't need to be a football fan to realise its loss would be an immense blow to the club. We head to the club offices and meet secretary Geraint Parry, who is one of football's nice guys, a lovely man who has put his shoulder to the wheel in the hard times. Neil pops in to collect a few more shirts for the collection he intends to auction. He is two-thirds of the way towards getting a shirt signed by their players from every Premier/Football League club. Most clubs have been good; others haven't quite got the point. They thought Wrexham would pay for the shirt. How naive! Neil is proudly showing off his Cornish Red shirt, hoping some of the people he exchanges emails with will now be able to put a face to the name and say hello.

We also visit a small shop the supporters trust has set up next to the Turf pub. Again, more willing workers are giving their free time to help the club. Fans are already eagerly buying things to swell the coffers, including some visitors from faraway clubs here to back the Clubs in Crisis day – a chap from Hull, someone in a Port Vale shirt and, most welcome of all, given their links, a fan from Brighton. A football family of sorts is about to assemble at the college. I recognise some of the speakers: Phil Tooley, acting managing director of the government-backed scheme Supporters Direct and chairman of the Chesterfield Supporters Society; Nic Outterside, a Brighton & Hove Albion fan living in Newcastle (why not?) who has been the prime mover behind Fans United and was named Radio Five Live's fan of the year; and my journalist colleague David Conn, who writes for *The Independent* and has chronicled the plight of so many of these clubs. Unsurprisingly, knowing some of these people, the bar is already doing brisk business.

There has been widespread publicity for Wrexham's Clubs in Crisis day, which has been organised by Fans United. The audience includes Wrexham fans involved in their supporters trust, some from clubs who have been through the mill, and others who just care. Neil Williams sits down with them. Like so many fans, he is new to all this. Most of them only become politicised when a crisis hits their club. I wonder how many more of these events writers like me and David Conn will have to attend before the game's governors close the loopholes that allow clubs to be ripped away from the supporters.

Days like today, when fans of many clubs gang together, are truly heart-warming. A cluster of fans who have travelled up from the Potteries – some Stoke City, others Port Vale – sum it up. 'We saw it advertised, Wrexham were in crisis very much like ourselves, so we decided, because we hadn't got a game today, to come along and support them.' Nic Outterside, who addresses the meeting, talks of the 'special bond' that exists between fans of his club Brighton and today's visitors, Doncaster Rovers, 'that has never weakened'. Both clubs experienced financial difficulties in the mid-1990s: Doncaster had their main stand burned down by their former chairman, for which he was convicted, and Brighton had their ground sold by a former owner who made lots of money but left the club homeless. 'It is now quite strange that a bond has stretched between Brighton and Wrexham,' adds Outterside, handing Wrexham Supporters Trust committee member Simon Johnson a 'token' Brighton & Hove Albion Supporters Club scarf. Phil Tooley urges Wrexham fans not to panic. 'Chesterfield have been there before. We were in crisis in 2001. We were minutes away from dying as a club, so if we, when we have a blank day, can't come along and support a club like Wrexham it's a poor show. Hopefully we'll be able to come back here in years to come as well.'

I chat to a Cardiff City fan who travelled from the south of Wales to the north to back the Wrexham cause. 'Every football fan should support Wrexham in this situation because it would be a pity if they went bust,' he says. I suggest it could be Cardiff one day. He looks slightly incredulous. 'I don't think so, but you never know. Look at Swansea and Leeds. You name them. It could happen at any time.' (A month later Cardiff announced they were £29 million in debt, which looked likely to scupper a new ground move.)

The consciousness is spreading. Steve Davis, a lifelong Wrexham fan, describes the way many fans now feel, a view that twenty years ago would have been heartily laughed at and deemed impossible. 'Yes, I laughed at the Doncaster chairman and the burning of the ground. The Chesterfield problems – they beat us in the quarter-finals of the FA Cup; you're not as keen on them as maybe you should be. Then all of a sudden something happens to you and you find people coming out of the woodwork to support you. I'll never forget the support we've had from football clubs. I'm sorry. I'm ashamed of what I didn't know before and what I know now. Thank you for the support of other football clubs, it means a lot.' The WST's Simon Johnson calls for stronger regulation. 'The time has come for the government and for the Football League and the FA to realise that football clubs are far more important to the community. They are not just profit-making organisations. We need to protect them for the fans of the future.' But you can hammer home the point too strongly. Looking behind me, I notice that Neil and Josh have slipped out. Neil tells me later that they went for a pre-match pie and to get into the ground in good time for the kick-off.

A pie and three points – well, they are kinda traditional, and very important. It's why we're here after all.

12.25 P.M.: LEAVING FOR ASHTON GATE Danny Coles shuts his front door and heads for Bristol City's ground. He is feeling his first nerves of the day. 'I'm usually fairly laid back. I don't tend to show my emotions, but I can feel it starting to build up now,' he says, as he packs some kit into his car boot and walks round to the door. 'This is a big game in our season. We've had a bit of a break [a fortnight: they didn't play over Easter because they had players on international duty]. Other sides have played in between and haven't particularly made the most of them. We need a win to boost our play-off hopes.'

It's a warm day after several weeks of poor weather. It might be an important factor. Danny has had a cold and a sore throat – not enough to stop him training, but he is coughing routinely. As he sits in his seat, he muses about today's opponents, Port Vale. 'They need a result to get away from the relegation zone, so it's an important game for both sides.'

Danny has started to bite his bottom lip. He has also looked at his watch several times. One of the most nerve-racking things for players is counting down the minutes to kick-off. There isn't much to do, or that the club actually want you to do. All he has to do is get to the ground, park up, sort out tickets for his family, listen to Brian Tinnion's team talk and then prepare to run off some of that nervous energy.

12.30 P.M.: THE SECURITY BRIEFING At Carrow Road Neil Doncaster is about to attend the pre-match security meeting. This is held at the same time ahead of every Norwich City home game and is standard procedure, as laid down by the post-Taylor Report regulations on ground safety. 'The chain of command is different on matchdays,' explains Neil as we head through a maze of corridors in the main stand, which is at the apex with the Barclay Stand. 'On non-matchdays you've got myself, as chief executive, reporting to the board of directors, and senior managers, such as Nigel Worthington, the football manager, Andrew Cullen, who is in charge of sales and marketing, and Shaun O'Hara, head of catering, who report to me. On matchdays it's the head of security who has command throughout the game, and before and after. Effectively he is running the game.' He smiles cheekily as he opens a door for me. 'It prevents amateurs like me thinking we've got a valid opinion to offer on running the show. He runs the game. If something happens and the police come in and take control of the game, then they can do that. That hasn't happened in the eight years I've been here, though.'

The control room is a fascinating area. It is the nerve centre for matchday security. Banks of CCTV cameras are laid out with operators staring intently at them. They can zoom in and out or rotate cameras in order to keep tabs on what is happening both inside and outside the ground, and maybe further afield. The control room has a radio link to stewards in the stands who can react to situations viewed from up high. In some ways it is reassuring: should there be an incident an instant response can take place. On the other hand, with observation comes inevitable intrusion. Don't think you can get away with surreptitiously picking your nose or getting something out of your pocket or hiding something away without it being noticed. This is actually a bit scary, but a price most fans would, on balance, concede is worth paying when you consider the lack of control in the past.

Control of the ground is now given to Norwich's stadium operations manager, Leon Blackburn, who issues a briefing to all heads of department in attendance, including head stewards in charge of different areas of the ground, police, transport police, catering, the public address announcer and the chief executive (Neil). He spells out that this is a high-profile game but that Chelsea should present few extra problems than most matches. This is a category B match, not a high-alert game; a bit of trouble may occur, but it isn't like a feisty local derby or a bottom-of-the-table six-pointer. Chelsea have a small kernel of troublemakers, we are told (though less so than in the past when they had well-documented problems), and the briefing on their supporters is incredibly detailed. Some will frequent city-centre pubs for several hours, but only two coaches are expected (most will come by train or car). And they have seventeen disabled fans.

The unique arrangements of Roman Abramovic are also covered in detail, including the time he is expected to arrive at Norwich airport, his journey to the game, where he will be dropped off and how his car will exit the main entrance. It's a bit like a royal visit. As a well-known Russian oligarch whose public appearances are few but whose enemies, according to various reports, are many, he will have four personal bodyguards who will have to be accommodated. They have not, as was feared, requested permission to carry guns. We are assured this would have been rejected. Nonetheless, Abramovic's appearance presents an extra security burden. Main stand stewards are warned to be extra vigilant. Delia Smith's intention to sit in the Barclay Stand is also dealt with. To say the least it raises some eyebrows. There will be understandable media interest, especially from photographers. Stewards in that area are warned to be wary of security implications. The stewards are also asked to keep an eye on fans near the front of stands because it's a snowy day and it may be slippery underfoot, inside and outside the ground. It is hoped fans will turn up, as requested, in good time to prevent any injuries.

Neil does not chip in. He listens intently. Another matchday meeting is ticked off.

12.32 P.M.: GROUNDHOP DAY II Bill Berry is heading south, through the Cotswolds across to the A41, to watch a game in the Hertfordshire Senior League Premier Division between Evergreen and Hadley. Evergreen's ground is north of Watford, just off the M25. It will take us two hours or so to get there. By Bill's standards, we're cutting it fine. 'I never leave it until the last minute,' he says. He usually plans his trips through the week, refining it down to two or three options on Friday night. He then checks the weather – 'no good going to an area in the country where they are predicting blizzards, frost or snow' – and gives the clubs a call on Saturday morning to check the games are still on. 'Even on a nice day like today – cold, but bright – you never know what might happen. The away team might not turn up for whatever reason and then you can be left without a game to go to. Sometimes you can be down to number six on the list, but it is up to you to decide where to go.

There's a lot of freedom.' Bill has to have a contingency plan and make sure he has enough time to act on it if need be. Even if our destination game is called off, he has to be there for the kick-off of Game B. Being late is not an option.

Let me explain a bit about the level of football we're going to see today. The FA has recently revamped the non-League pyramid, and in the structure of the English football game the Hertfordshire Senior League is ranked as level 12. And that doesn't mean it is the twelfth highest league in the country. *Au contraire*, it is the twelfth level of football. So the Premier League is level 1, the Coca-Cola Championship level 2, League One level 3, and so on. Take twelve steps down from Old Trafford, Highbury and Anfield and you cascade through the regional feeder leagues to county level, and clubs like Evergreen FC. 'This is their first season in this league,' says Bill optimistically about his choice of match. He has done roughly half of the grounds in this league and he is interested to see how Evergreen's ground matches up to those he has already visited.

Each level requires certain facilities. At this level – level 12, remember – that will probably be changing rooms, a club bar, and a hard-standing area, maybe with posts all the way round, for spectators to stand behind. They will have to offer set medical facilities too, and decent dugouts. Few countries peel back so many layers of the game or have so many individual clubs as Britain. On the continent it is far more common to have big sporting clubs that field several recreational sides, so the players find their levels and progress up and down through the club. Giants like Ajax in Holland and Barcelona in Spain operate in this way. They are true community clubs in a way that virtually no well-known, successful British clubs are. Almost half of all English clubs across all levels field just one team. We are not as sociable. It's sad, but it does give people like Bill Berry a lot more grounds to visit. So many, in fact, that seasoned groundhoppers like Bill, who has been at it for more than 30 years, stand no realistic chance of ever bumping them all off.

I have to confess this isn't the first time I've been to a game with Bill. During season 2000/01 I recorded a Radio 4 feature with him on the winter from hell for groundhoppers. Bill used the F word a lot. Three of them, in fact: floods, fuel protests and foot and mouth. All struck that season, so even if they could get petrol, even if they could find a fixture that was on, they weren't always welcome to take their city ways with them to country areas that had been closed to visitors. That day, Bill demonstrated an experienced groundhopper's skill and ingenuity. We headed to the East Midlands. It rained hard all day, and fixtures fell by the wayside. But Bill used his nous defiantly to steer us to a game in a Nottinghamshire pit village.

Although we don't get so much snow these days, global warming is wreaking havoc with groundhopping. Honest. More rain means more postponements, which means more late fixture cancellations. And if you routinely head for small grounds that can't cope you are going to find more abandoned games. And if you're a groundhopper, that simply won't do. We're a nation of softies nowadays. Whereas we once worried about little more than making sure snow or puddles didn't prevent us from seeing line markings, today we're more concerned about part-time or recreational players picking up injuries. We're also more litigious: players have sued referees for letting games go ahead during which they've been injured, claiming it could have been avoided – although I have never seen a referee cattle-prod a player on to a pitch against his will.

I like Bill, he's good company. As we cut through the Cotswolds and small towns such as Moreton-in-Marsh, Chipping Norton and Woodstock, he explains how he and Ann moved to Broadway in 1987 to escape the rat race in London. Initially a civil servant, Bill met Ann while working for a travel company in London. When the company folded, they took redundancy and moved out to the peaceful Cotswolds. Ann got a job working in tourism at nearby Sudeley Castle (she now works at the University of Gloucestershire in Cheltenham), and Bill set up the *Football Traveller* to provide an invaluable service for groundhopping, which, he says, was at its peak. I wonder why groundhopping grew, and indeed how this disparate, some would say desperate, group of individuals (bearing in mind the anonymity of their hobby) had developed and grown into a network.

Bill, who grew up in Putney, had been an avid Fulham fan, following them home and away in his youth and even watching youth-team games on Saturday mornings when Fulham were at home, plus midweek reserve-team games. There was no definitive moment for Bill. But when

Fulham, as they have so many times, fell into decline in the early 1970s he found himself less attracted to long, boring away trips – despite his hobby, he insists he isn't a good traveller – and he started watching games at other grounds around London. 'Evenutally I stopped going to Fulham home games too, and I went to watch the likes of Kingstonian, Corinthian Casuals and Tooting and Mitcham. It grew slowly from there. The distances travelled increased and I went to different leagues like the Southern League and Isthmian League, as it was then. It was fascinating seeing these clubs that had their own very interesting backgrounds. Some of them had lovely old grounds, like Tooting at Sandy Lane, which has now gone.' These clubs were a real throwback to the way football once was. And this was 30 years ago. Imagine the post-Premier League blues many fans have now. Some of the clubs were great names in the amateur and semi-pro game, and often something of a mystery to fans, who never bothered to check them out or learn more.

Bill soon realised he wasn't the only fan who felt this way. With some clubs staggering their fixtures in an attempt to draw a crowd, such as Southend, who played on Friday nights, as did Stockport County in the north-west, and Torquay, who uniquely played on Saturday evenings, he began to meet fellow fans who travelled to watch different clubs every week so that they could clock up as many grounds as possible. Bill found he derived more pleasure from watching matches at smaller grounds, where you generally found a friendlier welcome and where you could relate to the players who weren't earning exorbitant wages. 'You would group together to get fixtures for different leagues,' recalls Bill. 'There was no internet back then or magazines catering for groundhoppers [though before Bill's *Football Traveller* there was the *Groundhopper* magazine], so you each got the fixtures and shared journeys and stories.' A network of fellow souls developed, and as they began to seek out grounds further afield they linked up with others around the country. 'We seemed to be the first of a breed,' Bill observes. 'But there must have been people who were older than us doing it.'

Maybe not, if you listen to people who watched football either side of the Second World War. By and large they didn't travel long distances to watch football. In fact, despite the ballsy, fashionable breed of fans who make so many stupid and simply incorrect assumptions about what it is like to be an age-old diehard 'true' fan, our parents and forefathers did not laboriously follow their clubs everywhere. They didn't have the money and didn't have the inclination. What they did do more often than not, was watch their preferred club one week and their rivals the following week. My dad was a Wolves fan, but he saw plenty of West Brom and Villa games. It was the done thing. But he never dreamed of trekking to, say, Newcastle to watch Wolves. So maybe there *wasn't* a generation before Bill Berry's who groundhopped. Why would they? How could they?

'I've seen groundhopping grow from only a handful of people to maybe a thousand or more,' says Bill as we steer north of Oxford on to the A41. Getting a bit serious, I ask why he thinks groundhopping emerged. 'I think there was a lot of disenchantment with the experience of going to matches in the 1970s and 1980s – the hooligans and the measures to combat them. Obviously for some people, going and watching professional football at one club wasn't enough. There is rarely any trouble at non-League grounds. Where we go they are generally more pleased to see you. It means a lot, someone coming a long distance to watch. I went to one ground recently and when they realised I had travelled a long way they handed me my money back, halfway through the first half. Imagine a professional club doing that.'

Tales are told of legendary groundhoppers who clocked up more than 1,000 grounds. Many of them met up using public transport to reach remote grounds (oh, I forgot to mention this: some, albeit a small number of groundhoppers, will *only* use public transport to get to games – a fastidious logistical nightmare making arrangements much harder and lengthier, although for some it remains the only viable means of travel). But, unlike his most ardent readers, Bill is happy to select just one match every Saturday of the season, usually within a couple of hours' drive. He doesn't deliberately seek to pick off clubs one by one as some groundhoppers do. He's actually well past the 1,000 landmark now, even though he has never totted them all up, but he's nowhere near completing the 92 Premier/Football League clubs – a level of football he has little more than a passing interest in these days. To him, groundhopping is a casual hobby to be enjoyed. 'When I was younger I did get a bit strung up about it if I couldn't go to a game on Saturday. But it's not the end of the world. No one will know.' A couple of weekends a season Bill will actually do the decent thing: go out with Ann and miss a footy match altogether.

Groundhopping has taken him to a variety of locations, from downtrodden urban settings in the shadow of council blocks where you fear for the safety of your car during the match (these days Bill does not head for the inner cities), through to wonderful scenic venues. Rhyader in mid-Wales is one that readily springs to Bill's mind. There is something wonderfully, wistfully romantic about watching games in all of football's settings. Football is, after all, a true national game. I think of Stuart Clarke, the photographer who took the cover shots for this book, who with conspicuous success has turned his lens away from the action to the folks watching the games. I often think of his images when I am in some Godforsaken part of the country on a Saturday afternoon. It was Stuart who told me that when he lived near Coniston Water he would row a boat out on to the lake because there he could get the best reception for Radio Five Live. Now, whenever I hear the spine-tingling sounds of *Sports Report* and James Alexander Gordon reading the classified results, I imagine Stuart sitting in his boat, fishing maybe, wondering how Portsmouth are doing. There is something so beguiling about the image. All those urban grounds with the crowds squeezed in and the pungent smell of hot dogs, sweat, steam, smoke and petrol fumes, and then the peace of the Lake District. This is an all-embracing game that is consumed in a variety of ways in a host of differing locations. Bill has never been to a game in the Lake District, but he ought to. There are some fantastic grounds up there. Stuart has photographed them, and they fill his books. Groundhopping may sound like a strange hobby, a veritable psychological minefield ripe for analysis, but somehow it all fits neatly into place.

'How low would you go, Bill?'

'When I started out,' Bill replies, 'I thought I wouldn't go below the Southern or Isthmian League. But then you move on to the county leagues. There are so many of them so the line moves that bit further down.' He tells me about the annual Devon Hop, an annual three-day festival over the Easter weekend during which Devon league clubs stagger their kick-off times to accommodate groundhoppers, who watch three games a day. It started in the northeast, moved to Cornwall, and now into Devon. Other leagues, such as the Hellenic League in the Home Counties/South Midlands and the Central Midlands League (covering the East Midlands), organise similar gatherings. It boosts crowds and raises income. Several hundred groundhoppers descend on these venues, and many of the players in these games will never again get the chance to play in front of such big crowds. Bill talks of warm welcomes, clotted cream teas and home-made pasties, and asks me how many grounds I've been to lately with sun-kissed lakes or rolling hills behind them.

'Er …'

'How much does it cost to watch a Premier League game?' Bill follows up. 'Thirty quid? That's far more than I will ever spend on a day out. Today it'll be a few quids' worth of petrol, 50p to get in, and a half-time cuppa. What would that buy at Stamford Bridge or Craven Cottage or The Hawthorns?'

Not a lot.

With the price hikes at the top level of the game you may expect disillusionment with the professional game to have spiralled down to the grass roots and for groundhopping to have increased in recent years, but Bill believes it is in decline. 'It peaked about ten years ago, I would say. Maybe it's a generational thing. There aren't too many younger people getting into the hobby. The people I see are the people I used to see ten, fifteen, twenty years ago. A lot of people go by public transport, and the decline of train and bus services is well known. There are some people who have clocked up two or three thousand grounds, but you have to be a single man to do that and have time to travel to the continent where you might, say, knock off five or six grounds over a long weekend.' Hmm. Single men, old enough to clock up thousands of grounds – do the maths. We ain't talking about young bachelors here, but crusty crumbs-in-beard blokes. Though Bill isn't one of those. Nowhere near it.

Some people may be relieved about this decline – fewer oddballs walking the streets. On the other hand it also reflects a worrying theory that younger people simply aren't watching football matches. That the Sky Sports generation are content to watch the game at home in their armchairs and are rarely interested in darkening the doors of football grounds. Their parents are happy to dole out £40 or so a month to watch footy on Sky, or are just priced out of the loop altogether. A worrying implication, because as with so many other activities, if you don't get 'em when they're young you don't get 'em at all. Top clubs may be smug at the moment, but the longer term implications are dire. If more and more fans feel disenfranchised they may just want to search out small grounds, chew them up, tick them off, collect them like stamps, trains, planes or coins. Maybe.

Bill, for one, still gets a buzz out of going to see games, though he doesn't enjoy the travelling any more. 'It's the attraction of going somewhere different each week,' he says. 'Some you pitch up to and receive a nasty shock in terms of facilities, but for every one of those you get a pleasant surprise.' Recently, Bill planned a trip to a fairly local ground, Malvern Town, in the shadow of the hills and in the heart of Elgar country, only to find it wasn't a very pretty place at all. 'But that's the fascination – you don't know what you will find. I like a variety of grounds. And I don't like travelling along the same roads each week so I pick matches to suit. I don't feel the need to stay at one level. If I can get to a game along a pleasant scenic route and see a decent game of football, that does for me. Even if the football is a bit depressing, sometimes the scenery can be quite spectacular.' Visiting different towns, cities and villages, sampling different slices of British life, a bit of local culture with a footy match thrown in – it's partly the clichéd search for the soul of English football. 'It's different things to different people,' Bill says. 'I'm not particularly into the social side; I like to watch the games. But sometimes you have people stood next to you and they're not actually looking towards the pitch.'

As we head down the A41 past Bicester, I wonder what the promising-sounding Evergreen FC will be like – a pastoral setting, or next door to Watford's worst council estate?

12.35 P.M.: MIDLAND JUNIOR PREMIER FOOTBALL LEAGUE Bob Marley is late again. He's made his way from Hadley Rangers, the junior club, quickly picked up Seb's gear from the family home, driven on to where he is lodging at the moment, then on to Worcester City's junior development ground. Bob is chairman of the Midland Junior Premier Football League (MJPFL), a raft of football clubs set up this season (2004/05) for players aged twelve to sixteen in non-League club youth programmes. Not academies – that moniker belongs to the Premier/ Football League clubs who have seized control of the word, even over colleges and universities, despite an academy actually being a mythical grove where Plato taught his students. Not a centre of excellence for that matter either. No, if they use any term other than youth development programme the Football Association have threatened to come down on them like a ton of bricks. So they're youth development programmes.

The MJPFL is an ambitious project aimed at plugging the yawning gap between the professional club academies, funded to the tune of millions of pounds including significant slices of public/TV money, and the morass that is local junior football played mainly on Sunday afternoons, with poor behaviour egged on by the few ruining it for the many. The spark for starting the MJPFL came after one of Bob's players was repeatedly stamped on during a game. It fits neatly around schools football, which sadly has been decimated by the demands of professional clubs, which dissuade 'their' junior players from participating in schools football and even, when they can get away with it, other sports. The league is in its infancy but it has lofty aims: to provide quality coaching in small towns and cities across the Midlands, and the chance for local boys to pit their skills against rivals from fellow non-League clubs.

Despite the oft-held misconception that football's heartland is mainly the inner city, football is not solely played under the noses of the big clubs or within touching distance of their academies. It is often assumed that promising players who live in small towns or rural communities should naturally be ferried by their parents to large professional clubs without the club adhering to any obligation to keep them informed of their progress. The MJPFL may not offer the same facilities or quality of coaching, but it is on their doorsteps. A parent in Worcester, for example, sending their child to, say, one of the large West Midland academies – Aston Villa, Birmingham, Wolves or West Brom – will easily clock up a few hundred miles a week. Add the time involved, not least of all precious hours when they could be doing their homework, and it is an immense sacrifice. Bob Marley and the people running the MJPFL clubs realised there was a gap in the market. They can, and are, stealing a march where the professional clubs are failing. They may not have the same resources, but they have the same desire to develop players from their communities for their teams, and that is what is happening.

'The first-team games are important, but not *that* important to me,' says Bob as he unravels some goal nets. 'Last season we had a match arranged in Beverin in Belgium via our sponsors. A big game and an important night. Every one of our directors went except for me because it was our trials night for the U-14s. Where could I be more use to Worcester City? Drinking champagne in Belgium or helping our U-14s? No decision, in my mind.'

Worcester City's youth set-up is on a strip of land off the busy A38 which has changing rooms and enough space for four pitches. This is the very field where I played my first football. It used to belong to the local schools authority, and children from Stanley Road Junior School would be ferried here by coach every Friday afternoon. While Bob disappears to change, I look around, remembering it as if it were yesterday. A group of excited boys who had never played on a proper pitch before (we didn't have space at our school) would eagerly race on to the bus at school and jump off at the other end and into the changing rooms. Being here now as a forty-something adult approaching middle age is deeply moving. I can recall the smell of the freshly polished, warm coach; our rubber-soled boots with straps that were so difficult to untangle in the cold and that lashed against your legs; the difficulty of keeping shin pads on your ankles; the steam of the hot showers; the spattering of mud against the walls.

I recall playing here as a seven-year-old. Coldness and rain enveloped the field. And our bully of a PE teacher, an unkindly man called Mr Penny who hopefully wouldn't be let anywhere near a classroom these days, was in charge. He once hurled an ink bottle at a classmate for misspelling a word and never said anything remotely encouraging to any of us; he just issued bollockings when we did things wrong and carried out routine acts of physical abuse with total disregard for his obligation to teach. In fact, now I think about it, I don't reckon Mr Penny derived any pleasure from teaching at all. He certainly never smiled. Any poor unsporting boys were left to their own devices at the far end of the field. I bet you can sue for that kind of treatment these days. He once described my uncle, who had played in goal to a decent level of recreational football, as 'an idiot' when I optimistically tried to engage in a discussion about the finer points of goalkeeping and imparted what Uncle Bill had told me. Mr Penny wasn't someone to ponder the hurt he might cause children, but then neither was he particularly brave when I bumped into him in town when I was eighteen and asked him if he would like to try and ram my head against a cupboard door now.

Despite Mr Penny, on these fields I learned the rudiments of the game. Receiving the ball, trapping it, passing, moving on. It was an essential part of growing up. That hour or so on Fridays afternoons was great, but I was so jealous of other schools that had their own pitches and I remember the sense of inferiority when we played football or cricket at their schools. I am truly sorry this field is no longer available to the schoolchildren of Worcester, but pleased that Worcester City FC have got it, given it a lick of paint, refurbished the dressing rooms and made it available to hundreds of young players.

Bob Marley comes running out of the dressing rooms in a vaguely comical Corinthian sprint. As the chairman of the MJPFL, he could lord it up a bit if he chose. Stand back a bit, observe what is going on. Maybe he should. But now, in shorts, sweatshirt and socks, he's hands on. He marches around, putting the corner flags up, roping off an area for parents to stand behind. He is working towards a UEFA B professional coaching qualification, and although he is in overall charge of the development programme, he always coaches a Worcester City junior team every week. Today he's helping Andy Knowles to coach the U-13s, and he puts them through their pre-match paces. The team includes his own son, Seb. Mandy and Sam join the parents over on the far side of the field. Three matches are going on today, at U-12, U-13 and U-15 levels. It genuinely feels like a club.

12.40 P.M.: SOUP AND SANDWICHES WITH THE REVEREND John Boyers has mapped out his philosophy for sports chaplaincy and I have listened and learned. He has told me, quite graphically, about how he does his job; how he reacts, if not exactly in an emergency, certainly at short notice; how he tries to reach vulnerable young men on the cusp of fame and fortune, or those who fail to make it. But I'm troubled. There are several questions I want to ask. I sense John knows they are coming. I feel you may, too.

First, we break bread. John's wife, Anne, has prepared soup, sandwiches and freshly brewed coffee – hearty food for a winter's day, and greatly appreciated.

In theory, few people would disagree with the value of John's work. But should he be more proactive? What about the moral climate at football clubs? There are clearly people at all levels of the game – and one could run through any list of misdemeanours – whose words and actions are decidedly unChristian. So is there a need for chaplains to address these moral issues by confronting the guilty parties and condemning them? 'I think you need to understand the parameters of your role as a chaplain,' explains John. 'The behaviour of players on or off the field is the manager or coach's job. Sometimes a manager or coach may pick my brains on an issue. What would you say? What do you think? I try not to impose my moral stance on other people, but if an opinion is sought I will offer it.' In his work John throws issues at players, for example sexual ethics. 'I'll ask a group of players, "If your girlfriend says she is pregnant, how do you react? Do you know she is genuine or is she just trying to trap you? Should you pay for an abortion?" Throw that out to a group of young men and it is interesting what responses you get. I'm not there to say this is right, this is wrong. I am there to say, "Think about these issues and these actions and what may result."'

John's time at Old Trafford has coincided with some of the biggest sports news stories the game has seen, and some carry a moral dimension: Eric Cantona's kung fu kick at Crystal Palace; Roy Keane's lengthy ban following ugly remarks in his autobiography; Rio Ferdinand's failure to take a drug test and his subsequent ban; Ferguson's flying boot hitting David Beckham; indeed, the constant stories surrounding Beckham during his time at United; and, latterly, numerous instances involving Wayne Rooney. Then there are the boardroom manoeuvres: the so-called Coolmore Mafia 'war' with Alex Ferguson, the takeover attempts by Rupert Murdoch and Malcolm Glazer (now successful, of course). Major news stories. I don't insult

John by asking him to reveal confidences (he wouldn't anyway), but I do wonder whether he should actively express a view on such subjects, take a moral stance. Would supporters appreciate admonishment of immoral or amoral behaviour from the club chaplain? They might respect him for doing so.

John isn't convinced. 'To admonish is not a terribly helpful thing,' he says. 'Sometimes you do admonish, but I don't go around imposing my morality on people. It's a bit like the stranger asking the Devon farmer for the way to a nearby town, and him replying, "Well, if I was you I wouldn't start from here." If people ask for your advice I feel a lot happier, but I don't take the lead. You have to be very careful. You must be peripheral rather than integral to what is going on. What right do you have to speak on behalf of the club when you haven't been invited to? I'm concerned about that.'

John refers to a topical case in point. The previous week Wayne Rooney had returned to play for United at Everton in an FA Cup tie. There was huge speculation about the reception he would get. One of Everton's chaplains (they have two!) emailed John to suggest they should issue a joint statement with a clear Christian response in an attempt to draw a line under the transfer saga. 'I wrote back to say I didn't necessarily think we should do that. I wouldn't do anything without the club asking me to do so and I certainly wouldn't do so without the club affirming that is what they wanted. I feel there are probably only a small number of Everton supporters who are committed Christians. Are those most likely to be involved in abuse going to be committed Christians, and are they likely to listen to us? I see club chaplaincy as a low-profile thing. Some people try to make their mark via soundbites and photographs. They do things to promote themselves. I don't see chaplaincy as self-promotion. I think we are valued because we're genuine. We're not there blowing our own trumpet and trying to get in the limelight.'

These are deep ethical debates. John is well versed in them, and his views are thoroughly thought out. I guess there is another line: if he and his colleagues pushed their luck, would the door be slammed shut in their face? And what good would that do? To round off the conversation, John likens chaplaincy to mortar in a house. 'The bricks are what the house is made of, but the mortar hangs it together. The chaplain doesn't make the club work, but there are instances when you realise the job is hugely worthwhile. You can't help all of the people all of the time, but you can help some people some of the time.'

12.45 P.M.: DANGEROUS LIAISONS 'Worcester coach station, September 28th 1974. A young man stands alone.' So begins my best man's wedding speech. 'Long blond hair. And I mean long [points to below shoulders]. Crombie. West Brom scarf – a bit sad really.'

I could kill my mate Tim Lewis. Why's he mentioning this? Why now? It's not a picture you particularly want painted for your new in-laws. Do we really need to hear this?

'Then I looked down at myself. Long blond hair, Crombie and, yes, a West Brom scarf. Better.'

And so it goes on. A lifelong friendship forged through waiting for a Midland Red bus to a West Brom tie with Oxford United in the old Second Division. 'Big game,' says Tim, mockingly, in his speech. Huge laughs.

Even my best man's wedding speech was dominated by matchday. Tim recalled tales of a friendship essentially established and maintained through football. A tale of two lonely souls who had no immediate mates prepared to travel the 25 miles from Worcester to West Brom on public transport.

I had first been taken to the Hawthorns by my Uncle Jack, who was a Baggies fan but rarely went to games. He got us a lift to the ground from a friend at the printing company he worked at, a lovely Yorkshireman called Larry Licence – what a great name. I went lots of times with Larry's family. His son, Chris, went to my secondary school, Nunnery Wood. They had a small Triumph Herald. I don't think I ever travelled in Licence's Herald with fewer than five of us squeezed inside. It was like Doctor Who's Tardis – bigger on the inside than it seemed from outside.

My first game was a 2–2 draw against Don Revie's Leeds in October 1970. I had played my first match for Nunnery Wood U-12s in the morning, come home and proudly pronounced it the best day of my life. Playing for the school and watching West Brom. Life didn't get any better than that for an eleven-year-old boy. It took twelve games, all at home, before I saw Albion win. Eight of those round dozen were score draws, so when we beat Manchester United 2–1 in January 1972 with

46,000 shoehorned into the Hawthorns, I thought I had won the pools.

I could hardly be accused of having my head easily turned. My dad took me a few times, but he wasn't a West Brom supporter. He was very caring towards the end of the 1972/73 season when Albion were relegated. He drove me to night matches, and even though he was a Wolves supporter (he'd actually taken me to see them play on my ninth birthday in the vain hope of converting me), when we went to a match at Molineux near the end of the season, which Albion inevitably lost, he didn't cheer the Wolves goals, gloat in any way or say anything that wasn't totally sympathetic about Albion's plight. He hated driving to big congested places so it couldn't have been easy for him, but he loved his son, and I'm sure if he could have done anything to alleviate the misery of relegation for me he would have done it.

But by this time I was already a regular traveller on the Midland Red bus to matches, mostly on my own. The problem was, at fourteen I didn't really have any mates who wanted to stand near the back of the Brummie Road End, who wanted to be part of the special atmosphere of the terraces, to join in the songs and savour the general feeling of the crowd as it built, let alone someone who was into the same fashion or music. And Albion weren't a trendy team. Being relegated for the first time in 24 years didn't help. Most of my school chums supported other clubs, the usual suspects of the day: Man Utd, Leeds, Chelsea, some team called Aston Villa who had been a Third Division club. I was seen as a maverick, so I would usually troop into town and get the bus to matches alone.

That bus seemed to sum it all up. Most of the passengers were middle-aged men who had kept the faith but didn't or couldn't drive a car so travelled on a bus instead. I used to sit near the back, as teenagers do; they all sat near the front, as older folks will. When I went with a mate to Wolves on the Midland Red it was different: it was boisterous – they actually sang songs en route – and lots of them were pissed. OK, you'd get the occasional younger person on the Albion bus, and there were a couple of guys who would turn up for the chance of a ruck against teams they hated – mostly London clubs I seem to recall. They rarely seemed to come home disappointed, but there was no camaraderie, no spirit.

Still, I was desperately hooked and my matchday routine was

established. I'd walk into Worcester and, in what now seems a ridiculously formal process (and did so at the time, to be honest), buy a coach ticket from Midland Red's office in town. They would then keep the carbon copy and I would head off to the station a short walk away clutching my receipt, usually after wandering around the shops for a while, or sometimes scoffing pie and chips in Hutton's chippy across the road. The bus would arrive from Malvern scheduled for ten to one, then head north along the A38 to pick up passengers at Droitwich, and sometimes, depending on whether it was full or not, at Bromsgrove too. Then it would join the M5 to West Brom.

Then one day, nine games into the 1974/75 season with just two wins under our belt and a tiny crowd expected against unfashionable Oxford, this other blond-haired youth and his younger waif-like cousin turned up. Being the only people within a ten-year age radius, we naturally struck up a conversation. 'I had gone a few times on the bus but we hadn't met up,' Tim recalls. 'There was just something about it. We both liked the same clothes and music [soul], seemed to have the same sense of humour, and both of us loved the Albion.' I remember we flicked the obligatory V-signs to half a dozen Oxford fans outside a pub in Bromsgrove near to where the coach picked up. How brave we were! Inside the ground we stood together like lots of youngsters at the back of the Brummie Road.

That Oxford game drew a painfully thin crowd – 9,667. I'd never seen an Albion gate dip below 10,000 before. But it remains special. I'd found a friend. Unusually, West Brom were at home on consecutive Saturdays so we returned the following week for a 2–0 win over York City. In fact, we won three on the bounce, and there was something else: Albion were showing signs of promise. They brought some younger players in. An ungainly but game centre-forward, Joe Mayo, was back in the team for that Oxford game. There was England U-18 midfielder John Trewick, a Welsh forward, Ian Edwards, competent central defender Ian Rushbury, and talk of another promising player, Trewick's England U-18 colleague Bryan Robson, whom manager Don Howe seemed to be holding back. We couldn't decide if it was because he was special or just a bit crap.

Over the next few years, game by game, Tim and I became relative pied-pipers. The following season, Johnny Giles took Albion to promotion. One by one we each brought friends along on the Midland Red bus, and far from being the depressing experience I had once known it actually became the reason other boys came along. They liked the spirit on the coach. A group of us even went to the return fixture at Oxford on the train, just a few weeks after the Norwich football special that I went to with another bus regular, a gentle giant called Bill Harris who was also part of our gang, a truly lovely man, now sadly in ill health. We even got to know some of the older guys. One of them, Les, was only in his late twenties but seemed old and grown up to us. He would get us a drink from the bar underneath the Brummie Road End. Crazily, they used to serve drinks in old half-pint brown ale bottles (yes, glass). On the terraces he celebrated more wildly than we did, which struck me as a bit unhealthy. I mean, he had kids, a house and a job and stuff. But after one defeat I remember him saying, 'It stays with you for an hour or so, then you get over it.' Christ, I thought. It ruined my weekend. All week in fact. Indeed, if Albion couldn't repair the damage the following Saturday, even longer. I was psychologically scarred by defeat to the extent that these days I'm sure I'd have a good case for compensation. And Les was fine after an hour!

As Albion established a foothold back in the First Division, Midland Red could no longer really cope. The bus was full each week; you had to get a ticket in advance or miss out. Then something odd happened: the Midland Red stopping running buses. Either that or they lost the franchise. I can't remember. Either way we were gutted.

Sometimes we went on the train from Worcester to Birmingham New Street then caught a bus the four miles to the Hawthorns. Then, early in the 1977/78 season, we decided to set up a supporters club. I put an advert in the club programme and another in the *Worcester Evening News*. I was chairman, Tim ran the travel. His memory (more faithful than mine) is that we had 230 members that first season. We ran coaches everywhere – great days with a group of lads watching some fantastic football (we were into the Three Degrees/Ron Atkinson era). We also enjoyed what Tim described later in his wedding speech as 'the occasional shandy' along the way – understatement indeed. For home games we picked up opposite the Midland Red depot, but at one o'clock, not ten to one.

We had effectively become tour operators. It was all part of the routine I had grown up with – you played, you watched, you organised. Only this, especially for youths into punk at the time, was a thankless task. For all the nights I recall going to gigs and drinking in pubs and having a laugh, there were Friday nights spent fielding phone calls from ungrateful souls who wanted a place on an already full coach the following morning, and bad-mouthing you for not reserving a place for them. However, the biggest drawback, which I am not particularly proud of, is that I stopped playing sport, or at least I made no more than a half-hearted attempt at playing Sunday-morning football. I often had a hangover, so it was a truly pathetic effort.

Later, Tim and I travelled together in our cars. Much more civilised. As a youth you spend so much of your time either on public transport or waiting for it to arrive. Hours. Much of it is boring, but sometimes it is where you meet lifelong friends. Sometimes, too, it is how you learn to love your football club.

12.45 P.M.: STEWARDS' BRIEFING At Norwich Neil Doncaster is attending another briefing. Leon Blackburn is once again the deliverer, but this time it's the club's head stewards. Each section leader is handed a pack of specific instructions. Neil is there to offer support more than anything else. Another tick.

He returns for a quick bite to eat – the remnants of last night's curry. I make my way to a bar outside the ground and have a vegan burger – the first time I have ever seen anything like this sold at a football ground, and with real proper cooked chips too, much more appetising than those stringy fries served elsewhere.

A short while later Neil shows a group of friends around the main stand – the press box, control room, PA booth and directors' lounge. We joke about the lack of legroom in the press box. Well ahead of kick-off, several radio men are already there, some even on air, but squeezing past is impossible. I'm not picking on Norwich here, for the lack of space is a common design problem in UK football grounds.

Soon, Neil, clipboard in hand, will have to start his pre-match rounds.

12.50 P.M.: BRIGHTON – WITHDEAN AND I The drive into Brighton on the A23 is unlike any other in England. There isn't really another seaside resort that from so far out offers such a feeling of space. As you drive along the M23 and, later, the A23 over the South Downs on a clear day, the only thing you can see in the distance is sky.

Brighton is infamous. It has been the venue for mods versus rockers riots, it is England's gay capital, and it is home to an eclectic mix of people. It has palaces and piers, it's where the saucy seaside postcard was invented, and where Margaret Thatcher and the Tory party bigwigs were bombed by the IRA in 1984. Sometimes it is thought of as the home of Brighton & Hove Albion. Except that they haven't really got a home. Well, not a permanent one anyway, and their attempts to find one have been tortuous.

They used to play in Hove. Back in 1997, the week after the Labour government came to power, their well-liked but dilapidated home of 97 years, the Goldstone Ground, closed. The club was made homeless by a businessman, Bill Archer, who gained control of the club then sold the ground to a property developer. With nowhere to go, Brighton have been nomads ever since. Initially they moved 75 miles east to play at Gillingham FC – not the most enticing of options. Two seasons later they moved back to Brighton on a supposed temporary basis, to the Withdean Stadium, an athletics track which has a limited capacity of 6,973 and comprises mainly temporary uncovered seating. Their goal is to build a new community stadium just off the A27 to the east of the city at Falmer. Plans were submitted to Brighton and Hove City Council in October 2001 and approved by eleven votes to one. But a subsequent planning inspectorate report said it went against the City of Brighton and Hove's Local Plan and summarily dismissed the proposals, stating that the stadium lacked 'national interest' and that it was partly on an Area of Outstanding Natural Beauty. The application was 'called in' for a public inquiry, which concluded in October 2003. The final decision rests with the Deputy Prime Minister, John Prescott, who is First Secretary of State (formerly for the environment and the regions, which is still his remit). There is immense public support for the stadium – 45,000 people voted in favour in a local council referendum, over 100,000 have signed a petition, and football knights such as Alex Ferguson and Bobby Robson have backed the campaign – so Prescott hardly needed to employ one of New Labour's infamous focus groups. In the summer of 2004 he bottled it by asking for all other options to be fully investigated. Another public inquiry is due to report in late 2005.

In the meantime, Brighton & Hove Albion's fortunes have rocked back and forth. In 1997/98, the season after they were ejected from the Goldstone Ground, they survived relegation from the Football League on the final day of the season with a win at Hereford United. They then hauled themselves up the Third Division and were champions in 2001. A year later they won the Second Division title, but were swiftly relegated from the First Division in 2003. In 2003/04 they bounced back into the now renamed Championship via the play-offs. Irony alert: some 30,000 supporters travelled to Cardiff for that final – five times the number who can watch matches at the Withdean Stadium. In 2004/05, a city with 250,000 residents and an estimated catchment area of 438,000 had the smallest stadium in the Championship. Quite simply, without Falmer there is no hope for Brighton. Their temporary, rented home provides limited income, and losses year on year have been inevitable. Added to this folly or misery (you choose), they have so far spent £2.5 million on the planning application – which could, of course, have been spent on the new ground.

I am intrigued by the situation at Brighton for many reasons. I have never visited the site and fully appreciate the rights of residents, and the environment, not to be trampled over merely by the whims of a football club, but there are several things I do know. The first is that Brighton & Hove Albion and their long-suffering supporters are so desperate to find somewhere to play I cannot believe they would fail to look elsewhere if there were any other suitable sites available. Second, their application has not been shaped by a lone nutter running the club, it has been fully thought out, prepared and argued. And third, if the local council(s) or wider government can't find them a home they should look harder, and actually help rather than hinder the process. Given that football is the socially important national game I am describing in this book, surely government, local councils or maybe even the football authorities should assist a Football League club that has one of the largest geographical areas in England to itself. Their local derby, for heaven's sake, is Crystal

Palace in south London, 44 miles away; the nearest club east is Gillingham (75 miles away), and to the west, Portsmouth (53 miles away). Is someone seriously trying to tell me that land is so precious that nowhere can be found near Brighton that is suitable to house a football club? In the meantime, of course, any number of Premier League clubs have seen applications to build training grounds and/or academies in the countryside waved through with ease – not to house a community club but so that well-heeled footballers don't have to sully themselves by driving their expensive cars through inner-city communities where the club's main stadiums are based.

From afar, it looks ridiculous.

In spite of the obstacles that have been thrown in front of them, Brighton & Hove Albion's supporters have not done what many surely expected: turn their backs on their local club, give up, sit back with their Sky TV subscriptions and watch some live footy on TV. Instead, they have engaged in good-humoured debate, from peaceful demonstrations to forging unique links with fellow ailing clubs already mentioned, such as Wrexham and Doncaster Rovers. I have also heard that the Withdean is, frankly, crap. A joke, wholly unsuitable for staging Championship football. But I want to see it and experience it for myself.

The club's PA announcer has also been in the news. Attila the Stockbroker, the celebrated punk poet, and a motley crew of local musicians are in the charts with a remake of The Piranhas (a Brighton band, of course) classic 'Tom Hark', called 'We Want Falmer', recorded under the guise of 'Seagulls Ska'. It was number seventeen in the charts the week before my visit in January 2005 but had slipped out of the top 50, although there are hopes that a reissue will send it spinning upwards again. Attila is also not your average PA announcer, and his choice of music is somewhat different to most, but in these times of uniformity that is to be celebrated.

I have been reliably informed that I won't be able to park anywhere near the Withdean, indeed not even to try because it will only irritate the neighbours, and that is certainly not the aim of my visit. The club has installed park and rides to whisk in and out of the vicinity the relatively few fans who successfully clamour for the tickets on offer for Brighton home games. Today they are playing Nottingham Forest, who are struggling one place off the foot of the Championship table. They are, of course, yet another club who have hit hard times – unshaven, tie-loosened losers looking uncomfortable in the world of the Premier League's high-rollers.

I like park and rides. Football clubs, as ever, have been slow to use them. In theory, they should provide a safe, fast, cheap way of avoiding the horrendous congestion problems surrounding football grounds. Brighton, more than most clubs, have to think about the residents. But even though it is late January when there are surely few tourists about, there is calamitous congestion at the first roundabout into the city. I check my directions – turn right. A few cars are going down there, but it resembles a country lane – surely some mistake? There are no signs marked 'park and ride'. A few hundred yards along, after you pass under a railway bridge, the road is blocked off. There are no signs explaining why. It looks vaguely like the sort of scene you get in a TV drama when mad scientists have cordoned off land so some grisly experiment can take place.

I walk up to the barricade and ask. This is the park and ride. It is about to open. I am told to sit in my car. I look around and see a queue down a small lane to my right. I can see the other drivers saying, 'Cheeky bugger, who the hell does he think he is?' On the stroke of one o'clock, the barrier is pulled back and I am directed to park my car sideways on the road. Not on a park, on the road. Others file in beside. I get out of my car and walk, as others do – a smattering of home and away supporters – to the waiting buses maybe a quarter of a mile or so up the road. You have to show a match ticket to get on board. I am about to enter the Withdean.

12.55 P.M.: BEHIND THE SCENES AT BRISTOL CITY The one thing that always surprises me about Bristol when I drive through or around it is that a city of this size hasn't got a Premier League club. It should have. Period. Ashton Gate, all for the want of rebuilding the away end (the Wedlock End), is a Premier League stadium.

I meet Danny Coles in the players' reception. He is sorting out pre-match tickets for his family – eight of them are coming to today's game, which is about the norm. 'It's a pain to be honest,' he says. Like all players, he only gets two complimentary tickets ('two if you are playing, one if you are a sub, none if you don't get a game'). It seems a bit mean as Bristol City are hardly selling out each week. They have been averaging around 11,000 a match this season, and Ashton Gate holds 21,500. Being a Bristol lad his family are 'well into it' and Danny tries to get them seats together.

He quickly shows me round the inner sanctum underneath the Atyeo Stand, named after the club's record scorer, who netted some 314 goals between 1951 and 1966. From the players' reception area, with the manager's office and gym on one side, a long corridor leads past a kit room and mini-launderette on the left with the home-team changing room and treatment room annexe to the right. The changing room is square-shaped, the players' pegs are on two sides with their red kit neatly laid out, and two beds occupy the other corner. There are showers, loos and a bath in a gap that leads to the treatment room which has several tables, sinks and cabinets containing medical supplies. The walls bear snippets of articles or diagrams of body parts.

'The modern game is to have a quick team talk, a stretch and maybe a massage,' says Danny, 'but there is a lot of hanging about.' Danny seems more nervy now we've got here. I'm not helping. The more questions I ask the more concerned he seems. I am wary about putting doubts in his mind. He tells me who he'll be marking today: Lee Matthews, a former England youth international who didn't make it at Leeds United and spent four seasons at City before leaving for Port Vale last summer. 'One of my best mates,' says Danny, who is expecting a rough, tough battle against his chum. 'He's a character. I was on the phone to him last night having a laugh. I'm sure we'll have an *interesting* battle this afternoon. It is going to be strange playing against a mate. I've never really done it before so today will be a good test of character. We'll have to put friendship aside and kick lumps out of each other for 90 minutes, then have a big hug when we come off.'

I leave Danny, who sits reading the matchday programme waiting for Brian Tinnion to enter the dressing room to issue his team talk.

1 P.M.: DOCTOR IN THE HOUSE Dr Ralph Rogers arrives at the Bescot Stadium, Walsall's functional home near the ever-rumbling M6. A huge advertisement hoarding at the ground aimed at passing motorists earns the Black Country club some much-needed revenue. Ralph pulls up in his ice-blue Rolls Royce. Poor, he isn't. He is regally welcomed. Everyone knows 'the doc'. He puts himself about and is courteous and friendly.

As we get out of the car he spots a familiar face leaning out of a 4x4. It is Walsall's former goalkeeper Jimmy Walker, who left a few months earlier for West Ham. He leans out of his car and slaps his hand into Ralph's. 'How ya doin', man?' says Ralph, admiring Jimmy's car. 'They paying you too much?' They are genuinely pleased to see each other. Real comradeship. This isn't some distant doc dutifully turning up to make sure his name is in the matchday programme, here to pocket his cheque and lean on the bar enjoying the hospitality. Ralph is here to do a job for the players. And he is impressive – well built, smartly dressed, with stature and poise. He has professionalism and presence, and Walker's welcome is emulated by Walsall's players as we enter the changing rooms. He is an upbeat member of the team, maybe even bringing a bit of American pizzazz to proceedings.

'What's up, doc?' jokes a reserve-team player. Ralph grabs him in a head lock and rubs his head.

'Hey, Jimmy's back,' Ralph tells everyone. 'Where are West Ham today? Is he suspended or something?'

Another former player is back on trial. He pops in to see Ralph. 'Hey, you back?' says Ralph.

He is their mate as well as the doctor. He has built up a rapport. He introduces me to the club physio John Whitney, a witty, flat-nosed Northerner, an ex-pro whose work dovetails with Ralph's. For the next 30 minutes Ralph simply makes his presence known. A couple of players sneak in for a private word; they respect his professional opinion, and they know he won't blab to all and sundry. 'It's a comforting thing,' Ralph remarks. 'Maybe they'll discuss a problem and ask about an injury.'

His treatment room is small – certainly compared to Bristol City's, who play at the same level – and not particularly well equipped. Walsall couldn't be called an extravagant club, but they do pay the going rate for players' wages and transfers. Bearing in mind the Bescot is a fairly new stadium, built in 1990, it seems small and not the sort of place Ralph Rogers would prefer to work in.

As we sit on the single bed on which he has to treat players, he explains the cultural differences between sports medicine in the USA and UK. In the States even college sports teams have a team of physicians working with the players and facilities that resemble mini-hospitals. It is taken seriously. It is not considered a waste of money because the players are investments. British football has been an eye-opener for Ralph. In this most professional of sports – the national game, no less – where fans pay large sums of their expendable cash to watch players on fantasy wages at the top levels, medical treatment is left to inexperienced or ill-qualified physios and jobbing GPs working in often poor facilities. Small wonder that with his wider approach Ralph has built up a loyal band of players, and indeed other sportsmen. 'Former players call me up all the time for advice,' he says. 'Not just football but basketball. To ask questions or get things checked out.'

Ralph doesn't break medical ethics by diagnosing injuries or clashing with the professional opinion of the people treating the player, but all too often he believes they are receiving poor advice. He talks about an ex-Walsall player whose current club doctor is a cancer specialist. 'Maybe they are somebody's friend. There are probably 20 or 30 guys who will call on the phone or drop by because of the way I have treated them. I've seen three guys in the last few weeks. They will say the treatment isn't as good as when they were here so they end up coming to my private clinic rather than being treated by their club doctor.' I ask Ralph how he feels about that. 'I like to help out obviously, but overall?' He chooses his words carefully. 'Sad and disappointed.'

1 P.M.: LUNCH AT GRETNA At Gretna Paul Barnett has packed his pitchfork away and is tucking into lunch: traditional Scottish pie, chips and mushy peas. He has prepared everything for the game. The gates will soon open and he will welcome the referee for the pre-match pitch inspection.

1 P.M.: THE SOUPER CLUB Kidderminster Harriers' home, Aggborough, is only a five-minute walk uphill from the town centre. It is a sunny day and the sun gleams off the red seats, but it is bitterly cold. A biting wind whistles across the pitch. The only notable activity in the stadium is in the corner marked 'Kidderminster Harriers – the Souper Club'. Brian Murdoch and his staff are busy setting up.

The sad fact is that Kidderminster aren't quite so 'souper' at the moment. They are bottom of the Football League, and following the recent departure of the Danish ex-Liverpool midfielder Jan Molby, they have a new man, Stuart Watkiss, in charge for his first home game. Brian would like the club to prosper so that he has happy customers, but the psychology of supporters is interesting. For all their flipcharts and branding and pious assumptions about 'marking up' – one of the chancers at the catering conference I'd been to tried to convince me that fans actually liked it when prices were hiked up because they didn't want the change in their pocket – Brian's world-weary observations are nearer the mark. When you've sold hot dogs in rain-soaked town centres, you tend to know all about the sharp end of catering. 'Fans tend to wander a bit when their side is losing,' he notes. 'Something goes wrong and they kick the ground and come over to us complaining. But at least they buy something,' he smiles.

We walk around the ground, over the East Stand. His daughter Helen is busy setting up. She serves the Kiddy fans in this stand, but at the far end, the corner diametrically opposite Brian's 'souper' kiosk, we meet his son David, a pukka chef who has been to catering college. David has his own small team who are busy cooking food on site. This is where Brian's main culinary efforts are concentrated.

Any seasoned supporter who has followed their club home but especially away will know that there are some clubs that seem proud that they treat away fans as inferior beings, almost to wear the attitude as a badge of honour. When they can get away with it, some clubs try to charge them more to get in; they have stuck fans behind pillars; and catering-wise the facilities are rarely as good as those for home fans. There is a smug underlying assumption that they are getting one over on them, an attitude particularly prevalent in the dark days of hooliganism when the away contingent was hardly full of angels either, and serving food to some of these fans was an invitation to be abused all afternoon. But it makes little commercial sense. 'Ninety-five per cent of away fans will buy food inside the ground,' Brian claims confidently, 'whereas only one in five home fans will.'

I let this nugget of information sink in. 'Ninety-five per cent? Are you sure? I mean, how do you know?' I don't mean to 'dis' Brian, as they say in modern parlance. He has been at this game for 40-odd years and all that. But, well, frankly it seems a lot. He explains the rationale. 'Let's say you've come from Rochdale. It's, what, 100 miles or so? How long will it take to get here? About three hours, maybe four if you've got stuck in traffic or had to stop. So if you leave half an hour or so to park up and get in, longer if you fancy a pint, you leave at what time?'

'Ten o'clock, eleven maybe?'

'That's mid-morning. You might have a late breakfast, but the chances are that will be five hours ago. You'll fancy something to eat when you get here.'

'Ah, but you might stop on the way,' I chip in.

'Where? On the motorway services? Bit pricey. And coming down the M6, you'll probably want to make sure you've reached the M5 first, just in case you get stuck in traffic. By then you're virtually here.'

'What about a pie or a sandwich in a pub?' I venture.

'Maybe, but where are you going to eat around here? If they know they can get good food inside the ground they won't go looking for a chippy or a café, they'd sooner get in here and have some food before or during the game. Same with going home. They know they've got a similar journey home – three or four hours – so they will want something mid-afternoon for sure.'

'So why are the home fans so mean by comparison?'

'The home fans will eat at home. If they've eaten at home they will have snacks, but not meals.'

Hence Brian focuses most of his efforts on those most likely to buy – the away fans. The corner kiosk at the away end is shaped so it can serve fans from two sides, under the seated stand or outwards for those on the College End 'away' terrace. Brian's estimate is that one kiosk can serve 1,000 fans. Today he has four covering 2,500.

He shows me the menu for away fans. I've never seen anything like this inside a British football ground anywhere. Here is what is on offer:

Hot drinks £1.20
The Famous Aggborough Soup £1.50

Hot dogs/beefburgers/cheeseburgers £2.50
Bacon and egg bap/roast pork (with stuffing) bap £3
Cottage pies/cheese and onion pies/sausage and mash/
    balti pies/chicken chow mein/barbecue chicken £3.50
Veggie soup £1.50
Cheese and onion salad bap/egg, mushroom and tomato bap/
    veggie burger £2.50
Cheese and tomato pasta/vegetable curry £3.50

There is also a selection of chocolate bars. The cheapest thing you can buy is an Irn Bru chewy bar for 10p. You may notice there is one thing Brian doesn't sell – chips. This isn't for ethical or dietary reasons. 'To do them well you have to griddle them. A griddler costs £10,000, and there are the associated problems with getting a safety licence. It isn't worth the expenditure.'

Brian has laid down the theory. He has, quite literally, set his stall out. The proof will be, when the gates open, in the eating.

1 P.M.: HOVERING WITH INTENT I'm outside Wigan Athletic's JJB Stadium. I'm here to interview Five Live's legendary broadcaster Stuart Hall. I want to see how he does what he does – those inimitable reports.

Leeds United are in town. And on a roll, moving quietly and ominously up the Championship table. Wigan, however, are top, and have been there all season. It's a big game, and there is menace in the air. Lots of police around. As I park up I pass a pub so reminiscent of the old days of football hooliganism: ranks of visor-protected police together in a tight unit. Judging by the numbers, it looks like all police leave in Wigan and the surrounding area has been cancelled. (Later, this becomes a bone of contention. Wigan refuse to pay their police bill because they believe it is excessive; the police refuse to offer their services, which would mean Wigan playing games behind closed doors. They pay up, reluctantly.)

I am going down with something. I feel very cold but loads of weather-beaten Leeds fans are wearing little else but club shirts (and doing a damn good job of promoting White & Mackay whisky) – their sponsors. The word is they have sold more than 5,000 tickets, though none will be on sale today. It is a huge, amazing, dedicated following, and it will be Wigan's biggest gate of the season thus far. But a lot of Leeds fans are hanging around the main entrance. Why?

1 P.M.: AT SINCIL BANK Chairman Rob Bradley arrives at Lincoln City's ground, which is approached via a confusing array of terraced streets. Before we actually got here he stopped to show me a new entrance they are planning – access via the city's fire station. As long as it doesn't prevent emergency vehicles from going out speedily they should get permission. Anything would be better than meandering around these speed-bumped streets.

There are plenty of parking spaces at the ground. At most grounds pride of place usually goes to the chairman's car, whose space is clearly marked out. Not Rob Bradley. He parks in the street. 'I don't want to be seen to take a penny out of the club,' he says. This may befit someone who is the fans' elected representative on the board, but surely no one would begrudge him this perk? You could even argue it is essential: chairmen are the first people whose cars are likely to be broken into or damaged. But Rob is accountable to his trust and good to his word. His car stays on the street where he always parked.

On the short walk to the main entrance he greets lots of fans. This is the way it should be – an accountable chairman in touch with the fans, the paying customers. He is apprehended by a fan who asks if there any plans to build a club museum, somewhere for precious mementos to be stored and viewed by visitors. He has over 400 player autographs (and without being too unkind, looks like the sort of person who would have 400 Lincoln City player autographs). It would be easy to give a glib reply and move on, but Rob has a chat. Yes, he has thought about it. They are stuck for space but could convert somewhere. It is a good idea, welcomed and written down by the chairman.

Rob heads for the club office where I meet the football secretary, Fran Martin, and chief executive, Dave Roberts. The aim of his appointment, according to Rob, was to bring a bit more expertise to the running of the club, which was 'essential' in Rob's view. As a self-employed architect, Rob runs a small family firm – his son Matthew works with him – so being thrust into the role of managing a large, high-profile, ailing business was a challenge, and not one, I think with hindsight, he was quite prepared for or able to meet initially. But 2000/01 was the club's hour of need, and Rob is very much one of the fans rather than a businessman who has put in a wedge of cash and wants to be thanked for doing so.

He collects some routine post – he has been in every day this week so not much has arrived that is pressing – and then he is off. Time to meet some more supporters.

1 P.M.: WORCESTER CITY U-13s 2 RUGBY UNITED U-13s 3
Worcester U-13s are a depleted outfit. Some of their better players are doing other things, like watching Premier League clubs whose kick off times often coincide with times when youngsters are scheduled to play matches, effectively discouraging them from taking part ('At least they'll hopefully learn something,' muses Bob). Others have less compelling reasons. They don't acquit themselves well. At half-time they are losing. Much of their play has been sloppy, the body language is all wrong, and their coach Andy Knowles is understandably annoyed.

Bob tells the lads to get a drink, runs them up and down the pitch a few times, and then gathers them in a huddle. 'Hands up who thinks he is playing well?' Silence; no movement. 'Who thinks he can do better?' All hands shoot up. 'That was appalling,' emphasises Bob, before accentuating the positive. 'Now go out there and prove you can do better. Show me that you want to win.' He turns to the captain. 'How many times have I heard you shout? The answer is not enough.' He points to the armband. 'What's that? The captain's armband. So take charge then.' The skipper sheds a few tears – he knows he's not done enough. There is no shouting, just some much-needed geeing up.

It has an effect. Worcester hit the post virtually straight away and look like they have the will to win. They pull a goal back – 2–1. But their legs sap energy on a heavy pitch on which they train twice a week. They concede again, then pull another back, and press for a late equaliser which doesn't quite come. It would have been unjust on Rugby United, who were the better side throughout.

Bob doesn't allow the players to dodge the cold and slip back into the snuggly warmth of the dressing room. After shaking hands with their opponents, he gathers them together once again. He chooses his words carefully. 'You don't need me to tell you that that was unacceptable. You don't need me to pick out those who didn't do enough because you know yourselves. You may feel you've let the club down. You might think you've let your mates down. But, worst of all, you've let yourselves down. You're all better players than I've seen here today. Let's go away and come back with a better spirit because the second half was much better and we have to build on that.'

There are more sniffs to stifle tears, but there is little else to say. Football can be a tough game, and it gets no tougher than being told you've let yourself down. It's a phrase that will hopefully sting their pride but not destroy their passion for the game. When games start kicking off around the country in a couple of hours' time far harsher advice will be shouted into the faces of players. They've also had to come through the 'letting yourself down' phase.

It has been a mixed day for Worcester City. The U-12 and U-15 sides have won, 6–3 and 6–1 respectively. Three matches side by side have ebbed and flowed. You can see the development of players, the difference in physical capabilities of the age ranges. The U-12s are full of tricks, but the U-13s would overpower them. The step up to U-15s is massive. Worcester's U-15s have been together for a few years. They play as a cohesive unit and haven't lost for two seasons. Bob recognises their rough-and-readiness – some are from the notorious Tolladine council estate. 'They don't need geeing up. They don't have fancy boots. They just want to get on with it and win.'

1.10 P.M.: RIDING TO THE WITHDEAN The park and ride bus to the Withdean Stadium departs. Most of the passengers are red-shirted Nottingham Forest supporters. The bus rumbles forward, and at a roundabout about half a mile or so down the road enters a housing estate to our left. A rather posh-looking housing estate in fact. The houses are huge. It is leafy and wealthy. Indeed we are snaking through some narrow roads barely suitable for 4x4s (of which there are many parked on drives) let alone buses ferrying football fans. The bay windows and bedroom windows on some houses are wide, designed for sea views, although we must still be some miles from the front. There is a bit of 'fur coat, no knickers' about it all. These are not seafront properties, but I bet they are sold as seafront properties. You can almost feel the fingers twitching on the lace curtains, being pulled back to reveal the shocking horror of the great unwashed weaving their way through this *Daily Mail*-reading community, fuelled no doubt by outdated images of belligerent bovver boys seeking to rip up their houses and defrock their daughters. I feel like a refugee. I glance at my fellow park-and-riders: take off the football shirts and add a few more women (although there are plenty onboard) and it could be any collection of British people. One woman clutching a 'Come on the Albion' teddy bear doesn't look like she is about to be part of a riotous assembly.

We reach the ground in the valley of this housing estate. Its unsuitability is obvious. OK, there is a pub, the Sportsman (how original!), but none of the usual collection of shops that have sprung up around most grounds. There is no food on sale, indeed nowhere to shelter if it rains – which looks likely given the colour of the sky. This relative 'invasion' of football supporters – albeit only once a fortnight, maybe 25 times a year – isn't what the local community envisaged when they moved here. It does affect the peace and quiet of the area. I may take the piss out of them, but I do sympathise. My point is: why are their views, as they clearly are, given more consideration than those of inner-city communities, like the disenfranchised ones near Villa Park or the Hawthorns in the West Midlands? Certainly, you wouldn't get such a vast cluster of cones or a half-mile car-exclusion zone, such as surrounds the Withdean, elsewhere. As we disembark, I ask the driver where I can pick up the return bus. 'Right here,' he says. Remember that 'here' – adjacent to the stadium.

I am early, but I but feel hopelessly outnumbered by stewards. Again, I assume, another stipulation: man-to-man marking outside the ground. I have a good mooch. The sign says 'Withdean Athletics Track'. Everything belonging to Brighton & Hove Albion is temporary – the ticket office, the toilet block, the club shop, all the seating I can see inside. The Sportsman backs on to the ground. Next door is a pre-school nursery, the Pumpkin Patch.

The ground opens and the fans file in. The burger bar does brisk trade. I opt – well, as a veggie it's the only thing I can have really – for a cheese and onion pie, which is filled with the usual mashed-up gunge. I make my way to the press area, which is ill equipped, outdoors and too small for this level of football. But everyone is very friendly, and Brighton & Hove Albion are to be congratulated for being so helpful in their temporary home.

A Brighton fan persuades his son to approach former Forest captain John McGovern, working here for BBC Radio Nottingham, for his autograph. It is duly given. The chuffed dad then says, 'That man lifted the European Cup for Nottingham Forest once.' The child looks unimpressed. It wasn't that long ago – 25 years – but you can see what the boy is thinking. Nottingham Forest? European Cup? It's the Champions League, Daaaaad!

1.15 P.M.: GRUMPY OLD MEN So Tim and I started our supporters club and began travelling all over the country with the Baggies. On long trips to places like Norwich, Ipswich, Southampton and Middlesbrough you get to know people. We were mainly youngsters who shared an interest in the same football club and liked a beer. Some of those people I have never spoken to in years. Others, well, I feel I grew up with them. We're still good mates. We drank spectacularly, and often with the abandon of youth. We met in pubs before home games and drank too much after them. Away games were usually bawdy affairs that involved stopping en route – sometimes for several hours, sometimes in danger of missing the kick-off – and acting irresponsibly, which alienated some fans and attracted others.

But there was poignancy too. The late 1970s were socially challenging times. West Brom, of course, had three of the first black British players to make serious progress in the game. Laurie Cunningham, Cyrille Regis and Brendon Batson were each brilliant in their own way, and Cyrille and Laurie were virtually our age. We just loved them as footballers. 'I never thought of Cyrille as a black footballer,' Tim said to me recently. 'Just a fantastic centre-forward.' We'd grown up with black role models – Muhammad Ali, Basil D'Oliveira. The music we liked, other than punk and glam rock bands, was soul, reggae and ska. Hating black people made no sense to us. Other fans weren't so tolerant. At West Brom it was OK, but other fans could be vicious to the Three Degrees. They were booed at, jeered; they had bananas thrown at them; they even received death threats. We were hugely defensive of them. Without being too melodramatic, politically and possibly even culturally, the experience shaped some of us.

'We lived through the worst time to watch football,' Tim once said, talking mainly about hooliganism which was rife. To be eighteen and a regular fan and not in one way or another a victim was difficult. Sometimes you had to become a perpetrator just to get home. We used to meet up with other Worcester-based football fans on Saturday nights, and some of them, like a group of Chelsea fans we knew, were rancid and racist. But they had shocking role models at the clubs they followed. We didn't.

For separate reasons, but mainly because we grew out of it, as we moved into our twenties both Tim and I stopped going to matches on the coach and largely went our separate ways. But those memories last for ever. The beery camaraderie, the commitment to the cause, literally supporting the players through thick and thin, the humour, even the songs we used to sing on the coach – other than football ones, all mates-together songs by bands of the day: 'White Man in Hammersmith Palais' by The Clash (hard to do, but we managed it), 'Martin' by the Tom Robinson Band, 'Down in the Tube Station at Midnight' by The Jam. None of this ever leaves you.

In recent years we have started going to the football together regularly again. Nowadays, Tim and I have different matchday rituals. Usually Tim will pick me up, though we do share the driving. Sadly, I am always waiting for him, peeking through the curtains to see his car enter the close. I don't do this for anyone or anything else. I'm always ready. A quick goodbye to the missus – 'Hope they win!' says Teresa, usually in vain – and we're off. Tim will have his son, Jamie, and a mate in the car. They will talk to each other about transfer speculation, mobile phones or whatever fuels the minds of young teenage kids.

Tim and I, however, are venerable grumpy old men. They should have had us on the BBC2 series.

'Do you know what makes me sick?' I said once as I got into the car (no hellos or anything).

'If it's like me,' Tim replied, 'everything.'

It's four roads, 25 miles and roughly half an hour to West Brom from **my** house. In that time we will moan about the club's predicament. Some culprit or other in the team will take the blame. There have been dozens down the years, but take a bow Neil Clement, Jason Van Blerk, Brian Jensen, Micky Evans, Gary Strodder, Graham Harbey, Paul Williams, Daryl Burgess and co. You deserve it. Oh, and we whinge about everything else. Much of this behaviour is, for grown-up men, extremely childish. Wisdom, I have found, does not come with age.

Tim is the only person I feel truly comfortable sitting or standing with while watching West Brom. I don't have to apologise for my language or for ridiculous heat-of-the moment remarks; likewise, I know he doesn't talk rubbish about linesmen failing to spot split-second decisions (like we can tell at an angle), and he's not foolishly in love with the players. In short, he doesn't talk bollocks, and that is the best you can hope for in a football friend.

1.20 P.M.: IN THE CENTRE CIRCLE Rob Bradley enters the Centre Circle supporters club bar to meet some members of the Lincoln City Supporters Trust. Rob is still a committee member, and we stand at the bar chatting with a few other members, including Rick Keracher, Chris Ashton and Geoff Dams, who runs the Lincoln City Ladies team. There are also a couple of blokes from the supporters band who will, literally, drum up an atmosphere inside the ground later. It's the usual talk – concern about other clubs, articles in newspapers, how the game may go today. This is much more Rob's natural habitat. A fan complains to him about an allegedly aggressive steward who is out to enforce his own ban on fans throwing ticker-tape (in truth, little more than tightly ripped-up newspaper) when the players come out. Rob will sort it out. 'It's part of the atmosphere,' he says in flat Lincolnshire tones.

Not many chairmen would bother straying into the supporters club bar (some dare not). Rob has other glad-handing to do, but he sees this as an essential part of his role – a chance to put his face around, to make himself available so fans can tell him what they think, occasionally even putting his neck on the block. 'If people want to have a gripe, that is fair enough,' he says. 'It is partly what I am here for. It's no good being the fans' rep on the board if I don't find out what is concerning them. This is something too many club directors fail to fully understand. The supporters are not to be taken for granted, they are to be appreciated.' This seems the right thing to do. He will have to meet and greet sponsors and members of the local business community soon, and fair enough: lots of Lincoln businesses have stuck by their local football club despite their financial problems. But on matchday Rob never forgets the fans.

Until fairly recently, Rob used to run a minibus to away games with his mates. They would pitch up at a local pub, have a drink and a bite to eat, enjoy the crack, and at the ground, while Rob went off to carry out his dignitary duties as visiting club chairman, his mates would head for the away end. He misses it but believes that travelling on the coach is the right thing to do. It is, but I bet it isn't as much fun.

1.30 P.M.: GETTING DOWN TO BUSINESS At Ashton Gate Brian Tinnion has assembled his coaching staff for a quick meeting. Then he gathers everyone together in the dressing room for a team talk. The countdown to kick-off starts here; after all the waiting it is time to get moving. Danny Coles looks relieved.

Brian spells out the importance of the game and what is at stake – a win to push them near to the promotion places. 'This is a cup tie for us, a massive match in our season. We need to get at them early on – push them back, set the tempo of the game.' He has already done his tactical talk, on Thursday and Friday. 'They can't take too much information at this stage,' Brian tells me. 'We have worked on playing against a 4–5–1 formation, which is how we think they will line up.' As a team, they need to 'get in the faces' of Port Vale as early as possible. Brian wants them to keep it tight at the back – he specifically urges Danny and his central defensive colleague Louis Carey to mark tight – and for the midfield to win the ball and get it forward quickly to use the width they have (Scott Murray on the right, Joe Keith down the left). He also wants them to pay particular attention to attacking and defending set-pieces. But before a more detailed talk, he orders all those who need massages to get them and for everyone to stretch out properly and do their warm-ups on the pitch with purpose. Also, as it is a warm day, to make sure they drink enough water. Above all, to focus on what they need to do. Suddenly there is urgency about the place. The four medical staff are literally on hand to give the players their massages. Danny Coles's sore

Achilles needs special attention. Most players seem to have a niggle of one sort or another. The changing room echoes to the familiar sound of studs, footballs being bounced around and aerosol sprays. There's an early whiff of that most familiar of dressing-room smells – Vicks.

'They know their jobs and what is expected,' Brian tells me. 'They know their strengths and why I have picked them. It is just a matter of going out there and doing it. They should be prepared from a diet, health, fitness and tactical point of view to go out and win the game.' He is still dressed in his suit and doesn't change. He will not take them through their warm-ups on the pitch; he leaves this to his coaches. He is pretty laid back. A few weeks earlier he met supporters across the road before a game. 'I love talking about football otherwise I wouldn't do the job,' he says. 'The chairman [Steve Lansdown] was holding a meeting with supporters and I went over to join them. If anyone has any questions I'll do my best to answer them, whether they are good or bad, positive or negative. I'm prepared to stand up and be counted.'

As the players go about their business I meet a matchday steward whose job is to take corporate sponsors behind the scenes. He shows me a 1909 cup final loser's medal worth, he estimates, around £6,500, 'because it was against Man U'. It has been a long time since Bristol City have distinguished themselves in such a way.

1.30 P.M.: ANY QUESTIONS? Neil Doncaster, clipboard in hand, starts his rounds by walking along the Barclay End, where Delia Smith intends to sit today, and through the section for away fans, who are starting to turn up, in the new Jarrold Stand. He walks along the back and into the Norwich and Peterborough Building Society stand behind the other goal, and then back around to the Main Stand. He wanders underneath, looking in all the bars to make sure everything is ship-shape, then drops into the plush club restaurant, which is only open on matchdays and booked up well in advance. All seems to be in order. Back outside, he notes a blocked drain at the Barclay End which he hopes his security manager will also have spotted and will raise at Monday morning's briefing. It's one for Norwich City Council to deal with, and certainly a safety issue on a snowy day.

His main reason for deliberately walking around slowly and noting

171

things as he goes along is to be seen to be taking an interest. He also makes himself available to fans: having completed his rounds, he stands at a point where most of them will pass, on the corner of the Main Stand and the Norwich and Peterborough Building Society Stand, just over the bridge from the city centre. He is quite conspicuous, and many fans nod in recognition and say hello as they breeze past. Some come over and exchange more elaborate pleasantries. One thanks Neil for helping to arrange a recent event.

To Neil, it is all part of being the chief executive of a community football club. They do lots of studies and surveys, but sometimes away from the stats and number-crunching you just need to listen, plain and simple. 'If they have a view, I'll listen to it,' he says. 'If they have a question, I'll try to answer it. We're absolutely transparent in what we do and that makes it easier to go out and be available because most of the answers to the questions are already out there.' But does it come with its problems? 'It's more difficult when they are frustrated, but then you just listen, be attentive and concerned. And if that helps, then fair enough.' Ironically, it was worse last season when Norwich were topping the First Division and going well rather than this term when they are struggling in the Premier League. 'The main topic was, are we going to buy Darren Huckerby, and if not, why not?' This season, fans have had the odd rant, but most have been educated to realise that the club cannot and will not spend beyond its means. Still, it can be a challenging part of the job. 'The chief executive at Charlton was picked up and thrown over a hedge a few years ago,' Neil tells me. 'That hasn't happened to me yet, but I've had some fairly robust views expressed. It hasn't always been successful at Carrow Road. We've had our ups and downs, and people like to express their views in a forthright way. But that's fine. It's part of the job.'

As we wait for people to raise queries, Neil points out a block of flats being built opposite the ground on land sold for £3 million. It raised valuable funds. They've bought a strip of land downriver to use for car parking; fans are ferried in on special trucks sponsored by Norwich Union. He also mentions a hotel joint-venture that will fill the gap between the Jarrold and Barclay Stands. These would be trifling issues for today's opponents. They have Chelsea Village – the commercial complex that surrounds Stamford Bridge – and if Jose Mourinho needs money to strengthen his squad he only has to look to see if his Russian bank is open.

Norwich fans can be quite parochial. Most are from Norfolk, the only county in England without a stretch of motorway, and quite cut off, in some respects, from the rest of the country. But they are, by and large, well behaved and pleasant. They are unlikely to give Neil a hard time, and there is little in the way of boisterous behaviour on the way to the ground. Inside it is different, full of passion, but hooliganism from the home fans has never blighted this friendly club.

The temptation on days like today, with the Premiership big boys in town, must be for Neil to dispense with his clipboard and stay inside to do some glad-handing. Neil isn't so sure that is his true role. 'To be successful in the long term,' he says, 'you have to be run in the interests of supporters first and foremost. And I'm not sure many clubs in the top level of the game in England can claim that.'

1.30 P.M.: BARNEY MEETS THE REF At Gretna groundsman Paul Barnett meets the referee for today's game against Elgin, Jamie Downie, who may want to check any number of things. 'I tend to keep the nets up until just before kick-off,' Paul tells me. 'He might take them down to inspect them at this stage. He might say the line markings are not bright enough. It might even be a question of discussing when he wants the lights on; there is no point doing it too early if he doesn't want you to. I just like to communicate with the referee. You just want him to have a good feeling about things. It's the polite thing to do.'

Today, there are no problems.

1.30 P.M.: PITCH INSPECTION AT PORTMAN ROAD At Ipswich Paul Taylor walks out on to the pitch with his assistants, fourth official and match assessor. There are no problems with the playing surface: the grass is cut short and is in pristine condition. Alan Ferguson, who has already said hello, has been groundsman of the year twice.

Instead, Paul conducts a pre-match briefing in the centre circle. 'The expectancy of this game is high,' he begins. 'It's the A12 bragging rights at stake.' Paul wants his assistants to stay what he calls 'tight' for the first fifteen minutes. 'Let's encourage them to play,' he says, then lightens the mood by describing himself as 'excitable'. 'I'll rush in to sort out any incidents. If there is a scuffle, just pick out two individuals,' he tells his assistants. Turning to the fourth official, he asks him to spot just one player. 'Then I'll deal with it,' Paul confirms.

1.35 P.M.: GROUNDHOP DAY III I sense Bill Berry isn't amused. I was late to start with, and then we'd had a coffee, and frankly I had chatted too long to Bill's wife, Ann. Although we haven't encountered any awkward traffic and nothing has been said, I've noted his glances at the dashboard clock. We need a clear run to get there well in time. And now I need a pee. We pull into a petrol station in Aylesbury.

'All right now?' asks Bill when I get back in the car. 'Anything else?' This seems to amuse Bill, who obviously doesn't stop for much. He explains how games are sometimes cancelled late in the day at the sort of leagues he visits these days, where the 'crowd' is mainly family and friends. Sometimes they can be called off for strange reasons, but to Bill that is just a lost Saturday. He not only needs a contingency plan (another ground to reach) but time to act on it. Rolling up at a quarter to three isn't good enough. I start to feel strangely guilty for wanting a wee. I haven't had any lunch either. I thought we might stop for a snack en route; indeed I had planned to dovetail into Bill's normal matchday routine, thinking he might know his way around the chippies and cafés of Britain. Not so. Bill has a big breakfast and eats when he gets home. I'm starving. I could ask to stop again, but …

Bill has never failed to make a game, although earlier in the season he did struggle to reach a destination in North Wales because a bridge was closed and he had to double back through Shrewsbury. The game ended 0–0.

1.45 P.M.: THE THEATRE OF DREAMS John arrives at Old Trafford. We park in one of the huge car parks outside the North Stand – the old Stretford End. His priority today will be to head for the tunnel area and to meet people who knew Roy Unwin – especially, if possible, players and management. Hopefully, everyone will soon know about tomorrow's gathering in the museum. All staff are welcome. John will be there to talk and to listen. But frankly, most people are now pumped up for the game or doing their jobs. Players nod in recognition, they share a quick joke. Like Doc Rogers at Walsall, another professional, 'Rev John' is a familiar, reassuring face. But this is no time for ethical discussion.

It is impossible for John to meet everyone on matchdays at Old Trafford. 'At Watford we had 40 players and 30 admin staff. If you're doing a day and a half a week, you soon get to know everybody. You come to a club with 550 full-time staff on a two-and-a-half-days-a-week basis and you can't get to know many of them as well. It is a challenge, and frustrating.'

1.45 P.M.: THE SIGNATURE OF SENHOR MOURINHO Image-wise it hasn't been the best of weeks for Jose Mourinho. Chelsea may have won the Carling Cup the previous Sunday, but all the press talk has been of their manager's alleged arrogance: shushing the Liverpool fans (Mourinho insisted it was aimed at the press), boasting about his team winning the title, undermining opponents. I'm not going to enter into a debate about those things here and now, and notably the journalists making these allegations, who have ample time at the post-match press conference to take these matters up with Mourinho, choose not to do so. But there is something I spot Mourinho doing before the game as he comes out to look at the pitch and imbibe the Norfolk air. Lots of youngsters flock to the tunnel for autographs. Mourinho, with his own pen, signs dozens. I don't know if other top managers do this (I doubt it), and I'm not saying it necessarily atones for his other actions. But he did it. And that says something about his character too.

1.45 P.M.: SUPERSTITIOUS MINDS Back at Bristol Danny Coles has a strange superstition. Rather than clean his boots after each game, he runs them under the tap and does them himself on matchdays just before going out to warm up. 'I've been doing this for two years,' he explains. 'It wasn't something I did when I was really young. Maybe it was something I started doing when I had a particularly good game.' But it can't have been that notable as he can't remember a specific match. 'I have just got into the pattern of doing it. It would seem odd to stop now.'

Danny claims that most players have similar routines. His defensive partner Louis Carey has to walk around a post in the changing room before walking out on to the pitch. Very bizarre. 'It gives you a psychological edge,' explains Danny, remembering another habit. 'I always put my shirt on as I'm walking out of the door. I don't know why.'

1.45 P.M.: WE ARE LEEDS I've found out why the Leeds fans are hovering with intent. As the team coach draws level with the main entrance at the JJB Stadium, a hundred or so fans crowd around it. When the doors swing open the familiar 'We Are Leeds' chant starts up.

The odd thing is, the people singing and shouting this song of encouragement to the players are in their forties and fifties. Many of those eager to get the briefest glimpse of their heroes are at least twice the age of some Leeds players. I find this disturbing. They aren't accompanying their own autograph-hunting children. In some cases it is clearly the opposite: some children or teenagers are simply with their dads. They are acting out age-old habits, probably developed during the Don Revie era of the 1960s and 1970s. They will have continued through Leeds' last decline in the 1980s, been joined by bigger numbers when Howard Wilkinson took them to the title in 1991, and, as with Bremner, Hunter, Giles and Lorimer a decade or so earlier, in the 1990s they had stars worth queuing to watch amble off a coach (if you are so inclined) – Ferdinand, Kewell, Viduka, Keane, Smith and Robinson. Quite why they feel the need now to dog the footsteps of a group of players who could lodge themselves easily at the bar in most pubs in the land without fear of recognition is hard to explain. Perhaps I'd sooner not know. You have to admire their dedication and devotion, not to say resilience and sheer bloody-mindedness for not walking away from a club that has hit hard times after famously living a dream it couldn't pay for. I'm all for keeping the faith, I just wish they'd grow up a bit and keep a sense of perspective.

1.55 P.M.: BOLT-CUTTERS AT THE READY Ipswich Town's stadium manager, Trevor Kirton, pops his head around the officials' changing-room door. 'Ready for the stadium briefing?' he asks. He is beckoned in by Paul Taylor.

This should be just another chore. The ref gets shown the normal gubbins, what to do in an emergency, etc., all very important if a disaster occurs, which frankly and thankfully isn't likely to happen, but you never know. It is right that procedures are explained. And today it is actually a bit more interesting than that.

First, the referee is told there will be a minute's silence for those who have recently lost their lives in the Asian tsunami disaster. Second, if it is a heated game he will arrange for stewards to walk Paul and his colleagues all the way in from the halfway line; just the last few steps if it is a normal match. Third, the referee and his assistant are to wear plain black rather than any other colours. Fourth, there are a few police spotters in the ground keeping tabs on well-known hooligans. But the main news out of the norm is that intelligence has been gathered suggesting that Fathers for Justice are planning an incident at a football match. No one knows quite where, but clubs have been told to be alert as it could involve any number of possibilities, including protesters chaining themselves to a goalpost, referee or player. Paul is told Ipswich have bolt-cutters on hand if such an incident occurs.

It's a murky day, so Paul asks for the lights to be on from the start. There is no need to wait until it starts to go dark. 'Put another shilling in the meter,' he quips as Trevor leaves.

2 P.M.: GRETNA'S GRASS Paul Barnett is now prepared to allow the players on to his precious pitch. At the stroke of two o'clock he bends down and removes the 'keep off the grass' sign.

2 P.M.: MEETING 'MR LINCOLN CITY' Rob leaves the bustling Centre Circle bar and heads over to the Executive Club inside the ground, where the sponsors and other dignitaries meet. We go via the ground. Rob wanders across the pitch and meets a few people to check everything is OK: the stadium manager, the groundsman and the first-team manager, Keith Alexander, a tall, amiable, popular man in his second spell in charge at Lincoln. Rob calls him 'Mr Lincoln City' – respect indeed.

In 2004 Keith underwent life-saving brain surgery after feeling ill and nearly died. Everyone is happy to see him back. He is still operating on a post-ITV Digital collapse budget, and Rob and his fellow directors have reduced players' wages to more equitable levels. Indeed, the Football League (unlike the Premiership, which is yet to follow suit) has introduced a salary cap: league one and two clubs cannot spend more than 60 per cent of their turnover on wages – a measure implemented to bring financial stability to lower-League clubs that so often in a genuine attempt to achieve success spend beyond their means. Alexander is reputedly a good coach who is able to get the most out of his players, and the proof is here at Lincoln. After going into administration he was installed as manager and rebuilt his squad mainly by bringing in new players from non-League clubs, yet Lincoln's form improved. They reached the play-off in the next two seasons.

Rob also introduces me to David Beck, chairman of the Lincoln City Supporters Trust, and a few fans who have won an executive day at the club. Being a fish out of water, I feel we are kindred spirits, and we chat a lot. Lincoln is a friendly club, and there are few unnecessary airs and graces behind the scenes. As a supporter-chairman, Rob has helped break down any 'us' and 'them' divides.

2 P.M.: EXCHANGING THE TEAM SHEETS It is a formal ritual that must take place at the right time. Exactly one hour before kick-off, unless there are genuine extenuating circumstances, the teams must hand their team sheets in to the referee.

Ipswich manager Joe Royle and captain Jim Magilton come in first, full of seasonal greetings to all. There are handshakes all round. I dare say it is all very routine, and it certainly befits a club like Ipswich, one of the game's renowned friendly clubs, but it still strikes me as a bit too false, a bit 'be nice to me, ref'. A contrast to the way in which some managers scowl and bad-mouth referees afterwards. Joe Royle has always seemed a personable chap though, and Jim Magilton is an experienced, intelligent pro.

A minute or so later, Peter Grant, West Ham's assistant manager, and club captain, the extremely polite Nigel Reo Coker, bring in their team sheet. A few moments later manager Alan Pardew comes in, again all smiles. Can he make a decision on his fifth sub who needs a pre-match warm-up? For pedants, this would be a red rag to a bull, a chance to do some petty law-enforcing. Paul just says OK.

Of course, what the clubs really want is each other's team sheets so they can size up the opposition and assess any tactics. All the other parties will need the teams pronto too – the PA announcer, press, dignitaries – and they duly get them.

The officials scour the sides for potentially difficult players.

'Kuqi?' asks Trevor Pollard, who will wave the yellow flag.

'Oh, Shefki's OK,' says Paul. 'Horlock can be trouble.'

'Repka?' Hmm. West Ham's Czech defender, who is on the subs bench, has a reputation for poor discipline. No one says anything.

Time for the officials to get changed. Now, I'm not suggesting anyone gets tape measures out, but it strikes me that the officials' changing rooms at Ipswich, which are considered to be a good size compared to most, are a bit small. There are, say, sixteen players in each main dressing room, and having peeked inside I know each of those rooms is more than four times bigger than this one. 'You should see some of them,' moan the officials, who consider this to be relatively palatial. As they administer the liniment and Deep Heat – Trevor rubs some on to his boots, which I have never seen before, though it strikes me as a good idea – I glance at the loos. No towels, and just a single cubicle shower. Room to swing a cat? I would suggest only a very bashed-about moggy could be wielded in here.

2 P.M.: FOOD GLORIOUS FOOD … AT WALSALL Dr Ralph Rogers goes in search of food. On the way we meet Walsall's owner, Jeff Bonser. 'Don't take any notice of him,' he tells me, laughing. 'Money for old rope.' The reality, and Bonser knows it, is that Ralph saves the Saddlers money.

Walsall have their previous boss, Colin Lee, to thank for recruiting Ralph. As he tucks into a burger with loads of salad, Ralph explains how he got the job – standing in for a colleague who soon moved on. Lee was impressed by Ralph's '24/7' approach, that he sees players whenever necessary regardless of the time of day or week. 'That's the job,' says Ralph, taking a drink. He either visits the players at the club, or if they drop into his practice he can direct them to one of his specialists straight away. For many smaller clubs this approach is unheard of. Walsall have a small squad and they need as many of their players available for selection as often as possible. Both current manager Paul Merson and Colin Lee said they would sooner lose a player from the squad than lose their doctor. This is a huge testimony to Ralph's worth. Other clubs have been sniffing around, but Ralph is an honest man. 'Walsall have been good to me. I gave them my handshake. I told them I would only move on with their blessing.' One rival manager who tried to tempt him into a move told Ralph to 'remember you have no friends in football'. It is a cynicism Ralph has little time for. 'I do what I think is right,' he says. 'I'm not interested in the normal practice of this industry.'

The food we are eating is excellent. Walsall is another renowned friendly club, and their corporate catering has just won an award. Jan, who is in charge, has 700 diners to look after tonight after the game is over. It's a logistical nightmare, but she still manages to give Doc Rogers and me some personal attention in the players' lounge. All this, plus the conference facilities, help to generate the extra income Walsall need to compete. Ralph is more than a guest, he is part of the team. He gives Jan a pat on the back and heads off downstairs for business.

2 P.M.: THE PRESS ROOM AT WIGAN Press rooms on matchdays. When I became a sports journalist I never really did settle in as a matchday reporter. I used to work for my local radio station, and although I enjoyed it at non-League level I often found it difficult to fit in at bigger grounds. The problem was the other, often seasoned, journalists. I found too many of them excluded you from conversations. In fact, most would barely speak. Actually, some openly made it their job to be difficult. I just couldn't see the point in this. I also found that although they espoused all kinds of views in their column or when chatting, they just lacked the bottle or guts directly to ask awkward questions. They often hid behind the radio or TV boys and hovered in the background taking notes. At a big press conference they would bitch and moan, and then when the player, manager, chairman or whoever turned up they would say nothing or ask only harmless questions about the length of contracts or, bizarrely on one occasion – the launch of Chelsea's sponsorship deal with mobile phone company Orange – what Frank Lampard thought about mobile phones.

The press room at Wigan is packed, but all journalistic eyes are on the Arsenal v. Sheffield United cup tie on the TV in the corner. I try, in a friendly, gentle way, just to be polite, to engage in a conversation about the game with a man standing near a coffee table. He looks at me with disdain as if someone has waved an unpleasant smell under his nose. I decide not to bother him again.

If, like me, you're not here with any obvious kindred spirit, you are exiled. No one helps. No one tells you when the pies are due. I didn't even know they doled out pies – even though Wigan (the town, not necessarily the FC) has a reputation for them – until I saw all the others scoffing them. No one speaks unless they have to. As a breed, they can be a sour, dour bunch.

The club stewards are different – helpful, friendly, a good laugh. They show me to the seat where Stuart Hall, doyen of BBC radio reporters who has covered games in the northwest for *Sport on Five* since 1959, has set up his gear. He indicates that he might go for a pre-match snifter in the Wigan boardroom. I wonder about the ethics of this, but then he clearly doesn't need to mix with the undistinguished journalistic hoi polloi below (and, indeed, doesn't). So I sit and watch the JJB Stadium slowly fill up, waiting for Stuart Hall.

2.05 P.M.: WOOD LANE, SHEPHERD'S BUSH There is nothing like actually being at the place where matchday happens. The buzz, the feel, the smell, the sound of a football ground; the seats filling up, the fevered anticipation, the expectation; the game itself ebbing and flowing, the run of the ball, the aftermath; even the trudging back to the car or bus on rainy, windswept days when your team has lost. There is nothing quite like it. Not to be there is to be square. But if you can't – because you've got the kids, the car to wash, or, like me sometimes, you follow the footy on the radio while gardening (I've sent a few spades flying in my time, I can tell you), or if you simply can't afford it – the media are essential.

For football fans, there is nothing like the matchday minutes themselves. All 90 of them. To me, there are two essential options. Forget text messages or any of that nonsense – it's radio or TV. The latter is a decent option these days, especially since Sky Sports started their *Soccer Saturday* programme, presented by the excellent, unflappable Jeff Stelling with a studio panel of old lags and more expert reporters around the grounds, not to mention an innovative ticker-tape of results and a strapline running along the foot of the screen. It is a wonderful way to watch the unfolding drama of the day. BBC and ITV have tried to follow suit. But radio has the edge. It's portable for starters: you can listen wherever you like. Then there are all the local and regional stations. I switch between BBC Hereford & Worcester to check out Worcester City and other local clubs, and WM, for Albion and the West Midlands teams. But for an overview of all the top action, you can't beat Radio Five Live's *Sport on Five*. It is comprehensive, the reporters are succinct and impressively word perfect, and although you may suspect the odd bit of sucking up to the big clubs, it is usually straight down the line.

Some of their reporters are, of course, legends. Stuart Hall, for instance, the barmy ex-presenter of *It's a Knockout*, whose reportage I will follow on a matchday. His reports are wonderfully witty and off-the-wall, usually peppered with literary references, which probably whizz over the heads of his sports-minded audience, though they probably get the general gist of what Hall is opining. As one interviewee (who will, of course, remain nameless) said, 'Stuart Hall is either an institution or he should be in one.'

Another thing I like about *Sport on Five* is that it feeds into *Sports Report*, which starts, as it has since 1948, bang on five o'clock with the stirring tones of Herbert Bath's 'Out of the Blue' played by the Central Band of the RAF. De dum de dum de dum de dum de diddly dit de der, diddly dit de der, diddly dit de der, de dum de dum de dum de diddly dit de der … The days' headlines are summed up, and then come the scores, those classified football results read by – well, you know – James Alexander Gordon. Who else? Another broadcasting legend.

And I'm here in Television Centre where it is produced. I've driven down on to Wood Lane, the thoroughfare between the A40 Westway and Shepherd's Bush, in glorious ignorance of the fact that in an hour Queens Park Rangers are kicking off against Preston North End. Their blue-and-white-hoops-shirted fans are starting to turn up, exiting the Tube opposite the BBC's Television Centre and clogging the already busy roads with their cars.

At Television Centre I'm greeted by Audrey Adams, who has produced the classified results with James Alexander Gordon for the past twenty years. They are a veritable double act. Their office, a small workshop, is at the end of Five Live's news and sports room, which, strangely for a Saturday, is disarmingly quiet. In fact, despite this being the hub of the BBC's television output, the building is largely unoccupied. Actually, you can wear a footy shirt, shorts or anything really. Aud has on a Saracens rugby top. The nine-to-five office wallahs are long gone. No one really cares on Saturday.

I can barely believe it is from this small office that those infamous classified results emanate. Where is the microphone? Audrey nods at a small mic with a yellow shield on a tiny stand. 'What, that?' I ask. There is barely room to place a pile of papers, let alone spread out the football scores. 'That?' It's a major disappointment. I had expected, or hoped, that James sat behind one of those huge cast-iron microphones with an old-style BBC logo stamped across the middle. I have this image of him sitting there in a smoking jacket and bow-tie, all echoes of Reithian ethics and Bakelite gramophones rather than digital radios.

James doesn't actually turn up until just before the games start. Audrey has a host of minor chores to undertake prior to match time when she feverishly gathers all the results together, so she shuffles me off down the corridor – about half a mile's worth, it seems – and downstairs through a maze of corridors to the *Sport on Five* studio.

2.05 P.M.: AMONG HIS FLOCK John Boyers walks into other departments. The control tower is again busy, but at least they are assured John is around if a disaster happens. He has calculated that the worst incident would be two planes colliding and descending into the stadium. They need a contingency plan for all circumstances. It's not just idle thinking. 'At SCORE we are trying to give our sports chaplains critical incident support management training,' John explains, 'so if something horrendous happens at least we know that they have had some training. If there is another Hillsborough, Bradford fire or Heysel, they know what the procedure is.'

The likelihood of a disaster, especially on a 9/11 scale, is slim. Stadiums are safer than they have ever been – belatedly so if you look at what happened at Hillsborough and Bradford. John is more likely to be needed on a one-to-one basis. 'It might be that someone in the stand has a heart attack,' he says, pacing around to the disabled enclosure. 'A couple of seasons ago there was an announcement saying "Would the club chaplain please report to the stadium control room" at eight minutes to three. A member of staff was at home with depression. He was desperate and didn't know who to turn to, but he did know there was a club chaplain and rang the club.'

2.05 P.M.: BLINKING INTO THE SUNLIGHT Danny Coles is one of several Bristol-born lads who have progressed through the youth system; the others in today's squad include Louis Carey, Dave Cotterill, Tommy Doherty, Scott Golbourne, Cole Skuse and Leroy Lita. As a local lad he is cheered louder than most when he steps out on to the pitch for the warm-up. Danny responds by clapping his hands.

The warm-up is methodical and well planned. Lots of stretching, some shuttle runs and casual ball play, then a small-sided game with players forming a circle and one in the middle trying to intercept passes. Danny does lots of heading practice with coach Shaun Taylor (himself a former defender) and some passing with fellow central defender Louis Carey.

Danny says he can't imagine not warming up thoroughly. He is reading a biography of Rio Ferdinand at the moment, and in it the England centre-back recalls playing with Julian Dicks, a hard-as-nails left-back who came up through non-League football and who would sit in the dressing room with a can of Coke before going out. No warm-up, nothing. As recently as ten years ago players didn't or wouldn't warm up. Paul Merson, who surely needs to now he is in his mid-thirties, doesn't. 'I don't think I could do that,' says Danny. 'It wouldn't seem right somehow.' His warm-up continues until twenty to three, when he comes off the pitch looking, frankly, more knackered than I had expected. In the dressing room he takes off his shirt, which is wringing wet, and slumps in his seat with a towel over his shoulders.

Brian Tinnion's real pre-match team talk will soon start. I wonder if Danny is now experiencing real nerves before a game his manager has described as 'massive'. 'It's funny,' Danny replies, 'you don't always get pre-match nerves for big games. In the play-off semi-final last year we were losing with two minutes to go. I came over to the bench. Danny Wilson, our manager then, said, "Keep believing, keep believing," and we equalised and got a winner. I wasn't at all nervous then. But for the final against Brighton at Cardiff I was very nervous. It was shit or bust really. It was such a big game for both clubs.' Danny wants to and clearly feels he can play at a higher level. Earlier in the season he went on the transfer list. He has had his disagreements with Brian Tinnion, but says that now 'the vibe is all right'. Just before kick-off, a player cannot afford to think in any other way.

2.10 P.M.: THE INNER SANCTUM We move into the Lincoln City boardroom. Within these four walls some very difficult decisions have been made in recent years. For Rob Bradley there is more glad-handing to do – mainly welcoming the opposing club directors from Bristol Rovers. Local MP Gillian Merron, who is a genuine fan and not merely here looking for support, tells me about a fund-raising effort she is helping with having been approached in Parliament by a member of the Wrexham Supporters Trust. His name is Neil Williams.

2.10 P.M.: BROOKS MILESON – THE PHILANTHROPIST At Gretna there would be no promotion chase, no full-time playing squad, no full-time groundsman if it wasn't for the investment of Brooks Mileson. Paul promises to introduce me. As we walk into the club bar, he says, 'There he is.'

He isn't the person I'm expecting – loud, cocky, showy. Instead, Mileson is perched on a bar stool, smoking a cigarette and sipping a pint, wearing jeans and sporting a pony-tail (which frankly suits a younger man, but there you go). You would never pick him out as the man who has bankrolled this tiny club. 'My best signing' is how he describes Paul, grabbing him around the neck. Mileson is the managing director rather than the chairman. He prefers to donate rather than carve out an official role. 'You spend all your life making lots of money and then you piss it up the wall in a couple of years,' he remarks with a laugh.

He has also given money to Scarborough, Carlisle United and Berwick Rangers, and to charities in the north too, but it's Gretna where he is out to make his mark. He aims to take the club into the Scottish Premier. 'That's no problem,' he insists. 'Staying there is more difficult.' He plans to turn the Raydale into a 6,000 all-seater stadium. Gates have risen fourfold in two years but they are still under a 1,000 a game and he knows that has to improve rapidly. Much, he admits, depends on whether they can steal fans who currently watch Carlisle United or Queen of the South, but he is also committed to developing a huge community programme that will draw local support. He wants the club's academy to prove its worth too, by developing local role-model players rather than having to pay to buy them in. He wants to build a family base, to get the kids along. Later, he proudly marches around the terracing with his own grandson, looking much like any other granddad. Today, to celebrate the Chinese New Year, they have hired a Manchurian band. The club mascot, Robbie the Rooster, is also drumming up interest among the juniors.

This all sounds like a cohesive plan. So far he has given Barney £60,000 worth of equipment. There are 40 players on the books at Gretna, most full-timers on good money. Rebuilding the ground will cost millions – time will tell if it is achieved. But Mileson isn't in it for the personal adulation. He doesn't go in the directors' lounge or watch from the stands, he just blends in with other fans, which I kinda like.

2.15 P.M.: STUART HALL HA HA HA In the Wigan press box, or rather the radio points, I am going to have to straddle one leg then another to fit in between the seat allocated for Stuart Hall and a reporter from BBC1's *Football Focus*. An Asian Network reporter sits in front of us. If you are over, say, fourteen stone you are going to cause your colleagues a lot of discomfort.

This isn't unique – far from it: the facilities here are positively palatial compared to some. I once delivered reports for a first-round FA Cup tie between Cinderford and Bromsgrove Rovers with my feet immersed in six inches of water, with only a poorly tuned-in radio for a cue and a shared microphone I had to wrestle from a colleague working for BBC Radio Gloucestershire. That venerable sports columnist Frank Keating, who lived in the Cotswolds and was naturally drawn to the fixture for its cup magic potential, commented, 'You'll look back on this and laugh.' I didn't, and I don't now. I was wet through. So Wigan is a luxury. But this is still going to be a closer encounter than it needs to be.

Stuart Hall is not hard to spot. Sports journalists are hardly a dapper bunch. You might get the odd person who is suited and booted or sporting a snazzy winter sports jacket or a neat blue Crombie, but no one else would wear a full-length, deep-brown fur coat with a contrasting yellow scarf, which has echoes of Rupert the Bear. Stuart is invariably tanned and genial – all smiles for the fans occupying nearby seats who exchange pleasantries with him. They know it's a big game when Stuart is here, although he no longer gets the pick of the northwest's big games: these days Five Live will inevitably have a commentary team covering one of those (Manchester United usually). But Stuart still does plenty of matches at Liverpool, Manchester City, Everton, Bolton, Blackburn and Everton, with the occasional dip into the Coca-Cola Championship, to Wigan, Preston, Burnley or Crewe, maybe even Tranmere if they are going well. The fans at these grounds know and love him. I'm here to see how he delivers those marvellous, witty, distinguished reports with their twinkle-in-the-eye and cultural references.

Many people are flattered when you come to spend an afternoon with them. Stuart is ambivalent. Disappointingly so in some respects. It takes some time to squeeze the rudiments of an interview out of him. This is partly understandable because he has to keep an ear on the output in his cans (headphones) – he will need to deliver pre-match reports for both Five Live and the World Service before kick-off – but also because those waving to him from further down the stand are his true audience rather than journos writing books. They are tangible, they are real, they are here. Some may even have trannies pressed to their ears to listen to his summaries of the match. Maybe they'll let him know what they think.

No journalist is afforded such respect, except perhaps the odd ex-player commentating for a local radio station. Norman Hunter is here today, for instance. A few others may earn marginal recognition, but not many. There is only one Stuart Hall, and I'm about to find out why.

2.15 P.M.: BRIGHTON ROCK I venture into the Brighton & Hove Albion PA box, where I can imagine that the results of many a 400-metre race have been announced down the years. It is dead level with the finishing line, which means a long look up the pitch to the far end where the Nottingham Forest fans are in a temporary stand at an angle. We are at the back of the only permanent seating, which is about ten rows deep. There is just a grass bank to our right, and straight ahead, on the opposite side of the pitch, is a big temporary stand, or several clustered together, uncovered and with dark green seats, looking rather like the sort of thing you see at big golf tournaments.

I shake hands with Attila the Stockbroker, real name John Baine. He is a familiar face. We have met before, many moons ago, when he was championing a football anti-racism campaign. He's also got a benefit gig lined up for the tsunami appeal. But he can only loosely be described as a pop star: he writes poetry, sings, plays the mandolin and the violin, but rarely troubles the mainstream charts. However, he certainly isn't an artist who has belatedly found football or been wheeled on to the Soccer AM sofa to proclaim a lifelong love of footy only to fail to remember much past last season. He is 100 per cent Brighton & Hove Albion and has been a fan all his life. Like me, Attila is a 46-year-old ex-punk who is losing his hair badly. And what do old punks wear? Attila sports a Bad Religion T-shirt, leather biker jacket, narrow jeans, pointed shoes and a chain looping around his belt. All a little too tight, if truth be told.

On the face of it, asking Attila to play the music at a football ground is a bit like asking Hannibal Lecter to mind the kids while you pop out to a movie. He's not going to be satisfied playing Kylie or Rachel Stevens tunes. And what about football's much-vaunted ageing audience, the people who are steadily filing into those plastic seats opposite? How old are they? What music will they relate to? Attila's answer, on his debut for Brighton when they were exiled at Gillingham, was to slap 'Anarchy in the UK' by the Sex Pistols on the turntable. The chief of police on duty had a fit. By that I don't mean he started pogo-ing; rather, he raced to the PA booth and ordered Attila to stop it immediately.

'Why?' asked Attila.

'Isn't it obvious?' replied the policeman. 'It will cause a riot.'

Attila's riposte was stunning: 'I have heard this record played hundreds of times in public. I have seen people leap around to it, but I have never seen it lead to violence. On the other hand, if you order me to play "In the Air Tonight" by Phil Collins I will turn into a raging psychopath and cannot be held responsible for my actions.'

Point made. The policeman scurried off.

'We haven't had any problems here like that,' says Attila. Noise is a problem though. They can't play music at night games, and they have to be careful after the game too. I can imagine the Withdean residents armed with their tape recorders and notepads. Some would, apparently, love to get Albion moved. Best not to play into their hands.

The pre-match, half-time and even post-match music at football grounds is usually dire, thoroughly predictable and depressingly familiar. It used to be all Elton John and Diana Ross; now it's Daniel Bedingfield and 'Amarillo'. The songs played for players to walk out to aren't much better; Queen's plodding 'We Will Rock You' is a favourite. What has that got to do with football? 'I play a fairly eclectic mix of punk rock-type stuff', is how Attila describes his selections. 'There is no way of telling whether people actually *like* what we're playing. It's not like you're going to see people jumping around in their seats, but I'm sure they would complain if they didn't like it. Checking out the discussion in the North Stand internet chatroom, people seem to be three to one in favour. They prefer it to the normal boring mainstream dross.'

Not that Attila bombards Brighton fans at Withdean with a limited repertoire of seventies punk tracks. Today he opens with the Scissor Sisters, then the Libertines, closely followed by a couple of ska tracks. The Clash's 'I Fought the Law' is the first punk oldie. It's familiar. I'm not up with the new stuff. I hear the rumbling tones of a CD and look quizzical. 'The Killers,' Attila offers helpfully.

On matchday Attila is helped by Richard Lindfield, who also works for Southern FM, and Paul Samraha, an accountant by trade who is chairman of Falmer For All, the group campaigning for the stadium move. Various other people float in and out of the PA box.

'The PA speakers are poor,' admits Attila.

'Yet the emergency announcements are perfectly clear,' adds Richard. 'The best place to actually hear the music is in the toilets beneath the away fans.' I decide against checking this out.

Paul says Sheffield United also have a good musical selection.

'Do they?' asks Attila.

Paul furrows his brow. 'Didn't you go last week [Albion had been there the week before]?'

'Oh, yes,' replies Attila, 'but I didn't get into the ground until kick-off.'

Richard adds that Sheffield United's fans had even released a version of 'Tom Hark' that sold 5,000 copies.

'Did it get in the charts?' asks Attila. It didn't, and he is reassured.

Attila has a problem with other clubs' supporters singing 'Tom Hark' to Brighton fans when the Piranhas were a Brighton band. He puts on Babyshambles. 'The thing is,' he says, 'away from home, the atmosphere among our fans is brilliant. We always take 2,000 away and it's fantastic. But here it's crap, and anything we can do to lift it helps.'

Most clubs now, it seems, have songs they celebrate goals to. It's another Albion, my team West Brom, who are responsible for this sort of thing. In 1993 a small section adopted a trance-dance track called 'Poing' by the Rotterdam Termination Source. It is immensely repetitive but contains what sounds like a nose flute making a boing sound. At away games Albion supporters started singing 'boing, boing', while jumping up and down – for ages. The atmosphere built and built. 'Boing, boing, Baggies, Baggies!' Eventually it became something the fans sang only when Albion scored. It was a matter of spontaneity, but soon other clubs began to adopt tunes for when their teams scored, usually led by the limited imagination of people housed in PA boxes armed with their Phil Collins CDs, or 'Tom Hark', or Pigbag, or, latterly, 'Amarillo'. These are the sorts of tunes now played by clubs when they score. It is routine, flat and a bit boring. But it began with a posse of Baggies fans on a holiday dance floor.

Attila and co. are lovingly disorganised.

'We're not on here,' Attila announces, confused by the array of buttons in front of him.

'The good thing is,' says Richard, laughing, 'even though we've been doing this for several years we're still grappling with the technology between us.'

2.20 P.M.: BUCKETS At Wrexham the Clubs in Crisis meeting has disbanded, and I am on my way to the match. The atmosphere outside the Racecourse Ground is what you would expect: the sizzle and smell of fried onions and ketchup from a burger bar, programme sellers shouting for attention, and ladies urging spectators to buy half-time draw tickets.

But there is another, more recently familiar sound: the rattle of buckets. The Wrexham Supporters Trust is at it again, trying to do all it can to raise some money for the club. The majority toss coins (their spare change maybe?) into the buckets outside the away end. Doncaster Rovers fans have trod this path before, so they are generous. The bucket-rattlers thank each and every contribution. Glancing into one of them I can see a couple of fivers – some have been big-hearted indeed. And already, by the colour of the scarves and shirts, you can tell that they have come from all over the country.

But there is sadness too. This is what our national game at professional level has come to. Not just here at Wrexham, but elsewhere. Clubs kept afloat by generous donations, by the goodwill of fans prepared to rattle buckets under the noses of fellow supporters. What hurts is that it has been planned to be like this. Such struggle is inevitable as the Premier League creams off the game's wealth and leaves the rest to flounder. Clubs have always lurched into financial crises, but there are now so many of them that they can't all be cock-ups. This is systematic.

When Newcastle United chairman Freddy Shepherd, a man who has revealed his thoughts on many subjects on several occasions, said he didn't care about life outside the Premier League, he said it all. Self-interest – don't care. One day the buckets won't rattle. The game itself will suffer a death rattle instead.

2.30 P.M.: RED DEVIL WORSHIPPING As John Boyers does his rounds, I slip away to take my seat. I spot a 'Manchester United – The Religion' banner. This seems deeply ironic bearing in mind the person I'm spending the day with. It strikes me as a bit arrogant really. I don't like all these comparisons between football and faith. The mores and values of the Church stand in stark contrast to those that hold sway here, and elsewhere. I suppose the banner is more a statement of commitment and belonging, a boast about the dedication and devotion of these fans to this club.

I'm troubled by the idea held by some Manchester United supporters – too many in fact – that somehow their support is worthier and all the greater because they have made the sacrifice to get here. Martyrs to a cause. Naturally, I am excluding local fans here, those you might reasonably expect to follow a Mancunian club. It's the glory-hunters I have a problem with, not just at Man Utd, but currently Arsenal, Chelsea, Liverpool and maybe Spurs too: those who, frankly, are too chicken-shit scared to support a local team that might, gasp, lose too many matches; those who always have to side with the winners, who are too emotionally unbalanced to accept that in sport, sometimes you win, sometimes you lose; those who take the piss out of the loyal fans who support 'losers' – ordinary clubs, small clubs, local clubs, fiercely proud clubs, going-bust clubs, the clubs whose grounds they pass to reach this 'Theatre of Dreams' every time they visit.

So, come on, impress me. This is going to be the biggest crowd the Premier League has ever seen; I want to see how manic and persuasive the support can be. 'There's nowhere quite like it, Chris,' a friend told me. So, how religiously fervent does it get? Will I need ear-plugs? Outside there are a few anti-Glazer protests, but not the salvo promised in the media, and they are being ignored by the vast majority. United are doing rather well at the moment: they are into the FA Cup quarter-finals, and will go second in the Premier League tonight with a win; Van Nistelrooy is back from injury, Rooney is looking sharp, Ronaldo is proving an ideal replacement for the ageing Giggs, and Alan Smith and Louis Saha are waiting in the wings. Struggling Portsmouth should be a walkover. I'm expecting goals, noise and, particularly as I am sat in the family section, lots of jolly bonhomie – irritating children bursting into song and bubbling about the skills of their heroes.

But the signs aren't good. The ground seems to be filling slowly, dispassionately. There is little in the way of expectation. Half an hour before kick-off the Theatre is filling up much like any other Premier League or Championship ground. I try downstairs on the concourse. A juggling children's entertainer is failing to drum up much interest there. He makes the most of those kids who do glance his way. A few dads and lads are having a beer, served from the six identical food outlets in this corner of the West Stand. Each one sells the same food and drink, the usual suspects too: pies, hot dogs, chocolate bars, crisps, Cola. This is a world away from Brian Murdoch's 'quality fayre' and is nowhere near as enticing. You'll have to work hard to get a smile from the acne-troubled staff here, and the proof is in the non-eating. Ten minutes before kick-off you can walk up and be served straight away. Needless to say, there are no healthy options available. Jamie Oliver would, rightly, despair. I look around again, and sadly there are lots of overweight children. Manchester

*Worcester City director Bob Marley contemplates the meaning of life …
and non-league football. © Chris Green*

*Walsall doctor Ralph Rogers … at the
ground. © Chris Green*

*John Boyers, Manchester United
chaplain. © Manchester United PLC*

A fan's chairman: Rob Bradley sits among the supporters at Lincoln City. © Chris Green

Wrexham fan Neil Williams with some of the replica shirts he has auctioned. © Chris Green

Quality Fayre in Kidderminster. Brian Murdoch (far left) and team. © Chris Green

The fans are revolting: Clubs in Crisis Day at Wrexham. © Chris Green

A level playing field. Paul Barnett flattens the pitch at Gretna. © Chris Green

Danny Coles in action for Bristol City. © Press Association

Norwich City chief executive Neil Doncaster with daughter Grace
… and clipboard. © Chris Green

Referee Paul Taylor sorts out a dispute. © Empics

James Alexander Gordon – about to read the classified scores. © Chris Green

*Kevin Brookes (centre) and WPC Alison Geddes (right)
at the Handsworth Positive Futures programme. © Chris Green*

Phil Hamilton coaching in inner city Aston. © Chris Green

Mr Afan Lido, Phil Robinson, pulling post match pints. © Chris Green

The irrepressible Stuart Hall. © Press Association

Bristol City boss, Brian Tinnion, explains how the match was won. © Chris Green

United are not unique in failing to provide more imaginative catering, but if they won't do it, who will? The catering companies call this sort of thing 'brand awareness': punters know what to expect when they walk up to a kiosk. It is a scene replicated across the entire country. But the clubs are losing money. Check out all those different accents. These people must have travelled miles, maybe all day, to get here. Why aren't Man Utd hitting Brian Murdoch's 95 per cent mark with away fans? The answer is because the food isn't worth getting into the ground early to eat. The clubs are denying themselves extra income.

Back in the seats, the kids and their parents are soaking up the atmosphere with their heads stuck in magazines or chatting on mobile phones. This isn't a special occasion, it's just another game. Another thrashing to be handed out. It's the joyless pursuit of winning. They aren't religious converts, they are mainly consumers of football. They know how to watch a winning team, but do they really understand and fully appreciate the game?

2.32 P.M.: RALPH ROGERS RETIRES TO THE DRESSING ROOM Off comes Ralph's jacket, and into his room step a couple of players who have already been outside warming up under the guidance of coach Frank Barlow. Now the serious stuff begins.

Much-travelled defender Neil Emblen has a stiff neck that has been giving him some problems. He is having trouble turning it and has already been to Ralph's morning surgery. It sounds like an old man's illness, but it's one of those weird, unaccountable injuries that can be picked up as easily from a draughty window as a centre-forward's elbow. It is causing concern, for Emblen is no hypochondriac. There is even a hint he may miss the game. He wants a painkilling injection just before he goes on to the pitch.

'No worries, man,' Ralph says. 'Let's freeze it. We'll get you into the clinic in the week. OK?'

It's reassurance and diagnosis in one, on the spot. Emblen, a 33-year-old grizzled pro whose judgement these days compensates for his lack of pace, feels fine.

2.35 P.M.: GROUNDHOP DAY IV Bill Berry and I arrive at Evergreen's ground in Hunton Bridge, just north of Watford, a few hundred yards off the A41, near junction 20 of the M25. Despite the promise of the club's charming name, it isn't the idyllic setting I'd hoped for.

Let me paint a picture of the sort of ground Bill and his groundhopping colleagues tick off. Evergreen's ground is opposite a council estate. The car park has some twenty-odd spaces. There are two buildings, a changing block and a social club. Both have seen better days. In fact, they are badly in need of a lick of paint. There is also an astroturf five-a-side pitch with floodlights. Overall, it seems a well-equipped if slightly weather-worn set-up. The pitch is in the distance; it has bars all the way around it and a concrete path snakes behind one of the goals to the dugouts. 'It's probably taken quite a bit of organising just to get this done for a club like this,' says Bill. This is so true. For Evergreen, finding the money just for the pitch perimeter fencing will have been an enormous task. They would probably have had to do it themselves, and would almost certainly have needed planning permission too.

The people who organise football at this level of the game are gems. There is no reward or kudos for them. They do it to assist the club, to help the players and coaches, who are often friends and family. There is no payment involved.

This next bit is awkward. In fact, I realise in advance I am going to hate it. There is no entrance fee as such in leagues such as the Hertfordshire Senior League, Premier Division or otherwise. Instead, you have the option to buy a programme. They cost 50p each. Bill is pleasantly surprised: usually it is more, a pound maybe. Again, unlike many programmes at this level of football, this one is designed just for this match. Many clubs simply, and practically, issue one programme to cover the entire season. They only get occasional visitors, usually groundhoppers.

The club secretary is quite accommodating. Realising we are strangers, he shows us to the tea hut and offers Bill the pink and blue forms of the home and away teams, which Bill ordinarily has to seek from the referee. You see, watching the game isn't enough; Bill has to log all the details. He looks at me in despair as I fold my programme in half so that it fits into my jeans pocket. Sacrilege. It should be kept for posterity. But why? Who cares? Groundhoppers do.

All this could be extremely embarrassing. Bill is the nutty

groundhopper, and I am his socially challenged mate, too shy apparently even to ask for the team sheets or programmes. Added to which, Bill has told them he's coming. He has to so that he can ask if the match is on. Word may have got around that groundhoppers are in the area. You sense eyes boring into your back. The madmen have arrived. Frankly, I would have felt more comfortable scooping the entire collection of pornography off the top shelf of the local newsagent's and swanning off down the road with them tucked under my arm.

'A bag, sir?'

'No, not I, for I am a wanker, and let the world know it!'

But if they are feeling this way, they are hiding it well. Everyone is extremely friendly. The girl in the tea hut runs off to the social club to get me a cheese roll. She dunks the tea bag with tongs. 'That's a neat trick,' I say by way of conversation. She smiles sweetly.

I ask Bill if he fancies a cuppa; he looks back with barely disguised disgust. 'What, it's not half-time, is it?'

No, Bill.

So we've travelled 80-odd miles to watch two groups of strangers kick a pig's bladder about. Evergreen warm up vigorously with a five-a-side match. As we wait for the players to make their way over to the pitch, it's mainly family and friends milling around. And me and Bill. And then there were three. Bill's mate Dave, from Leatherhead, turns up.

As Bill disappears to find the loo – unsurprisingly, he won't risk missing a moment of the match – I chat to Dave. He works for the railways. Many groundhoppers do, doubtless attracted by the many hours spent as youths on station platforms logging locos. A rail pass is also a big bonus for groundhoppers. Without any prompting, Dave explains how he's recently been to mid-Wales to knock off loads of grounds, and that he is flying to Europe soon for a four-day sojourn, with a game planned for each day.

Dave is a nice guy, I suspect in need of a good woman. He asks if I am going to Devon (for groundhoppers, the Easter Devon Hop is an annual event akin to Glyndebourne for opera buffs or Edinburgh for arts lovers, hence its linguistic shortening). I explain that I am actually a journalist, someone mildly fascinated by groundhopping, and that I am writing a book. He is doing the Island Hop soon. I thought he said Ireland and quipped, innocently, 'Enjoy the Guinness!' But he means Jersey, Guernsey and Sark. Something of an organisational feat transport-wise. Dave looks slightly amazed that I could have made my way up journalism's greasy pole without knowing this event existed. Before I have time to conjure up an excuse, and with Bill back in tow, he's on about another trip to the Shetlands.

Before the game kicks off, I wonder whether Bill can actually recall any of the games he's been to. Yes, he can. He saw a game that finished 7–5 once (my highest aggregate in 40 years on the terraces and in a press box is a 5–5 draw between Bromsgrove and Woking). 'At Dawlish in the Western League,' recalls Bill. 'I was going to Torquay United in the evening.' Doubling up – sensible. Martyrdom and sacrifice may be an essential part of groundhopping for some, but Bill seems to have it just right.

2.40 P.M.: HARRIERS GET THEIR END AWAY As that doughty midfielder Oscar Wilde once said, 'I can resist everything but temptation.' At last, Brian Murdoch finally asks, 'Chris, what would you like?'

The agony of food choice is an unusual feeling inside an English football ground. I opt for the cheese and tomato pasta, and twenty minutes before kick-off I'm tucking in with a plastic fork. Actually, I think Brian is underselling this pasta. It's much more than just cheese and tomato: the foil dish is packed with carrots, mushrooms, onions, celery and whole peppercorns, which dissolve in your mouth. It tastes wonderful and wholesome, perfect alfresco food for a freezing cold day.

But never mind what I think. What about the away fans, Rochdale's barmy army?

The gates are open and, to be honest, I am just a bit sceptical about whether the Rochdale fans from pie-land are going to be experimental enough to venture away from the tried and trusted burgers and hot dogs. 'Bloody hell, what a choice!' exclaims a burly fan with glasses in the sort of Lancastrian accent that could curdle milk. His mates are equally awestruck. They stand back and take a look, letting others order first. One has heard about the soup and opts for that – it could just be for starters. He's telling everyone about Brian Murdoch's reputation and seems happy with his choice. Another goes for a burger. Safe ground. Boring. Another plumps for a pork and stuffing bap, which is attacked with gusto. No one says much. They are too busy chomping.

Rochdale have brought maybe 400 fans, and as I look across at the away terrace I see that most people seem to be getting stuck into the food. It looks like Brian is going to hit his 95 per cent. Some have waited to let the steady queue die down; others look like they might wait for the game to start. I decide to do what we journalists call vox pops (shortened Latin for 'voice of the people'). I go up to one fan, Neil, who is circling a finger around the base of a cup of soup.

'What's it like?'

'It's [slurp] the nicest [slurp] thing [slurp] I've ever [slurp] tasted.'

His mate, Stewart, is attacking a cottage pie, smothered in ketchup. The verdict? 'Superb. They're known for it, aren't they? It's always mentioned how good the food is.'

Another couple of lads, in their mid-twenties, admit it probably tipped the balance between their coming to the game or not. 'If you can get something good to eat it adds to the game,' said one of them. They'd made a late decision. They left Rochdale at 11.30 and came straight to the ground; no reason to walk the streets in search of edible food. 'And it's good value,' the other lad points out. 'Three and a half quid, that,' he adds, nodding at his cottage pie. 'You'd pay a lot more to eat something like that in a restaurant.' Another fan, John, is waylaying some chow mein. He doesn't want to be disturbed, but gives me a thumbs-up sign. 'Speak to you later,' he says between gulps.

2.40 P.M.: THE REFEREE LIMBERS UP At Ipswich Paul Taylor and his assistants, Tim Howes and Trevor Pollard, are ready for action. They go out for a warm-up with just their training tops and shorts on. I've seen people laugh at this, officials jogging around to loosen their limbs. Why wouldn't they?

For Paul, it is a chance to absorb the atmosphere and to run off some nervous energy. Only for ten minutes or so, mind. I ask if he is getting nervous as we move closer to kick-off. 'It's a cliché, but if you didn't get nerves you wouldn't deliver the goods,' he replies. 'It's exciting. It's what you train for and what all the preparation is about. I am getting a bit edgy, but that gives you an edge. It gets you alert.'

Oh dear. As the words trip off his tongue, I can feel a disaster coming on. Edgy. Excited. Penalties, sendings-off, incorrect decisions. I hope he is right: on edge rather than toppling over.

2.45 P.M.: JIMMY GORDON The big clock on the wall in the *Sport on Five* studio is ticking down slowly towards three o'clock. The show has been on-air since midday, taking in early kick-offs. Mark Saggers, the programme's cool-as-a-cucumber presenter, is effortlessly guiding us through the afternoon's action. On the other side of 'the glass', producer Adrian Williams is also calmness personified. Reporters have been dialled up and they are ready to deliver their pre-match spiel – ten to twelve seconds of precious airtime during which pieces have to be delivered with sublime accuracy.

Saggers spins around the grounds – all the main football matches, as well as today's key race meeting at Newbury, the Six Nations rugby international between Italy and Scotland, and athletics from Sheffield. Within two minutes, eight footy matches and the other events are covered. It is awesome. Ten people are packed around Williams, willing helpers poised over reel-to-reel tape machines, which for all the technical innovations of recent years is still the easiest and most tactile way to slice out reports of goals so that they can be played back at opportune moments.

Outside, a lone figure wanders down the silent corridor, a grey-haired man with a limp called Jimmy Gordon. He slowly makes his way up the stairs to the Five Live production office. No one notices him. He is largely invisible in terms of the action, but the man is a broadcast legend. Possibly the most treasured voice you can hear today.

Born in Edinburgh, Jimmy's mum died giving birth to him. He never knew his real father and was duly adopted. At six months he contracted polio and endured the sort of childhood that could make you weep. He had both legs amputated and had little formal education because he spent so long in hospital and in a special school. His face was so deformed he couldn't speak clearly, and because of facial paralysis his lips skewed at angles across his face. His adopted family were poor. He can remember his mother crying because they couldn't afford to buy Jimmy the special shoes he needed in those pre-NHS days. His father worked in a factory and brought him up the hard way. When he fell off his prosthetic legs he was told to pick himself up. 'Get up – you can't lie down there,' his father would say.

His only escapes were books and the radio. Jimmy was self-educated. He disappeared into the world of Dickens and Shakespeare (for fun!). In hospital, and encouraged by his parents when at home, he would write radio reports and read them out. His father would say, pointing at the radio, 'He'll read the news on there one day.' In jest.

Thirty-five years later it came true. Jimmy's face straightened. The pushiness of youth and the desire to overcome his disability and to leave an office job with ICI in Grangemouth forced the boy to seek out a living as a musician in London (his mates had gone down the seemingly more exciting route of National Service). Bold as brass, he walked into the Noel Gay Organisation in Denmark Street and ordered a meeting with the managing director, who was astonished and straight away took him on as a dance-band musician. He worked in music publishing and read the introductions to records, and became rather good at it. So good, in fact, that it was suggested he should audition as a continuity announcer for the BBC.

In 1972 he was taken on, to read the news as he had as a child, though now on Radio 2 rather than the Light Programme. 'The wee bugger's done it,' said his tearful father back home in Grangemouth. He had indeed. He had also acquired a new identity. There were lots of Jimmy Gordons around in music publishing, and many James Gordons too, so he inserted his mother's maiden name in between. James Alexander Gordon was born – JAG to all and sundry.

2.45 P.M.: PRE-MATCH ENTERTAINMENT At Wigan Stuart Hall has sketched out the basics of his pre-match report: who is in and who is out of last week's teams for Wigan and Leeds. He has barely noticed the pre-match entertainment taking shape – a display of self-defence techniques by the Royal Marine Commandos. Three different units are on different parts of the pitch. From afar it all looks rather brutal, but in reality it is being hammed up for the audience. Once he's noticed it, Stuart sweeps back in time to his *It's a Knockout* days. He lets out a belly laugh and tittering giggles as boots, fists and arms send would-be attackers to the ground. 'Great fun,' he says. He smokes like a trooper, but his reports are enthusiastic, vivid and atmospheric. When you are listening in the car or at home, you want to be where Stuart Hall is. Now I am.

I have to confess a fondness for Hall. My favourite report of his was when he likened the first half of a dull game to a surreal French new-wave film directed by the *auteur* Alain Resnais called *Last Year in Marienbad*. It's a challenging film that is not remotely entertaining; the action is repetitive and deliberately disarming. And let's face it, we've all seen football matches like that. Who else would have had the cultural knowledge or nerve to draw this comparison but Hall? That virtually no one listening would have understood is exceptionally poor radio reporting discipline. But, hey, for those that got it, it was classic Hall. It promises to be an interesting afternoon.

2.48 P.M.: A RACE TO REACH ST GEORGE'S LANE If Bob Marley and his son Seb don't get a wriggle on they won't make it in time for the kick-off. At the ground Bob assumes another guise – club director. He steps out of his muddied boots, socks and sweatshirt into trousers, shirt, tie and club blazer. He suddenly looks much older (the club blazer doesn't help), but Worcester City have a strict directors' box dress code. Bob also grabs a bite to eat and yet another coffee and chats to Sebastian, who makes the wise choice to stay warm and watch the rugby on the TV in the directors' lounge.

2.50 P.M.: RUBBING SHOULDERS WITH ABRAMOVIC Satisfied that he has availed himself to those who would wish to meet him, Neil Doncaster heads indoors. He goes off to deal with one or two matters, and I am left below the entrance to the directors' box and executive area. Suddenly, Roman Abramovic turns up. His bodyguards are sorting something out, leaving him temporarily alone. A few strangers shake his hand, including one man who was slating him seconds earlier in the toilet. The unassuming Russian clearly feels uncomfortable. He shakes hands and smiles but does not and cannot engage in small talk or conversation. In fact, it seems a joyless, indeed quite lonely experience for him. For a few brief moments, while his security men are presumably checking under seats for bombs or guns, he is lost and vulnerable. He looks at me fleetingly, a seeming kindred spirit: we are the only ones on our own in an apparently alien environment. He makes as if to speak. I simply shrug my shoulders in a 'don't ask me, I'm lost too' gesture. Then he has gone, whisked away into his seat. The supposedly fearsome security guards are tiny and not at all menacing, though I am later assured they are keen martial arts experts.

2.50 P.M.: CROSSING THE WHITE LINE Brian Tinnion is about to prove his worth. You can forget all the midweek training-ground detail; the pre-match team talk is when the gaffer earns his corn. He has to fire his troops up to go out and get a vital win. His laid-back, nice-guy demeanour must fly out of the window. Beforehand, he told me, 'We have prepared the players for this, they have put the work in, and if they do everything right and put 120 per cent effort in they have a good chance of winning the game.'

Tinnion and his assistant Keith Millen are a double act. Tinnion goes first. He doesn't mince his words or complicate things. He has been calm and rational, but now he stamps home the meaning and importance of the game. I'll leave out the profanities, football's industrial language, but basically it goes like this: 'Let's get in their faces. Get at 'em early. Set the tempo. Get the ball forward early.' Millen then talks tactics and brings forward the clipboard. Jamie Smith, a much-travelled full-back, is receiving some lower-back manipulation but twists around to see the position each player is expected to take up at corners and set-pieces, which must be defended, as planned, at all times.

There are observations of the way they expect Port Vale to play – one up front with another attacker playing just behind. His runs will need to be checked, and Danny Coles is told to keep a close eye on his 'old chum' Lee Matthews up front. 'Don't give him a sniff,' orders Tinnion, who prowls in front of his players, fists clenched. Coles is quiet. 'I tend to focus on good things,' he said earlier, 'like the way we felt after our last game [City beat Torquay 4–0 away] and how I felt at five o'clock, or just a game when I played well. But you have to stay focused on the task in hand, what we need to do to win this one.' In 2004, Danny worked with a psychologist on visualisation and hypnotism. 'If you visualise bad things, you do it. If you visualise good things, it is amazing what you can achieve.'

Some of the players begin to psyche each other up. It starts slowly. 'Come on, lads, let's do it!' shouts Jamie Smith while stretching his abductor muscles. Goalkeeper Steve Phillips joins in as he prowls up and down. He seems anxious to get out there. Young forward Leroy Lita, an England U-21 international who scored a hat-trick in the previous match, stalks the dressing room, loosening his neck from side to side. He is cocky and has a bit of flashy arrogance about him. Tinnion pulls him to one side for a quiet word, urging him to run at Vale's defence. 'Stay calm, but get at them,' he says. It is a lovely, quiet piece of motivation. 'We are trying to get a squad of players who will die for each other on the pitch,' Tinnion told me. 'At the moment we have a young squad and they are all fired up and wanting to be successful, because a lot of them want to play at a higher level and want to do it with us.' There is belching too as the players try to get everything out of the system. Then all the players and coaches shake hands and embrace one another, like soldiers going into battle. A few players, Danny Coles included of course, don't put their shirts on until the last minute. Most of them rub Vicks on their chests or on their shirts; some even snort it to shock the senses. There is also a late rush for the loos, and many pensive glances. This is put up or shut up time.

Many of them look smaller in here than they do on the pitch. Maybe it's me, maybe I am getting older and more worldly wise, but they look vulnerable too. Young, small, vulnerable and in some cases spotty. They are carrying a weight of expectation on their shoulders. Their manager is young too – this is his first season, remember. His future depends on them earning a result.

The bell in the corner rings, and there is a brief moment of calm. Hold that moment. Then suddenly the noise erupts again and there is a sense of urgency, of men on a mission. They march out purposefully, the staff behind them. Nerves are jangling. They line up alongside their opponents from Port Vale, a few pleasantries are exchanged, and then these young gladiators march out of the tunnel, blinking in the sunlight, with the noise of the fans enveloping them. Balloons float into the sky and the PA system pumps out loud music. It is spine-tingling. There is no going back.

2.55 P.M.: GAME ON AT WALSALL Neil Emblen looks like Bruce Willis's character Butch in *Pulp Fiction*. A tall, hard-looking guy, he nonetheless can't look at Ralph's needle. I strike up a conversation to help take his mind off it.

'Do you mind Chris seeing your butt?' Ralph asks, laughing.

'As long as I don't have to see the needle going in I don't care what happens,' replies Emblen.

Player-manager Paul Merson hasn't joined his players on the pitch. It's eerie in the dressing room because it's so close to kick-off yet all the players are outside, except for Merson, who is furiously pedalling on a battered old training bike. His warm-up looks like an afterthought. The perils of being a player-manager: you forget to prepare for the playing bit. 'I hate going out there to warm up,' the former England international tells Ralph. 'All that running about leaves you knackered.' It seems an incredibly outdated attitude. Merson's very public problems with his demons – drink, drugs and a turbulent personal life – are well documented. It has left him looking much older than his 36 years. More wrinkles than you'd think is healthy for a sportsman. He is clearly starting to struggle with his weight too, and his patched-up legs look battle-worn. He grimaces as he pumps faster on the cycle. 'I'm a slow starter these days,' he acknowledges. 'I'll be useless for the first fifteen minutes, but, tell you what, I'll still be going at the end when they're all shagged out.'

The troops return. As kick-off approaches you get the impression others would like something to numb the pain of anxiety that permeates dressing rooms all over the country. Backstage at the Bescot the nerves are starting to show. Players are pacing around. No one wants to stand still, they want to walk it off. They stretch in a large room outside the dressing room. 'They don't need calming down, they need pumping up,' Ralph observes. 'They've got to get the adrenalin flowing.'

Team-talk time. Ralph doesn't participate, he just strategically positions himself by the dressing-room door – a place where he can give a final thumbs-up to the players he knows are carrying niggles. The pumping up begins. Walsall are four matches unbeaten; they want to make it five. 'Be first – every time.' 'The biggest crime in football is giving the ball away.' 'That feeling when we score – remember what that is like.'

'Come on, let's do it!' Across the nation, team talks are following much the same pattern.

Walsall's dressing room empties as the warriors storm out. Physio John Whitney will be the medical man on the bench. He will stay in touch with Ralph, who will be up in the stands. He brushes by and scoops huge armfuls of ice into a basket without gloves on this cold, crisp day in December (aargh!).

2.55 P.M.: PRE-MATCH ANNOUNCEMENTS Richard does the pre-match announcements: 'Welcome to the Withdean to Nottingham Forest and Brighton & Hove Albion!' Big cheers. He turns away from the mic. 'Go on, John, do the teams.' Attila runs down the players. It's all a bit weird because there is a slight time delay. When Attila has finished, Richard picks up again. 'Let's make it fortress Withdean! We need your help. Let's hear you, South Stand, and let's hear you, North Stand! Get behind the lads!'

2.55 P.M.: SKA AT WREXHAM I have rarely been to a game like this. I'm standing pitchside at the Racecourse Ground and the atmosphere is wonderful. Football fans are a tribal breed, so this seems unreal. The Wrexham home end, The Kop, is festooned with banners from other clubs. It's more like an end-of-season party. The Pryce Griffiths Stand, where Neil Williams and Josh are sitting, has a fair smattering of shirts and the usual gang of scallies grouped together singing near the Doncaster supporters, who are also in good voice. 'If there is anything good to come from our situation it's the heart-warming response from other football supporters,' says Geraint Parry, Wrexham's secretary. 'I think they realise Wrexham is not a club that has been wild with its money and thrown it away. It is a normal football club, and that is why they have responded so well to us.'

Attila's 'We Want Falmer' floats through the air. It's an upbeat tune, and the mood is good. I look around again. There are fans literally from all over the country – from Rugby, Plymouth, Wolves, Brighton, Celtic, Bradford, Burnley, West Brom, Birmingham, Port Vale, Stoke, Macclesfield. It isn't quite the bumper gate Wrexham had hoped for, but it is an almighty effort. But where are the football authorities?

2.56 P.M.: BLINKING INTO THE FLASHLIGHTS For the first time in an age, Roy Unwin isn't there to lead Manchester United's players out on to the Old Trafford pitch. In fact, they probably never had anyone else to lead the teams out together before Roy: it is very much a Premiership/ Champions League thing. United's players are sporting black armbands in his memory.

Old Trafford comes alive, albeit briefly. Mobile phone cameras, and those of the professional photographers, snap at the same time. The effect is dazzling. It must be hellish for the players, whose nerves will already be on edge. But the atmosphere, given the numbers (some 68,000), is insipid. The Family Stand should be the most boisterous, with all those over-excited kids high on E numbers from fizzy drinks and crisps and whatever else they've eaten, but some can't even be bothered to stand up. A girl in front continues to chat on her mobile. This isn't the buzz and bounce of Manchester United – The Religion or the noise that used to make Old Trafford such a feared fortress. It is a theatre where people sit and expect to be entertained – and beware any actors who fluff their lines or stray off-script. I find this disappointing because, well, I've been to so many smaller grounds for this book where it is hard to create any sort of atmosphere. This is where I am expecting it to be loud and exciting, but it's all a bit flat really. Maybe the game will stir them.

At the other end, well in the corner, hidden away out of sight of the TV cameras, the Portsmouth fans are bouncing around and enjoying themselves. They seem really pleased to be here, not least because their fans are determined to make the most of their time in the Premier League. 'Living the dream', as it is called these days – more realistically, erasing the memories of darker days in the lower divisions. They want Pompey to, as the song goes, 'play up'.

2.57 P.M.: THE CHAIRMAN IN THE COMMUNITY STAND I'm with the chairman, right? My name is in the programme among Rob Bradley's welcome notes. I expected the best seat in the house, to just mosey outside and watch the match from the best possible vantage point. Instead, we're walking around the ground to the opposite side to sit in the Co-operative Community Stand, a big 6,000-seater stand where most of the crowd are assembled. For Rob, this is another essential part of being the fans' rep on the board: you sit at least part of the game with them, listen to their gripes and see things how they see them.

2.57 P.M.: LEADING THE GLADIATORS OUT It is *the* match in the Championship, first versus seventh, the table-topping Tractor Boys against the highly fancied East Enders. They met in last season's play-offs. West Ham went through to the final that day. Will Ipswich exact revenge today?

Paul Taylor leads the players out of the tunnel at the corner of Portman Road, through the haze of fireworks that explode into the afternoon sky. Music is pumping out of the speakers. It is a wonderful, colourful atmosphere.

2.58 P.M.: PHIL ROBINSON LEAVES THE BAR Things have been brisk in the Afan Lido club bar. It is one of their biggest gates of the season, Phil Robinson has been working double quick, and takings are good. Now he has come out to watch the match and is clearly delighted. Someone else has agreed to keep an eye on the bar. He heads off to the far side, to a point far away from the near end where a large wire fence allows children to kick a ball about without getting a whack from the ball in the proper game.

I watch Phil pacing around. I hope Lido win for his sake.

2.58 P.M.: TAKE YOUR SEATS Brian Tinnion makes his way across the right-hand corner of the pitch at Ashton Gate over to the subs bench/dugouts/technical area. His staff take their seats – subs, assistant manager, Keith Millen, and physio, Anna Easton. Other medical staff sit nearby. Brian remains standing, alone on the edge of the pitch. This is his side, he has prepared them, and now they are about to do battle.

2.59 P.M.: MISSING MATCHTIME I recall that early-January day in Carlisle when I was supposed to be going to Gretna to see Paul Barnett to witness his preparations for the club's cup tie with Dundee United but ended up marooned in the hotel. Just before three o'clock I was standing on one of a number of bar stools – the water having submerged the ground-floor area including the reception and bar – which had been arranged like stepping stones so that we could meander our way close to the doors for the boats coming to rescue us.

I glance at my watch. Players around the country will already be on the pitch. Spectators will be cheering them, referees will be staring at their watches. Bill Berry will be in some Godforsaken place; the steam will still be rising from Brian Murdoch's soup; Bob Marley will have been on the roof at Worcester City; Ralph Rogers will have given the thumbs up to Walsall's players; Rob Bradley will be worrying about Lincoln City; Attila the Stockbroker will have played his last pre-match punk record; Stuart Hall will be cheerfully constructing some last pre-match nuance; James Alexander Gordon will be on his way to the *Sport on Five* studio; John Boyers will have shaken his last pre-match hand; Neil Doncaster will have been among the fans at Carrow Road; Brian Tinnion will have rallied the troops, and Danny Coles will be champing at the bit; Paul Taylor will be poised to blow his whistle; Alison Geddes and Phil Hamilton will have overseen lots of inner-city kids playing football; Phil Robinson will still be busy at Afan Lido; Neil Williams will be hoping for a win for Wrexham; and Paul Barnett, on this wet day, will hopefully have his feet up at home in Dumfries.

Me? I'm stood next to a Scouser called Dave who has phoned his mate to ask if he can text any updates from Everton's game. 'Oh, and maybe West Brom too.' His wife, Tiffany, looks embarrassed – we have our bags over shoulders, holding on for dear life. No one fancies falling into the icy water below.

Some matchday, I think. Meanwhile whistles blow to kick off all the matches. Game on.

GAME ON

3 P.M.: GAME ON AT EVERGREEN There is no grand entrance for
the players at Evergreen. There is no Corinthian-style sprint on to the
pitch. Instead, they do the Sunday-morning skulk I know so well. The
only notable exercise is bending under the plastic perimeter fence
surrounding the pitch. Bill, Dave and I with assorted friends and family
wander around the concrete path, which snakes around the nearside
goal over to the tarmac area either side of the dugouts – probably
officially described as 'technical areas' in the FA handbook.

Evergreen, as you may expect, are ever so green: green shirts (with
white hoops), green shorts and green socks. Hadley, who are top of the
Hertfordshire Senior League, are dressed in red shirts and black shorts.
They look physically sharper than the home side, with a few more
youngsters, a couple of handy-looking beanpoles, and three or four
players who look like they have done the rounds and possibly played at a
higher level. Maybe even semi-pro.

Bill has his stopwatch at the ready. Major incidents are to be logged
with accuracy. The ref blows his whistle and we're underway.

Immediately you can see Evergreen are not as sharp as Hadley. Their
goalie resembles Fatty Foulkes, the legendary Sheffield United
goalkeeper from around the turn of the twentieth century who weighed
24 stone. This guy has a big round stomach and seems averse to bending
over or coming off his line. His speciality is bullying his defence and
younger members of the team. We share a giggle when, early on, he
mercilessly lays into a midfielder for not tracking back, seemingly
ignorant of the fact that had he wandered maybe four or five yards off
his line he could have snuffed out any apparent threat. Instead he
watches the ball drift perilously close to the near post without moving.
While shaping up to take the goal-kick, he slams his fist into his other
palm – 'Fackin' listen to what I say!' He is physically intimidating. I've
little doubt he could back up his verbal threats.

There is little in the way of camaraderie about Evergreen. They are noisy and loud, and they argue prodigiously. A bleached-haired defender who looks a little bit like a younger version of the actor Bill Nighy barks similar orders. 'Fackin' mark tight!' It isn't the last time he offers such frank advice. In fact, Evergreen are fackin' experts, with a usage for every occasion and incident. Like so many footballers, they swear like troopers, usually with little coherence.

Their manager, Gordon Wallis, bellows specific instructions seemingly unaware of his players' ability to stick to them and the lack of the skills required to manoeuvre the ball around with accuracy. The pitch, to be fair, doesn't help. It is hopelessly rutted. No one's fault – that's just life at grass-roots level. There are no Paul Barnetts at this level. Hadley assert their dominance from the start, but are slow to realise they cannot afford to play too much football on this surface. Evergreen's direct approach is more appropriate. Their goal doesn't come under undue early pressure.

3 P.M.: GAME ON AT ASHTON GATE I'm sitting beside the bench, in the shade at Ashton Gate. The sun makes it a vibrant sight. If you are a seasoned fan, it is sometimes easy to forget how stunning this can be. The contrasting strips – Bristol City in red and white, Port Vale in black and white – and the various colours of the mainly T-shirt-wearing crowd contribute to a dazzling spectacle. At ground level it also looks incredibly fast-moving. The players, like actors on stage, seem bigger than the nervy young men I saw in the dressing room minutes earlier. But it's a cagey start. No one wants to make an early mistake.

Brian Tinnion stands pitchside, hands in pockets, reading, watching, observing; examining Port Vale's shape and plan of action, and realising that his players will need to adapt to it. To assert their authority. An early goal would soothe the nerves.

3 P.M.: DELIA COOKS UP AN ATMOSPHERE Neil Doncaster is standing between the corner of the Barclay and Jarrold Stands at Carrow Road, sandwiched into a space separating the home and away fans. Other than a middle-aged, female supercook on one side, we have Norwich's younger, more vocal fans. On the other, Chelsea's 2,700 travelling contingent, a mix of new-found fans who have the money to snap up the relatively precious few tickets for these away games and older-style, scowling wide boys. The atmosphere in this corner of the ground is loud, boisterous and hostile.

The Chelsea fans launch into a chant: 'We've got Abramovic, you've got a drunken bitch!' (It had been widely speculated in the media that Delia Smith had been at the cooking sherry before her outburst the previous Monday.) It is vaguely witty, but not as good as the instant riposte: 'We've got a supercook, you've got a Russian crook!' Touché. It momentarily shuts the away fans up. They know Smith allegedly having a snifter isn't anywhere near the problems a Putin purge could impose on the finances of Chelsea. They reply with 'You're only here cos it's Chelsea!' Wrong. Fifty of Norwich's last 64 games at Carrow Road – most of those not in the Premier League – have been sell-outs.

On the pitch, the blue shirts have rather more elegance. Makelele, Lampard, Tiago, Cole, Drogba, Duff – these are world-renowned stars. They dance around in neat patterns; they have poise and seem to have more time on the ball. Norwich's players in their yellow-and-green shirts – Darren Huckerby their only star – are spirited but rushed. They work hard at keeping Chelsea at bay. But you wonder for how long.

Neil spots some stewards watching the game on TVs beneath the stand rather than doing their jobs and notes it down.

3 P.M.: GAME ON AT GRETNA Gretna's supporters are expectant, as well they may be. They have won every League home game here this season, and there have been some real thumpings: 6–0 and 6–2 against Albion Rovers, 8–0 against East Stirling, 5–1 against East Fife, 4–1 against Queens Park. Children behind the goal wave white and black flags proclaiming 'Raydale – home of Gretna FC'. A few older sages along the side, in front of the bar where I am standing with Barney, are unconvinced. They think there have been too many player changes of late and are concerned this lack of continuity will result in a dip in form.

Elgin's fans are on the far side. It's a decent turnout – maybe 40 or 50 – and there's a huge banner: 'Elgin City Supporters Club – Bolton Branch'. The people beneath are wildly enthusiastic and singing songs. 'They come here every time,' says Barney. 'They really enjoy themselves.' But their side is mid-table, and I am expecting them to go home with a heavy defeat.

3.01 P.M.: AN EARLY GOAL – IPSWICH 0 WEST HAM 1 The first goal of matchday! West Ham take the lead after 70 seconds. A shocking, lax mix-up between Ipswich's goalkeeper Kelvin Davis and defender Jason De Vos, who collide, results in the ball dropping to West Ham forward Marlon Harewood, who can't believe his good fortune and almost apologetically taps the ball into an unguarded goal. Davis throws his arms up in despair as if to appeal to a higher authority (the ref) to scrub it out in the way they do on these occasions, because it was a cock-up. Everyone looks to the referee's assistant, Trevor Pollard, but his flag stays down. Paul Taylor points to the centre circle as the jubilant West Ham fans to my right sing 'One-nil to the Cockney boys'.

3.05 P.M.: A CURRY IN THE CORNER – KIDDERMINSTER 1 ROCHDALE 0 At Kidderminster I'm still in the away end asking Rochdale fans what they think about Brian Murdoch's food. In the corner I spot a young couple tucking into curries. Darren's is topped with a pastry crust, freshly cooked especially for him. Sally has a chapatti. They have both helped themselves to the selection of Indian pickles on the counter next to the brown sauce and ketchup.

To say the least, they are impressed. Both are lapsed Birmingham City fans who follow the England national side home and away but are fed up with the way they feel their own club rips them off in a variety of ways. They moan about the weak beer, the food, the lack of ladies' loos, the cost, everything. They've been to Kidderminster before and know the ground. They are in the away end because this is where the best range of food is sold.

As we chat, Kiddy score a spectacular opening goal. A rasping 25-yarder in the fifth minute struck by left-footer Dean Keates. Just the start the home side need.

Sally is a vegetarian, and she's awestruck by the choice on offer. 'You just don't get this anywhere else,' she says. 'The number of people eating meat has dropped, but you wouldn't get a hint of that from going to football matches.' Darren is no veggie, and loves 'the poke' his curry has. I take a taste – it is very spicy. Just what I want from a curry, and on a cold day it is warming. They had a drink beforehand. Curry, beer and footy – what else do you want on Saturday?

3.08 P.M.: DUFF DENIED Chelsea are sublime. You can have all the money you like but, ultimately, it's all about the players, their quality and aptitude. They have pinned back Norwich, whose efforts have been fantastic, and they are being ripped open down their left. Blond-haired Irishman Damian Duff breezes into the penalty area, but chips rather than shoots towards goal over the onrushing Norwich keeper Robert Green. Jason Shackell does incredibly well to hook the ball off the line to safety, but the ease with which Chelsea have carved through the Canaries has worried the home faithful.

Ah, the contrary feelings of fans of so-called smaller clubs. They dream of seeing the stars on big matchdays – that special feeling of them strutting their stuff at their local club. I remember seeing George Best and Bobby Charlton at the Hawthorns in the early 1970s, for instance, and have never forgotten it. But you don't want them to win.

3.09 P.M.: WAYNE'S WORLD I – MANCHESTER UNITED 1 PORTSMOUTH 0 Old Trafford bursts into life. It should. They've seen the Bests, Charltons, Laws, Cantonas and Beckhams down the years here, and the latest is Wayne Rooney, who scores a quite wonderful goal, the culmination of the game's first meaningful move. Ronaldo ghosts down the right and pulls over a harmless-looking cross behind the line of attackers but in front of the Portsmouth defence, who allow it to reach Rooney, who strikes a controlled volley from twelve yards.

Old Trafford explodes. At last it's noisy. This is the intoxicating atmosphere they talk about. It crackles in a way few other grounds can. Rooney drinks in the applause – echoes of Best closing his eyes to absorb the warmth beaming down upon his soul, or Eric Cantona, spinning slowly like a triumphant gladiator, accepting the adulation of his admirers.

Rooney's is a perfectly executed goal, made to look astonishingly simple. But more concentration was needed from the Portsmouth defence. It could be a long afternoon for them.

3.11 P.M.: STUART HALL OVER THE WORLD – WIGAN 1 LEEDS 0
Stuart Hall is marvelling at Wigan's start. They have dominated Leeds and have moved the ball forwards, at fast pace, where their two lookalike forwards, Jason Roberts and Nathan 'Duke' Ellington, the Championship's leading scorers, are causing mayhem.

Hall has been a BBC matchday reporter since 1959, the year I was born (which I find a staggering, sobering fact), a period spanning six decades. Throughout, Hall's appetite has remained the same. 'Run him,' he orders as Roberts bursts into the box. 'Come on, give me a goal!' Roberts duly obliges by setting up the ball for Ellington. Stuart is ecstatic and can't wait to tell the World (Service) and Five Live's listeners all about it.

He writes very little down. I ask where those choice phrases come from. 'Imagination,' he replies. Today he is envisaging the Wigan chairman, David Whelan, sitting on the veranda of his Caribbean home while tuning in for Hall's reports.

He quickly recalls the move that allowed Ellington (Stuart will call him Duke, not Nathan, in every report today) to net his nineteenth goal of the season. 'I'm really enjoying this,' he says, bouncing in his seat while describing a fiercely competitive game on a typically chilly northern afternoon watched by 12,000 Wigan fans and 5,000 from Leeds. This is the passion, enjoyment and love of the game I associate with Stuart Hall. It's not something I see elsewhere in the press box.

I wonder where he draws this enthusiasm from. After all, I like my footy, but I got bored after a few years of local radio commentaries – using the same phrases to sum up similar games week after week. 'It's what you see here today,' says Stuart. 'The atmosphere, the great theatre, the draw of the match, happy, smiling faces – not always, but often. There's nothing like it.'

He has a fan club in Melbourne – students mainly. My mind's eye conjures up an image of them sitting around a radio somewhere in the south Australian city. I wonder if they have any idea of how cramped and cold the conditions are here (or if they care).

3.12 P.M.: WORCESTER WOE – WORCESTER CITY 0 STALYBRIDGE CELTIC 1 Bob Marley takes his seat in the directors' box just as Worcester

City go a goal down – to bottom-of-the-table Stalybridge Celtic, whose players can barely believe their luck when visiting forward Andy Hayward taps in their opener.

It's an old habit for Worcester City. They're on a seven-match unbeaten run. Keep it going until Christmas and they may get a couple of bumper gates, but they look like tossing it away to a struggling side. Worcester have a loyal band of long-suffering supporters and can easily tempt transient fans and double their gates when signs of promise flicker. But in recent times City have nearly always cocked up when a big game comes along. A crowd of 2,700 turned up for the club's centenary match against Stafford Rangers in September 2002 with City unbeaten in their opening ten matches. They crashed 3–0, and scraped a thousand for their next game. With Christmas coming and a couple of large seasonal crowds in the offing they look like pooping their own party.

It doesn't take long for discontented fans to air their views. 'They don't bleedin' care, none of 'em!' shouts a voice behind us. He could mean the players, but the comment implicitly includes the manager and the board. Bob slips off to deal with some routine business (he isn't a good spectator) as the natives get increasingly restless. 'Fucking useless!' shouts a voice from below. This is a not unusual comment at St George's Lane. This time it is hurled upwards at the board members.

The Lane is renowned as one of non-League football's more aggressive grounds. In the late 1970s a cage was erected leading from the dressing room to the pitch to prevent visiting players and officials from being attacked. Fans traditionally congregate there because it is near the exit. A well-worn phrase is that opposing players or errant referees will get 'a caging' – fierce hostility often involving fists banged against the metal cage. Pretty it isn't and not the spirit of the club I grew up supporting. But I can identify with the frustration.

3.14 P.M.: LITA LIGHTS UP THE GAME – BRISTOL CITY 1 PORT VALE 0 It's *déjà vu* all over again, as someone once said. I am just writing in my notebook that Bristol City have failed to get 'in the faces' of Port Vale, to steal the initiative that Brian Tinnion so wanted, when Leroy Lita, their livewire England U-21 forward, collects the ball on the left edge of the penalty area, draws his marker and unleashes a terrific right-foot drive, which is only going one place – the bottom corner of Port Vale's net. One–nil, and a sublime piece of skill well above anything else we've seen so far. Enough to win matches at a better level than League One.

Tinnion can't control his joy and dances on to the pitch. The rest of the bench jump up too, and fans around the ground take to their feet. It is a wonderful climactic moment. Lita races off to soak up the applause. Bristol City – the Robins – are rocking.

3.15 P.M.: 'GOOD REFEREEING' Things are getting feisty at Ipswich. The home side have had a dreadful opening to the game. Their defence in particular cannot seem to clear the lines. In frustration, the tackles are flying in. Paul Taylor has a quiet word with West Ham forward Bobby Zamora for pushing once too often. Many would have brandished a yellow card and would then have felt the need to keep balancing things out. No need.

Then comes the game's first real poor tackle, a desperate lunge by Ipswich skipper Jim Magilton that looks vindictive. Closer to the action, Taylor acknowledges it as a genuine attempt to reach the ball. The Ipswich fans, naturally, agree, but fear the worst. Taylor has another word. 'Good refereeing,' says a young man behind me. The situation calms down. Remember Taylor's pre-match dictum: 'Let's encourage them to play.' He does.

3.16 P.M.: A PENALTY … SAVED Brighton should be ahead. I mean, the players in the blue-and-white-striped jerseys have started better than their crimson-shirted opponents. Their nimble-footed forward Leon Knight nips into the penalty area and is tripped by Forest's much-travelled keeper Paul Gerrard. It's an obvious spot-kick. Gerrard could be sent off, but survives.

Knight opts to take the penalty himself. 'He missed last time,' Attila whispers. 'He always goes the same way – to the goalkeeper's left.' He duly taps this one to the goalkeeper's left, and nowhere near firmly enough. Gerrard guesses right and makes immediate amends for felling Knight.

Forest have lost their last eight away games, and on that kind of roll they are searching for positives. Their outfield players race to congratulate their keeper. The fans behind leap to their feet and applaud. Surviving a penalty is one of those galvanising moments in a football match, a chance to rally the troops. Gerrard urges his team-mates to focus. There is a long way to go. Will Brighton, the lowest scorers at home in the Championship, get as good a chance to score in the game again?

3.17 P.M.: TAKE ME HOME, COUNTRY ROAD You can't please me. I didn't like their silence, but now that United's fans are singing, I'm even more irked. They belt out their version of 'Take Me Home, Country Road' – 'to the place I belong … Old Trafford, to see United, take me home, country road'. Is this supposed to be irony? Man Utd's fans? Home? The place most of them belong? Where's that? Newton Abbot or Newton Heath? Biggleswade? China? Timbuktu? Surely the thing about Manchester United is their … well, they lack a sense of place. Their fans come, largely, from hither and thither. This is not their home, spiritual or otherwise. And it ain't no country road. Why don't they go to their local club ground and sing it? Better still, pay them a few bob and keep going back? Grrr.

John Boyers's son Jonathan, who is studying theology at a local college, joins us, having underestimated the tram journey from the north of the city.

United win a corner at the Stretford – sorry, North Stand End. At Old Trafford more than any other ground I've visited, you sense the frustration of balding middle-aged fans, people who no doubt passionately supported the club in their youth. Red, black and white scarves around their wrists, long hair, baggies, brogues and all that. And now they sit inside Old Trafford, which for all its grandeur falls periodically into deep long murmurs. You see them all around the stadium, old Stretford Enders I bet, springing to their feet, trying to urge their fellow fans into a chant, throwing 'wankers' signs at opposition players when they retrieve the ball. It isn't unique to this place, but it is sad. Our parents and their generation left the youngsters behind the goal to make the noise. Here, the kids largely seem to deem it uncool. It's what their dads do.

3.18 P.M.: NEIL'S NECK Ralph Rogers has been leaning forward on his knees for most of the match so far. He is keeping a keen eye on Neil

Emblen and his stiff neck. 'Get it, Neil!' he shouts, fidgeting in his seat, as Neil rises to nod a testing ball, which looks to loop over his shoulder near the edge of Walsall's penalty area. Ralph watches Neil's reaction to this neck-twister, which makes his muscles twitch and produces a grimace. Emblen's hand reaches up to his neck as the ball drops into touch. He won't want any lengthy bouts of head tennis or to be grabbed in a head-lock. Thankfully, so far it isn't a rough-and-tumble game. Ralph gives a thumbs-up to John Whitney, Walsall's physio, who is pitchside and has turned around to check with the doc. So far, so good.

3.19 P.M.: LIDO TAKE THE LEAD – AFAN LIDO 1 LLANELLI 0 Afan Lido have started well and take a deserved lead. Sacha Walters, a twenty-year-old sporting a bird's-nest haircut, races through and skilfully lobs the advancing goalkeeper. It's a pity it's at the far end of the ground where no one is standing; most supporters hang around the entrance, near the bar behind the nearside goal, or sit in the stand. Phil Robinson, who is standing incognito in line with the penalty area at the far end, claps enthusiastically and beams a huge smile at the well-taken goal.

3.20 P.M.: BILL BERRY COUNTS THE CROWD It's 26. I'm not sure if Bill has included the couple of boys on bikes over the far side who come and go, or the woman who has gamely pushed her pram on to the grass. I assume her partner/loved one/husband is either playing on the right for Hadley or on the left for Evergreen because she has stayed over there on her own. Another young girl stands dutifully behind Hadley's goal – the keeper's girlfriend, I assume. It must be love. He is everything Evergreen's outsized keeper isn't. Agile, jumpy, young. When Evergreen's first effort whizzes wide he leaps through the air even though his goal is not under threat. It is a rare moment of levity, in more ways than one.

Bill Berry likes to watch matches. I mean, he actually avidly watches the games rather than just attends. In the car on the way down, he told me how he hated people chit-chatting their way through games, often oblivious to the action. Dave, meanwhile, has barely drawn breath.

'Are you going to the Central Midlands Hop?' he ventures.

'Wouldn't have thought so.'

Four games in a day 'followed by therapy', he remarks with a chortle.

'You going?' I ask.

He drops his head to one side. Obviously.

Hadley are on top, but it's still 0–0.

3.21 P.M.: AN EDUCATED MAN Wigan are pummelling Leeds. It should already be game over. Lee McCulloch has shot tamely at the goalkeeper from a good position, and Jason Roberts, as I know from watching him at West Brom, can be profligate.

So, why does Stuart Hall chuck all these literary references into his reports? Is he showing off or what? The answer is in his background. The son of a baker, he was born in Ashton-under-Lyne on Christmas Day 1929 and went to Glossop Grammar School where he achieved high academic accolades, captained the soccer team and became head boy. He did an English degree at Manchester University and thought he might as well throw some of the things he learned into his reports. Initially, in the 1950s, he tried to become a professional footballer with Crystal Palace but realised there wasn't much money in it. He then flirted with a career as a racing driver. A natural extrovert, he went into the media instead, doing his sports reports and shooting to fame as an affable evening presenter on the local BBC magazine programme *North West Tonight*. In the mid-1960s he got his big break as Eddie Waring's ever-giggling co-presenter on *It's a Knockout*, his infectious humour endearing him to millions of TV viewers.

Today, he earns a living doing all kinds of corporate media work. 'Most of it I never see,' he says with world-weariness. His hobbies include clothes, cars, cooking and collecting antique clocks. Matchday reporting is 'my bit of fun – I don't do it for money, never have'. I ask what his bosses in London think of his uniquely verbose style. He simply doesn't care.

In his next report he over-emphasises words like 'rasping' and 'scintillating'. There is a lyrical flow to his enunciation, a seamless continuity. For Stuart Hall this is as natural as breathing air. It is how he has always done his reports. 'This isn't football, it's theatre,' he says. How true. What drama.

3.22 P.M.: COLE ON GOAL – NORWICH 0 CHELSEA 1 Neil Doncaster's ongoing audit of Carrow Road reaches the lower end of the Norwich and Peterborough Stand just as Chelsea take the lead. Joe Cole rides a couple of ineffectual tackles and pings a left-footer into the roof of the net. One–nil to the champions-elect. Silence among the home fans, and an apparent delayed reaction before the Chelsea fans clustered in the far corner respond with joy. A nearby Norwich fan drops his head in his hands. I know how he feels. Twenty thousand others feel much the same, I suspect. Is Norwich's season going to turn?

3.23 P.M.: DONNIE DOMINATE AT WREXHAM The atmosphere is convivial, quite unlike any other game I have been to, but the game is dire. Wrexham, who are desperate for points as they are hovering near the relegation zone, are eager to attack but they lack the aptitude. They fail to create a decent chance early on. Neil Williams follows every move. He is sporting a multicoloured topper and holding a Welsh flag in frustration. I ask him about Wrexham's players, and he runs through some of them, including midfielder Darren Ferguson, Sir Alex's son, who never quite made it at either his father's club or Wolves, whom he joined afterwards. In truth, he is struggling to make his mark at Wrexham.

Doncaster are in the top half of the table and look brisk and quicker. There is more purpose about their play, but they too fail to create chances. It's a disappointing match so far for this cosmopolitan crowd.

3.24 P.M.: SEAGULLS SAVED Nottingham Forest are finding their feet. Buoyed by their goalkeeper's penalty save they have gradually got into the game. Their Republic of Ireland international midfielder Andy Reid (shortly to leave for Spurs) curls in a free-kick that is pushed on to the bar by Brighton goalkeeper Michel Kuipers. It bounces down and out, but looked suspiciously as if it went over the line. There are collective sighs of relief around the PA box. Everyone looks at each other, eyebrows raised. That's the luck you get when you're in Forest's position. No luck whatsoever.

3.25 P.M.: WAYNE'S WORLD II The one thing I really like talking to my dad about is football. He can pick out the really special players. He rates Wayne Rooney very highly in the way he did the likes of Stuart Pearce and Paul Gascoigne. Not one to be fooled by David Beckham's lack of pace, for instance, my dad. I listen when he talks about the players he thinks are a bit special. I always have. Because they usually are. A delicious moment from Rooney at Old Trafford, superb skill you can only truly appreciate if you have played the game (and if, like me, you have failed to master the really difficult things). Most of the kids surrounding us missed it. Rooney receives a ball outside the left edge of the box, right in front of us, bursts into the area and on his wrong foot, in full stride and at full pace, whips over a wonderful cross to the far post which Ronaldo knocks back, resulting in a shot that is saved. That run – oh, that run! At speed. So difficult an art to master, but done with such ease, without a change of gear.

Wayne Rooney. Whatever his faults, whatever the taunts, whatever expletives he hurls at refs – call him Judas or Shrek if you must – but what an exemplary talent. Always, always cherish his natural talent. It is rare.

3.26 P.M.: A VITAL INTERCEPTION Danny Coles's visualisation is working. He has kept a keen eye and hold – sorry, Danny, I did spot a couple of inappropriate nudges – on his former team-mate Lee Matthews, but he allows him to briefly slip away. The ball is played into Matthews's path, he pulls back the trigger to shoot from twenty yards … and Danny slides in to tackle. It's a vital interception that had to be well timed.

His sore Achilles isn't impeding his game. A couple of times he has joined attacks down the left, usually after a one-two, and he does so again now, rashly allowing the ball to loop up in the air. He is fortunate to get a foul awarded in his favour. Danny rushes into the penalty area in the hope of getting his head on to the resulting free-kick.

3.28 P.M.: LACKLUSTRE LINCOLN There are a few nudges of recognition towards Rob Bradley, but little more. He blends in with the fans in the Co-op Community Stand, and in any case, it's no big deal to see the chairman sitting here. Some would court the media or seek praise for slumming it with the hoi polloi. Rob just wants to watch the match and get a feel for how the fans view things. I suspect Rob also feels he can be a bit more of a true fan over here.

This bit I really like. He doesn't want to talk idly during the match. I stick to asking about players and performances. He is edgy and grumpy – Lincoln haven't produced enough – and isn't slow to let his feelings be known. But he is strangely protective of them too. Football fans are. You can moan about the club yourself, but hate it when others do. Funny, that.

Anyway, Lincoln are generally on top, but other than an early effort, which grazed the outside of a post, it has been a quiet affair.

'We haven't created anything – rubbish Lincoln!' shouts a voice behind us.

'Except that one that hit the post,' Rob bounces back. He is taking it personally.

3.29 P.M.: THERE IS ALWAYS A BRUMMIE AROUND One of the things I like about non-League grounds is you can walk around. I often do this just to watch the game from different angles, sometimes enjoying a chat with people along the way.

At Afan Lido I leave Phil Robinson alone. He gets few opportunities to watch matches and doesn't want me hanging on his shoulder when the chance comes along. I have been to Albion games with people who aren't really into it, and I don't like it. If they don't share the passion it is inhibiting and ruins the game. I mean, it's a bit voyeuristic really. A bit like watching someone having sex or something. You don't want to talk to your mates while you're doing it (not unless you are particularly perverse).

So at Afan Lido I am walking around. At the far end, which has perimeter fencing but no terracing, there is a solitary person behind the goal. While I wander up there, Lido almost add a second goal, a well-worked move at the end of which the busy Sacha Walters shoots just wide. Everyone at the far end thinks the ball has nestled in the net instead of lodging in the side-netting. Joy turns to pain, and there is a groan when they realise what has happened.

'That was close,' I say.

'Should have done better,' comes the reply. I recognise the accent. West Midlands, Birmingham probably. 'A good move, though.'

We both think the same thing: where is he from?

'You're not local,' he says.

'I'm from Worcester,' I reply, and explain what I am doing.

Alan is an exiled Brummie (well, it is Wales). We start chatting about a club in Sutton Coldfield called Romulus he used to be involved with and how, now he has moved to South Wales, he gets around the local grounds just to watch a decent game of grass-roots footy and have a pint. Talking of which ... 'Do you fancy a pint at half-time?' he says. My flesh is weak. Could you imagine this happening at a Premier League game?

3.31 P.M.: ELGIN MARVELS – GRETNA 0 ELGIN CITY 1 Gretna have cracked in 80 goals in 23 League games – three and a half a game – but haven't created a decent chance so far today. The curse of Chris Green strikes again. The locals are grumbling about the things they suspected at the start: the manager is making too many changes in too short a space of time. Worse still, plucky Elgin deservedly take the lead, winger Andy Roddie curling in a twenty-yard free-kick.

Paul Barnett goes ballistic.

'Do you think the keeper should have got it?' I ask.

'No! Look at them, they're on my pitch!'

The Bolton crew of the Elgin supporters club on the far side have danced merrily on to Barney's pitch, and off again. Paul goes to get his pitchfork – not to seek retribution, but to press down the divots at half-time.

3.32 P.M.: FRUIT, AND SOMETHING FOR THE BOSS TO CHEW OVER 'Would you like to join our picnic?' asks one of the Bristol City medical staff. I don't know what they mean, but soon a serious-looking man arrives with a kit bag I assume is full of medical gear. 'Coffee?' he asks, pulling a cup out of the bag. 'With or without sugar?'

'Without,' I reply.

Out comes a plastic pint glass filled with sliced fruit. I choose some kiwi fruit.

'We have to eat in case someone gets injured and we have to be at hospital until eight o'clock,' says Heather Montague, the club's medical officer, whose munching is disturbed as soon as the words leave her mouth. Leroy Lita goes down clutching his leg, and the assistant referee in front of us suffers a pulled hamstring. Medically, all hands are to the pump.

The linesman is replaced, but Brian Tinnion faces a dilemma. A lump has appeared on Lita's ankle. He could play on, but he risks further injury. With big games coming along at promotion-chasing rivals Bournemouth and Brentford in the next week, Tinnion decides on a substitution. Paul Heffernan comes on, and Lita hobbles away down the tunnel behind the injured official. Heather follows both of them, and doesn't reappear until late in the game. Maybe the fruit is a good idea after all.

3.33 P.M.: MISDEMEANOURS AT BESCOT – WALSALL 0 BLACKPOOL 1

Walsall are trying to play neat one-touch football and are looking to get 'runners' – midfielders charging into the opposition penalty area in the hope of shooting or setting up chances – forward, but are cheerfully ignoring their pre-match motto that giving the ball away is a criminal act. Today they are serial offenders. Bad enough to do this in the opposing half, catastrophic outside your own penalty area.

Paul Merson is proving a priceless playmaker, setting the runners through. 'There's no substitute for class, man,' says Ralph Rogers, but the gaffer is as guilty as his team-mates for giving the ball away, and they duly pay the price in the 33rd minute when they fail to clear outside the right edge of their area and the ball is fed to Blackpool striker Scott Taylor, who punishes them with a neat finish.

Merson isn't a happy bunny. Time and again his players haven't been alert enough. When there is a lack of movement as he is standing over a free-kick a minute later just outside Blackpool's box, he explodes. As he waves his arms about the ball is touched on for a shot that catches him out, and it goes from bad to worse.

'Gonna be interesting at half-time,' shouts Ralph, who wraps his coat around him. He maintains thumbs-up contact with physio John Whitney at ground level, not least when defender Mark Wright is sent flying by an aerial challenge.

3.34 P.M.: SANITY RESTORED – GRETNA 1 ELGIN CITY 1

Elgin's lead lasts a mere two minutes. No sooner have their excited fans jumped back over the barriers than Gretna are stirred into an immediate response. They charge up the other end of the pitch, force a corner, and striker David Bingham levels from close range after a scramble in the Elgin six-yard box.

3.36 P.M.: SOUP, AND ALL SQUARE – KIDDERMINSTER 1 ROCHDALE 1 In the interests of thorough research, you understand, I decide to try some of Brian's infamous soup. Is it all it's cracked up to be? It's certainly thick with vegetables. Having seen other fans struggle to get the contents out, rather than drink it I decide to ask for a fork.

It is simply sumptuous. Brian's reputation is fully deserved.

I'm halfway through my soup when Rochdale score, against the run of play, Gary Holt hammering a left-foot volley past Harriers' helpless keeper Ryan Clarke and into the top corner. The sustained Rochdale fans are now in good voice. It is a good, open, even game, and on a crisp, clear day with some decent tucker inside you it's good entertainment.

Mine is only a small cross-section of fans, but I've spoken to people who have actually swelled the gate because of the food, not in spite of it. Brian's grub has added income to Kidderminster. Much-needed cash in the coffers. Yes, they could try to do it in-house, but would it work? Would they have the dedication of Brian and his team? Would they care as much as Brian so obviously does? I watch the Rochdale fans going back and back for more.

There is another factor in the equation: goodwill. Fans frequently moan about the welcome they receive, but the Rochdale fans are happy and genuinely affectionate towards Kidderminster. 'I hope they don't go down, we'll miss all this,' says one of them to me. 'Tell them that,' he adds, assuming I am from a local paper.

I speak to a steward who usually does the away end. 'They say the food is good but I've never tried it,' he says. 'What I do know is we never get any trouble, and the fans do seem friendly.'

Kiddy almost regain the lead, but are thwarted by some heroic defending, most notably by Greg Heald, blocking shots from Simon Russell and Tom Bennett inside Dale's penalty area. I decide to check out what Brian's regulars in the Souper corner think.

3.37 P.M.: WORCESTER GET LEVEL – WORCESTER CITY 1 STALYBRIDGE CELTIC 1 An equaliser at St George's Lane. Order restored, and the board, the management and the players are given respite from the irritated few. The scorer is club stalwart Carl Heeley, who has played some 400 games here, who headed in from a corner. Bob Marley, typically, has missed it. Away dealing with more minutiae …

3.41 P.M.: NO OLD PALS ACT AT ASHTON GATE Danny Coles flattens Lee Matthews. They've been tugging at each other all afternoon. Danny ups the ante by giving Matthews a good shove on the halfway line. Matthews complains long and loud with enough theatrics to suggest this is something they'll discuss later. The crowd love it: fans always like to see one of their former charges brought down with a bump. 'Lee Matthews, you're a wanker!' they chant. He would expect nothing less.

3.42 P.M.: A PENALTY CONVERTED – EVERGREEN 1 HADLEY 0 Quite remarkable (you do the Motty/Coleman impersonation). Evergreen, who have been under the cosh for the entire first half, have won a penalty. Hadley have conceded rashly during a rare Evergreen raid into their box.

Up steps their number 8, Dean Seabrook, a young, slightly scruffy midfielder, who plonks it to the keeper's left with aplomb. Everyone goes wild. In football, there's nothing quite like scoring against the run of play, when you've stuck to your guns and toughed it out against the odds, especially against the show-boating table-toppers. They see out the last couple of minutes and leave the field with a spring in their step.

3.46 P.M.: A GOAL AT HALF-TIME – WALSALL 1 BLACKPOOL 1 Why does this always happen? Doc Rogers and I sat watching the game for 44 minutes and 45 seconds before Ralph decided we should pop downstairs so we can be on hand to welcome the players back into the dressing room. The goals I have missed this way. Usually for nipping out to avoid the loo queues at the Albion. Needless to say, the goal comes from a Paul Merson cross; Jorge Leitão heads in a simple goal. 'That should ease the half-time pressure,' I suggest. Ralph isn't so sure.

The troops sweep into the changing rooms, and the door slams shut behind them. Bollockings are being roundly issued. Home truths are being told. It hasn't been good enough. Manager and coach rage. The unmistakeable smell of mud, damp and sweat hangs in the air. Ralph seeks out Neil Emblen, who is struggling but keen to continue. 'I'm OK,' he insists, sipping a drink. 'I just don't want too many high balls in the air over my head.' He smiles at that, subconsciously feeling his neck.

3.46 P.M.: A HALF-TIME PINT Phil Robinson is once again busy behind the Afan Lido bar. Half-time is his busiest period, and the sooner he gets everyone served the sooner they sup their drinks and leave to watch the rest of the match. Alan, the Brummie I have met, gets the drinks in. We are served quite late and have to bolt it down because I can sense Phil wants to shut the bar. The news on the TV from other games isn't great, but none of Afan Lido's rivals near the foot of the Vauxhall Masterfit Retailers Welsh Premier League is winning. Lido need to hold on to their lead for a precious win.

3.47 P.M.: HALF-TIME DOWN THE LANE I meet up with Bob Marley in the boardroom beneath the main stand at Worcester City. He vows to watch the second half with Seb and is as good as his word.

We chat about handling all these different commitments and whether it is fair to look after the kids around his work. 'Saturday is the day I get the kids as such,' he says. 'Fortunately they are football nuts, and sometimes it involves them playing and coming down here, bringing their mates. They sell programmes and they learn to interact with people, so they are an active part of it – which is good for them. It is hard work, but for me part of their growing up is learning they can't always do what they want. Sport teaches them to put a bit back, and that is equally as good as other educational experiences. Life isn't all about locking yourself away in a bedroom playing on XBoxes or PlayStations – they see plenty of life down here. If they grow up in an environment where it's good to help people they'll always have that in mind.'

3.48 P.M.: OFFICIALDOM AT HALF-TIME A fairly quiet first half ends at Ipswich. Paul and his officials swap stories. They discuss their own performance and, like fans, the flow of the game. They can't believe Ipswich's hesitation at the back. Time and again Paul has had to check his gallops upfield from their end of the pitch because they cannot seem to clear their lines. If he sprints off to the halfway line he will be in no position to spot infringements back in their area; equally, hang back too long, and suddenly the action is 40 to 50 yards away. It can be a tough call for a ref.

I mention the simmering frustration of the crowd. Paul hasn't noticed. He cuts the crowd out of his sight and sound. But they are simmering. Paul's team – for that is what the officials are – seem quite content with their decisions so far. They also know edgy Ipswich will have to up the stakes if they are going to get back into the game. You can hear them pumping themselves up down the corridor.

3.48 P.M.: 'ONE–NIL TO THE CHAMPIONS' Neil Doncaster heads back into the office, and I am left in the directors' lounge. Alone again, naturally.

For the second time that day, for a few brief moments the only other person on his own is a bashful-looking bloke with a faint beard and beguiling smile wearing faded jeans. For all his investment in Chelsea, in English football if you want to be kind, for all his attempts to buy success and maybe even respect, no one seems to speak to Roman Abramovic. People are deep in their conversations, and as I walk past he looks at me again in faint recognition. I wonder if he knows someone who looks like me. Maybe I have glanced longer than a millisecond at him. Maybe it's because we are the only folks alone. Either way I smile back and walk past. So many questions I would like to ask, so little time to realistically do so.

3.48 P.M.: A WEALTH OF CHANCES GONE BEGGING Stuart Hall is describing a lop-sided first half. Leeds fans, on a freezing cold day, swing their shirts above their bare chests and heads insanely, as if a manic display of courage will inspire their players and demoralise the opposition. It doesn't look like working.

Hall's half-time reports convey a wealth of Wigan chances that have gone begging, and he wonders whether they will come to rue them. Then he nips off for a fag and maybe a snifter.

3.49 P.M.: 'IMAGINE ONLY BEING GOOD ENOUGH TO PLAY FOR PORTSMOUTH' Half-time at Old Trafford. The floodgates didn't open. United looked hesitant, out of sorts. In charge, yes, but they rarely threatened Portsmouth's goal in the last half-hour. Polite applause echoed around the ground when the referee blew his whistle. Seconds earlier, after a one-two for Pompey failed to come off, a young voice had sneered, 'What a crap player. Imagine only being good enough to play for Portsmouth.' Out of the mouths of babes, eh? I turned around and smiled sweetly. The boy who smirked this comment was about ten years old. And fat. I felt like saying, 'Imagine *you* running across the car park.' But that would be cruel.

Only good enough to play for a mid-table Premiership club! Most people would give their right arms to play ten minutes at this level, for anyone.

I'm not picking on ten-year-olds here, and I may be doing the boy a great disservice, but the way I see it, this is the sad side of the glory-hunting brigade. You have to be raised a certain way to think like that – that all United players are great and Portsmouth's must be crap; that playing for any team other than United is pointless. You're certainly unlikely to be a player. Judging by his accent – southern England, obviously – he probably didn't play a game that day (this kid didn't look capable, to be honest) like, say, the several tiers of football I have seen already – mini-soccer, junior or youth leagues, school sides, even a kickabout outside a mate's house. It's most likely that this morning he was on the country road to the place he belongs – Old Trafford … to see United … getting fat … eating burgers … thinking Portsmouth's players are crap and that all his non-United-supporting school chums are tossers.

Sadly, I suspect his dad has bred Manchester United – The Religion into him. Just a theory. What would he make of Neil Williams and Josh?

3.49 P.M.: HALF-TIME COFFEE – A REAL ROASTING As we make our way around the goal, past the tea-bar – which is now, surprisingly, shut – and on to the social club, we walk past the changing rooms where Hadley's manager is giving his players a fearful dressing down. Ouch.

3.50 P.M.: 'IT'S ALL ABOUT THE SECOND GOAL' Bristol City's players left the pitch to applause. The City faithful are upbeat. Any sort of lead is enough to inspire belief among most fans. Here, expectancy is matched by optimism. They have been well worth their single-goal lead, and it might have been more.

In the dressing room Danny Coles is breathing heavily. He has whipped off his shirt (has this boy got a problem with polyester?) and has his head buried in a towel in a tennis-player-in-a-five-setter mode. It is a hot day, and the combination of the heat, his chest infection and his sore Achilles is taking its toll. He looked fine out on the pitch, but in here he is red-faced. Like his colleagues, he takes huge swigs from drinks bottles. Some sit with their hands clasped, physically drained for now. 'Get plenty of water on board,' they are urged before Brian Tinnion addresses them.

Tommy Doherty, a hard-running and -tackling midfielder, draws up phlegm noisily. There is something vaguely comical about the regularity with which he does this, but nothing funny about what he spits on to the floor in front of him. The gory scene isn't an image I wish to retain. Suffice to say there are huge lumps of the stuff on the floor, and his team-mates have to jauntily dodge around them.

Tinnion is delighted with the tempo. 'Excellent!' He loves the commitment. Turning to Danny and Louis Carey, he adds, 'They've created nothing. You've given 'em fuck all, and they got fuck all. Now' – he emphasises the word by clapping his hands – 'it's all about the second goal. If they get it, we've got a game on.' He urges Danny to stay tight for the next fifteen minutes in particular. 'They are still dangerous – they have to come looking for a goal.' There is no mincing of words. 'Let's make sure we get it. Keep pushing. Get the ball wide. Let's keep exposing their back line. Let's keep running at them.'

Both Tinnion and his assistant Keith Millen, separately, instruct right-winger Paul Murray to attack Vale's left-back, who, they've spotted, has a habit of drifting in-field. He is also on a yellow card; another caution means he will be sent off. There is no sentiment. 'Run at him. He can't afford to tackle because a reckless challenge means he'll be off. Make him foul you. Let's get him off, then we've really got them.'

Some players leap on to the treatment tables. Danny's Achilles is carefully massaged. Others head for the loos. Goalkeeper Steve Phillips doesn't take off his gloves and looks slightly comical stalking the dressing room ordering, 'Come on, lads!' He's had a fairly straightforward 45 minutes. He would like another half like that.

Tommy Doherty continues his earnest efforts to see what else he can retch up from his lungs and stomach. No wonder the fruit is left uneaten.

'Some players need bollockings, others need an arm around their shoulder,' Tinnion tells me. 'Knowing your players, that's the key. It's man-management. I've had to learn that, how to treat each of them differently. They all have their strengths and weaknesses.'

He has a quiet word with Leroy Lita. A blood clot has formed on his injured ankle. It is a freak wound, which may require minor surgery. Tinnion tells him not to worry about it. But when the troops march out for the resumption Lita is left alone in the dressing room to gather his thoughts. A shower? Some treatment maybe? This must be a lonely place when you can hear the action through the walls. Imagine the frustration of injury or the anger at being sent off. What goes on within these walls ultimately decides what happens outside.

3.51 P.M.: STREAKERS ON THE PITCH! At Gretna most of the crowd rush for the loos or something to eat while Paul and Selwyn hop out on to the pitch with forks and spades to flatten any divots, paying particular attention to ruts in the penalty area.

On the far side, three Elgin supporters – the Bolton branch, we suspect – are so delirious with their team's first-half display that they can't contain themselves. Off comes the kit and they streak across the pitch. This is hilarious and fairly bizarre. Paul and a steward chase and apprehend them, but no one seems to notice the ensuing pandemonium. The spectators are queuing for food, in the bar, popping to the toilets, listening for scores; some are just plain moaning about Gretna not playing well (you can't please some). They didn't miss much – it was a cold day! No one is thrown out. It is all taken as good fun and frolics at this level of the game.

3.52 P.M.: GOALLESS AT THE WITHDEAN In the PA box at Brighton Attila the Stockbroker is plugging 'We Want Falmer' for all it's worth. He tells the crowd which newspapers Seagulls Ska has appeared in: the *Guardian*, the *Sunday Times*, the *Sun*, plus national TV and radio. Paul says it has also been in a couple of trade journals he knows, *Accountancy Eye* and *Planning*, although it's doubtful how many copies of those will have been shifted. 'Believe it or not, we've sold out of the original pressings so we've now got to print an extra 1,500 copies. It has dropped to number 46 in the charts, but it might actually be back in the top 40, which would be something. So well done everyone who bought it.'

Amazingly, Attila doesn't play his signature song. 'Well done, John,' says Richard. They then hand over to Paul, who is now on the pitch with a community scheme.

Attila and Richard discuss a local resident who has started a campaign to get Albion ousted from the Withdean, even though he moved into the area after Brighton began playing there. 'He needs a slap and to be told to shut up,' says John. 'I'm fed up of upper-class twits trying to cause problems.' Richard concedes the resident may, legally, have a point. Albion had originally agreed to move on. And would dearly love to, of course, but not while this public inquiry lingers on. 'Well, I've had enough,' insists John. 'I'm just fed up of these people. We should picket his house.'

'You rebelling then, John?' asks Richard.

'Yes, I bloody well am.'

Then everyone bursts out laughing. If you didn't, you would cry.

Attila reads the half-time scores and the England cricket latest.

3.53 P.M.: THE CHAIRMAN RUNS THE GAUNTLET Rob Bradley walks around the ground back to the directors' lounge. 'You wanna get your chequebook out, Bradley,' shouts a fan from behind the goal, who clearly isn't happy with Lincoln's first-half performance. He gestures the familiar sign of implied tightness, rubbing his thumb and forefinger together.

'Mine wouldn't do a lot of bloody good,' he tells me.

Rob is thick-skinned, but this hurts. Most fans understand the background, some don't. Rob isn't chairman because he has money burning a hole in his pocket, he is there to represent the fans. Some, he says, 'think because we have made a profit we should spend it all on players. But that is how we got to where we were when we had no money.'

Administration has left an impression on Rob. Over half-time soup, he tells me how difficult and chaotic the process was. Lincoln had to go to the High Court in London twice a week. Approaches to buy the club were being made by all sorts of people, including some who proved wholly unsuitable and went elsewhere instead. Creditors have been offered shares instead of a percentage rate of payment in the pound, except the secured creditors like the brewery and bank. The players' wages were covered with a £150,000 'soft loan' from the PFA. Local businesses have stayed with the club, as have the Co-operative, which sponsors them, and generally the crowds have backed the board too. Today's gate is 3,900 – lower than average but 'not surprising' given that Rovers haven't brought many fans and last week Lincoln lost to Kidderminster, who, as we know, are struggling at the foot of the table.

3.55 P.M.: A FANS' LAP OF HONOUR This is far more dignified. Fans who have travelled to Wrexham but support other clubs are being encouraged to assemble in front of The Kop for a photo call. A huge banner sums up the camaradarie: 'Wrexham 4 Falmer'. Wrexham, a club seemingly about to lose their old crowd, want Brighton to get their new stadium. They walk around the ground, waving their scarves, showing their shirts as the PA announcer reads out the names of the clubs represented. It is a long list. They receive huge applause. A tingle of warmth runs down my spine. I clap heartily as they pass by. So does Neil Williams, who tells me 'he cannot thank them enough. Some of these people have been marvellous.' It is a moving sight.

Such a scene would have been barely imaginable twenty years ago, but fans are growing to realise that this is their game. The hell are they going to watch other clubs disappear and cheer as the coffins roll by; they don't all readily subscribe to the greed that has caused a situation where more than half of the Football League's clubs have fallen into insolvency in recent years. They care about the many and varied hues of English football. Can you really say that about the owners of most Premier League clubs?

3.56 P.M.: HALF-TIME AT THE HARRIERS Brian Murdoch is busy, busy, busy. And hot. Steam is rising, and not just from the boiler, the spitting burgers and the bubbling soup. The queue to his kiosk stretches some twenty yards, and it'll get longer before half-time is through.

I'm squeezed into the corner of Brian's kiosk. There is barely room to stand. They are a tight-knit, hard-working team. Steve is up front, Brian is to his right, the other three are behind.

Brian's soup is balm on a bitter day. It is served with a smile and a joke at no extra charge. One boy asks for a shot of brown sauce – it takes all sorts. There's a skill to serving the customers quickly and keeping hold of your smile. Brian is a past master.

'Notice something missing?' asks Brian. 'Tills. Slows things down.'

No one actually has to move their feet. Brian leans from side to side to show me. He is in charge of the pork and stuffing rolls and hot drinks. 'Nescafe, Typhoo and Cadbury's. No rubbish. You could serve anything and make more money in the short term, but they won't keep coming back.'

They whizz through the fans with impressive speed, handling orders a few back, talking to fans all the time, making them feel welcome.

'The food is always better than the game,' shouts a regular.

Brian smiles. 'Always 100 per cent here, you know that.'

The fans are forever shuffling forward. Along with his four assistants, he is ripping through one of them every ten seconds. The economics are impressive. Six fans a minute, with an average spend per head of £2. It'll stay this way for maybe half an hour or so. The other kiosks are also busy. And unlike kiosks at other grounds, Brian doesn't close: he'll stay open until after the match. It all tots up to a tidy income, even after the cost of the ingredients. When children give change for chocolate bars and chews, they don't even count it. 'Waste of time,' says Brian. 'The bloke behind may want a burger costing £2.50. Let's serve him rather than chase pennies.'

'Stuffing?' shouts Brian to someone who has ordered a pork roll.

'Not today, we ain't losing yet,' booms a loud voice with a chuckle.

'Yes please,' chirps the quieter voice of the person who has ordered the roll.

It isn't stunning humour, but it is convivial, and the quality of the food – well, I've mentioned that already. Without Brian, and, to be fair, Kidderminster's loyalty to him (I bet the smoothies from the catering chains have been down to dis him and his ilk in the interests of their own finances), football would have no soul. Fans thrive on ritual, routine and reliability, and Brian provides them all. 'Best part of the match,' says a smiling fan, soup in hand, with a wink. And I believe him.

3.58 P.M.: THE RESTART I can't imagine Evergreen FC's bar gets too busy too often. Or that there is a frequent demand for filter coffee. Amazingly, they haven't put any on in advance of half-time, so I watch the last two cups being served then have to wait for the fresh pot to percolate. It takes ten minutes. Yes, you can pass the time by watching the remaining half-times come through on Sky Sports on the super-sized screen, but it's boring, and when you are cold it adds up to misery. And it's a pound a cup.

Bill gives up. He won't risk missing a minute, and has gone before the players leave the dressing rooms. Just in case. They make substitutions at half-time. Bill has to log them. Dave is not so fastidious. And anyway, he's now on to real ale. He's keen to tell me all about being a member of CAMRA and how he always has the *Good Beer Guide* with him. Really? I tell him I'm from Worcester and that I like a good pint of bitter myself. Big mistake. He knows my city well. And its real ale pubs. Very well, in fact. Do I know the Dragon? He's a frequent visitor. What about the other side of the river? Do I know The Bush? Yep. The Bell? That's the one.

We'd better join Bill, I suggest. We do.

4.02 P.M.: STUART HALL'S FAVOURITE GROUND Stuart Hall has been espousing the merits of Wigan on air. The JJB Stadium is without doubt a nice, neat, modern stadium, functional and with all the right facilities. But he has worked this feverish football patch for 46 years. Which ground, I wonder, is his favourite?

'Anfield. On a big day. Has to be. In the sixties. Kop swaying. Cut the atmosphere with a knife. Wonderful stuff.' He talks in short bursts like that. It is what he loves about the game.

The JJB isn't quite like that, but it is rocking. A bit like the Leeds defence.

4.04 P.M.: THE SECOND HALF BEGINS AT CARROW ROAD Neil Doncaster is on the prowl again. Same route: under the Barclay Stand and around through the gates between the Barclay and Jarrold Stands. We watch briefly before going on to make our way through the away supporters to the back.

A steward is having a problem with Chelsea fans seeking to stand or at least perch on the backs of their seats. Neil looks on. I examine the Chelsea supporters. Few top clubs in the post-Premiership era seem to have such an uneasy balance of old- and new-type fans. I look closely at the mainly middle-aged, grey or balding old-school fans, trying to get a constant 'Chelsea, Chelsea' chant going with outstretched arms in an upward motion, beckoning their fellow fans to join in. Mostly it falls on deaf ears. Enough join in to keep it going, but the swanky new-money types in quality coats with their siblings in tow are not inclined to chant. They don't remember the days when Mickey Droy and his fellow game-but-inadequate team-mates would come to grounds like this and get a drubbing. Chelsea's hooligan fans were more than adequate at settling the relative score off the pitch. What do they do now? What do they think now? Can they feel comfortable supporting such a cosmopolitan club whose players are plucked from all over Europe and beyond? Who have a growing core of fans who are maybe a bit too poncey for their liking?

For many of the younger fans who join in the song with a single raised clenched-fist salute, this is not an issue. They are 1990s lad culture, the post-Cool Britannia breed – a bit more savvy. They read *FourFourTwo* magazine and like a midweek game of five-a-side with their mates. They can talk the tactics, too.

Neil clutches at straws. He has developed a habit of watching larger parts of the game here because Norwich do better when he does. He cites the 4–4 draw with Middlesbrough (City scored three times in the last eleven minutes to earn that point) and the 3–2 win against West Brom (thanks, Neil!) as examples. Reality is, Chelsea's players don't need support or superstitions to help them. They are doing just fine, thanks.

4.05 P.M.: 'COME ON IPSWICH!' The second half starts at Ipswich with the fans backing their team. 'Come on Ipswich, come on Ipswich' rings around Portman Road. It is awe-inspiring stuff. But with this comes pressure for the referee.

There is an early tumble in the West Ham penalty area. Paul Taylor waves his arms crossways low down in front of his midriff. It is a clear decision. No doubts, no hesitation, no weak signs for fans to pick up on. The pace of the game has quickened too. It could be a lively second half.

4.06 P.M.: HADLEY GET LEVEL – EVERGREEN 1 HADLEY 1 In the faraway field in Hertfordshire, watched by a crowd of just 26, Hadley restore parity seven minutes into the second half. It had been coming. The fat goalie's luck ran out. A cross was angled in from the right. He was required to jump and fluffed it badly. Rachatahr Hudson tapped it in almost apologetically. The goalie looks around for someone to slap, or threaten to slap, but Evergreen's outfielders troop back to their places in silence. I suppress a giggle while Bill writes it all down. It's no one's fackin' fault but the keeper's.

Evergreen's supporters have got noisier (some have probably been in the bar). They're not in the mood for laughs.

I'm warming to Dave. He's a bit keen, but well into his beer and curry. He watches football at all levels and … well, I get the feeling he just needs company.

4.07 P.M.: WALSALL TAKE THE LEAD – WALSALL 2 BLACKPOOL 1 The half-time rollicking has worked for Walsall. Neil Emblen's neck must be all right. He is now brazen enough to search for headers, and ten minutes into the second half he knocks down a corner for on-trial striker Marvin Robinson to tap in. The stand around us explodes. Ralph in particular. His jab has worked, and he admires Emblen's bravery. He has set it up, but you get the impression he might have thundered it into the net himself had it not been for his neck.

Ralph continues to watch intensely. He's noting the players who are looking tired.

'Would you recommend who should stay on or go?' I ask.

'Only if asked,' he replies. 'I'm not a coach, I'm a medic.'

4.08 P.M.: 'YOU DON'T KNOW WHAT YOU'RE DOING!' A spate of quickfire incidents test Paul Taylor's nerve. The pressure and frustration mount with each decision. Watching it impartially, it is as if fans think the ref is there to balance out the decisions rather than call each incident as he sees it. First, a yellow card for De Vos for a foul on Zamora. Then, after Ipswich's third foul in quick succession, this one committed by Magilton, there's widespread abuse. Three minutes later, Zamora crashes into Ipswich keeper Kelvin Davis. The Ipswich fans call for a sending-off, which is flatly ridiculous. Taylor has a quiet word rather than issue a card. So the familiar cries ring out: 'You don't know what you're doing!' A minute later the West Ham fans call for a penalty, again not given and, in my view, not deserved. A few seconds later Zamora backs into a defender and a foul is given against him, which earns mock-ironic cheers. Who would be a referee?

4.08 P.M.: POMPEY PLAY UP – MANCHESTER UNITED 1 PORTSMOUTH 1 Portsmouth haven't read the script. This wasn't supposed to happen. A minute into the second half they venture into United's half, whose defence, for once, fail to clear, and from twenty yards Gary O'Neill, a young midfielder, thunders in an equaliser. Cue the obligatory diving celebration in our corner. Cue the Pompey fans dancing in delight at the far end. Cue the two-fingered salutes and general disbelief. Is this going to be allowed to stand? Children look at their parents as if to say, 'Can't you stop this madness? You didn't say this could happen!' (OK, I am imagining this, but that is how it feels.) There is little of that 'let's get back at 'em' attitude you see at most grounds – a rousing of the troops. Here there are murmurs of disapproval; collective 'humphs' work their way around the ground; there is much tut-tutting, for the actors have fluffed their lines. You wouldn't be surprised if someone asked for their money back. To make it worse, Fergie has brought on Alan Smith and is playing him in midfield alongside John O'Shea. A defender and an attacker, in midfield. What is he up to?

4.09 P.M.: WALSALL WAVER, BUT THE DOC PRESCRIBES – WALSALL 2 BLACKPOOL 2 No sooner have we settled back in our seats, chipper that Walsall have scored, than they concede again. This time there is little they could have done about it. Blackpool equalise through a direct free-kick deliciously curled in by Peter Parker from just outside the box. Eat your heart out, David Beckham. 'No worries, man, we'll still win by two clear goals,' says Ralph confidently. 'We're flying.'

4.10 P.M.: EARLY DOORS IN THE SECOND HALF AT LINCOLN
Rob Bradley sits in the main stand in his seat in the directors' box for the second half. He tells me he still finds it strange. He has always preferred to sit rather than stand, but he never expected to end up here. He is refreshingly candid about Lincoln's pattern of play. A near-post header is cleared off the line; Rob moans like a fan. 'Bloody pathetic effort,' he fumes. A poor clearance is dismissed as 'madness'. Rob blows hard and twists his head away in abhorrence, digging his hands deeper into his coat pockets. You know how he feels.

4.13 P.M.: BUT WHO SCORED? – WIGAN 2 LEEDS 0 Wigan extend their lead, and you sense it is game over. The goal comes from a corner, but it produces a classic moment of confusion in the press box. It was McCulloch's header, but did Roberts get a touch on the line? He has certainly reeled away as if he has scored. But some Wigan players have gone to McCulloch. A collective decision, it is felt, is needed among the press corps. Roberts, 56 minutes, it is decided. Later, video replays confirm it.

The crowd sing 'We're going up, we're going up' to the tune of 'Tom Hark'. Attila the Stockbroker wouldn't be amused.

4.15 P.M.: KUQI-ING UP TROUBLE A major flashpoint at Portman Road. Shefki Kuqi, Ipswich's tall Finnish forward, lunges into a tackle in front of the West Ham fans. A major scrap ensues. Gavin Williams charges in. Paul Taylor tries to hold Kuqi back. 'He lost it,' Taylor would say later. Remember his pre-match words – 'Shefki's OK.' Not today, it seems.

It takes Taylor some moments to calm things down. He also has to get things right after an incident that exploded rapidly into chaos. He has a word with Trevor Pollard, his assistant, who was on hand. Decision: he books Kuqi and marches the free-kick ten yards forward for West Ham. It appeases both sets of fans. Ipswich must have feared Kuqi would be sent off; West Ham escape with no bookings and get their free-kick to the edge of Ipswich's box.

The incidents continue to come thick and fast. Fouls on Magilton and Bowditch are given but go unpunished, and at the other end Bobby

Zamora has a free header, which he should convert but nods straight at Davis. As at Ashton Gate, it's all about which way the second goal goes.

4.16 P.M.: TINNION GETS FRUSTRATED The gaffer isn't happy. Minor decisions are going against Bristol City, and they start to mount. It is frustrating, and he suspect his players are losing concentration. Tinnion steps on to the pitch to contest one particular decision and is hauled back by the fourth official. He then wanders outside his technical area to dispute another.

Looking back on this period of the match later, Brian recalls, 'I was getting annoyed that we weren't doing the right things. I felt we needed to get the ball down and play and work harder to win it back when they had it. This is was an edgy time and I didn't feel comfortable.'

The waving of the left hand has been furious. The start of the second half is a notorious time for players to take their foot off the pedal, or just fail to get going. At 1–0 down, Port Vale are still dangerous. An equaliser will change the mood completely.

4.18 P.M.: INTIMIDATION IS THE SINCEREST FORM OF FLATTERY Trouble is brewing at Evergreen. The Bill Nighy lookalike embarks on a couple of temper tantrums almost certainly influenced by reactions he has seen in a top game on TV.

Clichéd tantrum number one. He has just flattened one of Hadley's forwards. It was over the far side by the boys wobbling on their bikes, yet you could hear the sickening thwack as he hit the ground. Ouch. Sweeping his bleached hair back, Nighy is suddenly transformed into Roy Keane bawling into Alfe-Inge Haaland's ear after felling the Norwegian at Old Trafford in 2002 (an incident later recalled in Keane's autobiography and which subsequently earned a hefty ban). With great theatre, he makes allegations of diving by bellowing into his opponent's ear to get up. He's acting. Hmm. A brawl is inevitable. Fisticuffs follow. He aims the first few. The referee is amazingly lenient. He books him, but Evergreen boss Gordon Wallis wisely wastes little time in getting a substitute on and pulling the Nighy lookalike off.

Clichéd tantrum number two. Nighy hauls off his shirt as he walks off and hurls it at the bench, then storms away for an early bath. He doesn't return, not even to cheer his mates on. You have to smile. He must be in his mid-thirties, but he's still imitating his football anti-heroes.

Bill Berry notes it all. Dave too, and me, for the record, for this book. What a sight we must look. Three middle-aged men so fired up they have to write it all down. I mean, we could just go home. We're not playing, we won't be missed, no one knows us. It just doesn't, well, matter.

4.19 P.M.: SADDLERS SOAR – WALSALL 3 BLACKPOOL 2 Ralph Rogers knows his boys. On his home debut Marvin Robinson, who has recently been on loan at several clubs having been released by Derby County, heads in from close range from a corner for his second goal of the match. It is a poor goal to concede. Blackpool manager Colin Hendry, like Paul Merson in his first season in management, is apoplectic with rage. An international defender with a Premier League championship winner's medal with Blackburn Rovers in his cupboard, he cannot understand the slack marking. He is furious and soon rounds on the fourth official after a minor incident. His job, even after only a few months in management, is on the line. People aren't doing what they've practised all week. Learning to keep your cool is part of making it as a football manager.

Robinson, Leitão and Merson then waste good chances to put the game beyond Blackpool's reach. Ralph, with the optimism so readily associated with Americans, doesn't see the nervy end that is surely coming.

4.20 P.M.: AN EQUALISER AT CARROW ROAD – NORWICH 1 CHELSEA 1 After checking the disabled facilities, Neil Doncaster stands in the gap between the Jarrold and Norwich and Peterborough Building Society Stands as Norwich begin to assert their game on Chelsea, who are floundering in the late-afternoon cold. They look uncomfortable in the air. Peter Mendham, an ex-Norwich player, introduces himself and gives me a postcard – 269 appearances for Norwich, 31 goals between 1979 and 1986 and a League Cup winner's medal. He explains the tiredness that comes with chasing the ball and the silky skills of Chelsea. But then a Norwich cross from Darren Huckerby finds Leon McKenzie, who heads home.

Widespread jubilation. McKenzie raises his finger to his lips, imitating Mourinho's shushing gesture, but the crowd are having none of it. For the next five minutes there is real hope of Norwich grabbing an unlikely three points. The atmosphere is wonderful. They pin Chelsea back, but it's like a boxing bout. Norwich have had a good round and have thrown lots of leather, but Chelsea are only temporarily stunned.

Mourinho makes a double substitution. Eidur Gudjohnsen and Mateja Kezman come on for Tiago and Drogba. Norwich are presented with fresh problems.

4.21 P.M.: LINCOLN'S GREEN SCORES – LINCOLN 1 BRISTOL ROVERS 0 Y'see, if you are watching as a neutral, you can see a goal coming. But if you are a full-on fan, you view things with far more scepticism. Rob Bradley is unconvinced that a goal is coming Lincoln's way. But I can sense it. They are turning the screw, and Bristol Rovers are defending deeper. So when Francis Green volleys them in front it is fully deserved. The relief is palpable. Rob Bradley is out of his seat, as we all are, clapping eagerly. 'At bloody last,' he says. 'Now I've got the jitters.'

4.22 P.M.: A QUIET CUDDLE IN THE DIRECTORS' BOX Bob Marley is patiently watching the second half of the match with the enthusiasm a director should have. But you sense his mind is elsewhere. Sebastian has joined him, warmed up after playing and watching the TV downstairs. Now he watches his dad's team. Bob puts an arm around his son. It is a brief moment of solace. Dad and lad together, and the only time Bob has sat down for any length of time all day. It is a poignant moment too. Earlier Bob had confessed how his involvement with the club had contributed to the break-up of his marriage and therefore his ability to be the hands-on father he would like to be. That, and the several thousands of pounds a year he finds for this indulgence. For these brief few moments, though, he can be a normal dad with his son at the footy. Arms round each other, cuddling out the cold.

4.23 P.M.: BARNEY WATCHES THE BOUNCE OF THE BALL 'I don't watch the football, I am looking at the way the ball is rolling and bouncing, how it is playing, whether there are places I need to concentrate on,' says Paul Barnett, who is probably doing the best thing. Gretna are pushing hard but, for once, failing to score at will. It isn't a good game. 'I can see things you probably can't,' Paul continues. 'If someone miskicks, is it because of a divot? Silly things like that can cause a player to go over on his ankle and have a serious injury.'

Gretna get a penalty. But it is like Leon Knight's effort at Brighton early in the first half, struck too softly and easily saved. More work for the Borderers to do.

4.25 P.M.: TINNION KEEPS UP THE TEMPO Brian Tinnion wants the faster tempo to return. He can sense Port Vale are still dangerous as a 30-yard effort is tipped around his post by City keeper Steve Phillips. Somehow, it galvanises the troops. The effort to keep a clean sheet and resume attacking is overwhelming. Later, Tinnion calls this their 'desire' – a word often over-used, and frequently out of context, but called correctly here.

City have to drive forward. Football is a tough game. It requires sinew and effort, and it is fast-paced. They have to find the will to win. Young managers like Tinnion and his opposite number for Port Vale, Martin Foyle, have to learn to get the most out of their players. Anguish is frequently written over Foyle's face; he grimaces whenever things go wrong. You sense he would like to chastise his players but wonders what that might do to their confidence. They need building up at this stage of the game, not knocking down. The three points are there for Bristol City, for Brian Tinnion, for Danny Coles, but they have to earn them. Danny continues to blow hard but he still hasn't let Matthews in. He is doing his job.

4.26 P.M.: ALL SQUARE, BUT AGOGO GONE – LINCOLN 1 BRISTOL ROVERS 1 Lincoln City don't surprise Rob Bradley. Having nudged their noses in front, they meekly let their lead slip. It is woeful defending, casual and careless enough to enrage a stadium full of monks, let alone diehard football fans. But it is a strange, bitter-sweet moment. Poor defending it may have been, but, having rolled the ball into the net, there was no need for Rovers' scorer, Junior Agogo, to gesticulate to Lincoln's defenders as they despondently trooped back for the restart.

Not in front of the ref anyway. Especially when you've already been booked. Foul and abusive behaviour is an instant yellow, in this case followed by a red. Agogo stands in disbelief. The crowd wave wildly. 'Cheerio!' The Bristol Rovers directors around us are furious. It may have been a harmless bit of winding-up, but it could also have caused a ruck.

4.27 P.M.: FOREST ON FIRE Nottingham Forest's Marlon King forces Michel Kuipers into another save with twenty minutes left. Brighton are flailing. Rain has started to fall. Everyone sat over on the far side and behind the goal is getting soaked. It's just another part of the folly of the Withdean. Kuipers then suffers a shoulder injury while punching clear a cross from Reid as Kris Commons challenges him. He is replaced by youngster Chris May as Brighton look to stretch their unbeaten run in the Championship to six games.

4.28 P.M.: THE MAGIC OF MERSON I may be at Walsall to watch the work of Dr Ralph Rogers, but a word about Paul Merson. The former England forward may have his well-documented demons, he may be putting on weight and nowhere near the required fitness for the demands of the modern game, but all afternoon he's never stopped playing clever one-twos and give-and-go's, endlessly spinning the ball away with the outside of his foot into the path of onrushing team-mates who are learning to play off this gifted footballer. It is a joy to watch and an education for youngsters.

A ball is hammered with ludicrous ferocity in his direction. The instantaneous reaction from most players at this level (and higher) is to panic, maybe to attempt to chest the ball down, bring it under control and hopefully head for the line, or get a cross in, or lay it off. Not Merson. He uses his football nous, simply takes a step back and pings the ball on the half-volley, using the speed of delivery to whizz it into the corridor of uncertainty between the goalkeeper and back-pedalling defenders. No one quite connects, but it is a wonderful piece of skill, which earns a respectful ripple of applause.

There are doubtless many people who feel that top footballers demean themselves by playing down the divisions, that it is humiliating to play on a small stage with tiring legs and growing girths, that they should simply give up. Maybe, but the likes of Paul Merson may also have to play on because they frittered away so much of the mega-money they made during football's boom times. I grew up watching lots of former stars putting something back at non-League level. At Worcester City I remember the presence of the likes of Norman Deeley, Ivor Allchurch and Gerry Hitchens. Deeley, Eddie Stuart and Eddie Clamp had all played in Stan Cullis's championship-winning Wolves team. Hitchens was an England centre-forward who was one of the first English players to play in Italy; bizarrely, he joined Worcester from Torino. In particular, I remember watching Allchurch, a gifted Welsh international midfielder, spraying the ball around with precision. I learned a lot from him – how small the pitch can look if you pass well and into the path of team-mates, for instance. Later, when I progressed to watching West Brom and graduated to standing on the Brummie Road End, for the first time seeing the game from height behind the goal, I could appreciate the true value of width. Bobby Hope, an almost criminally under-rated left-footed midfielder, would use the full width of the pitch to supply accurate passes to wingers like 'Chippy' Clarke and Willie Johnston. They, in turn, crossed for Jeff Astle to score or provide knock-downs for Tony Brown.

My love and appreciation of the game began with the likes of Allchurch and John Charles at Hereford putting a bit back into the game as the sun set on their playing days. Loads of players used to. I would heartily encourage them to carry on doing so. Sadly, it seems fewer players are willing to take this option. It's a shame, and it's why I hope the young fans watching Merson fully appreciate what he is offering.

4.29 P.M.: TOTTENHAM HOTSPUR 0 WEST BROMWICH ALBION 6
It must be true. I have just listened to James Alexander Gordon saying it. Sadly, this memorable scoreline was uttered only for a pre-record.

Rather than hang around for the evening games to end (Albion are playing Spurs in a 5.15 kick-off), James runs through every conceivable option, from nil-nil to six apiece and optimistic-sounding sevens, eights, nines and tens, so the correct score can be cut into later classified checks.

But I can dream, can't I?

4.30 P.M.: THE EQUALISER – AFAN LIDO 1 LLANELLI 1 Oh, no. Lido concede to Llanelli. The children are still kicking the ball about and the adults are chatting (I'm still with Alan the amiable Brummie, talking about the decline of Midlands non-League clubs) when Peter Cheeseman taps in the equaliser. The mood at the Runtech Stadium changes. I see Phil Robinson, hands in pockets, in despair. Question is, can Lido regain the lead?

4.31 P.M.: CONTROVERSY AT KIDDY – KIDDERMINSTER 2 ROCHDALE 1 Brian's kiosk looks out across the pitch. It's a place where you can watch the game and have a chat. I've been here many a time for an evening game, chatting and listening to the locals, some of them long-standing friends of Brian's – he has known them for ages. They try to elicit information from him about the club and offer the various rumours they've heard, but Brian is a sly old fox. He never quite gives his hand away, rarely lets on what he is really thinking. He and Steve are experts at working their way through the customers while watching the match.

The kiosk is a beacon of light on dark winter nights. It offers comfort and warmth. It is the beating heart of Kidderminster Harriers.

The game itself is frustrating. Kiddy are piling on the pressure, but when the ball disappears up the pitch at the feet of blue-shirted Rochdale players there are the familiar groans from supporters whose team is anchored to the foot of the table. They fear the worst. Most expect it.

Then a promising move takes shape. The ball is slid into the path of a crimson-shirted Harrier. It's Dean Keates. His cross crashes against the hand of Dale defender Wayne Evans, who is only yards away, but his arm is raised. You see them given. There are desperate appeals for a penalty, and the ref points to the spot. Rochdale, who haven't lost in seven weeks, can barely believe it. Their players are furious, and surround the referee. But I've never known one to change his mind. There is a buzz around the crowd. A goal from nowhere, maybe? The ground falls momentarily silent. You can see the anxious faces. Don't miss, don't miss. Doubts creep in. Silently, I suspect many think Ian Foster, a diminutive striker, will fail, but he looks confident enough. You can see he really wants to tuck this one away. He looks to set off early, but the ref hasn't got everyone back. Wait, wait, you utter under your breath. From Brian's corner we watch him run up and …

The crowd punch the air. Foster peels away in our direction. 'Come on, come on!' he shouts. His team-mates follow. There is belief and hope again. Now they just have to hang on.

4.32 P.M.: CHELSEA BACK ON TOP – NORWICH 1 CHELSEA 2

Chelsea regain their composure and their lead. For Norwich it is a soft goal to concede after working so hard to get on level terms. Gudjohnsen heads on and Kezman reacts first to tap the ball in.

For ten minutes, Neil Doncaster has been a fan, joshing with stewards, absorbing the game. Disappointed, of course, but in a lighter mood. The day has, despite the scoreline, gone off OK thus far.

4.33 P.M.: THE SECOND GOAL COMETH – BRISTOL CITY 2 PORT VALE 0

The second goal arrives at Ashton Gate, and it is the one Brian Tinnion wants. The supply line was predictable, the one the coaches spotted at half-time. Paul Murray has taunted and tantalised his marker Craig James to the point where he cannot cope (James is later substituted). This time Murray gets a cross over to the near post at the Atyeo End, and Paul Heffernan, who has had a poor game since coming on for Lita, scuffs his shot past the goalkeeper. There is immense relief. Brian Tinnion leads the bench celebrations. Everyone is on their feet, and Brian punches the air in the direction of the fans in the stand above.

As the fans start singing 'Feed the Heff and he will score', Keith Millen quickly grabs Tinnion's arm. They discuss something quickly and look to get an urgent message on to the pitch. 'It was to tighten up our midfield,' Brian told me later. 'We felt we had won the game but we didn't want to let them straight back in. We wanted our midfield to sit slightly deeper and thought maybe we'll bring another midfield player on to tighten it up, and then cruise through the game.' They duly brought Murray off (to thunderous applause) and Bradley Orr on, to play a central midfield role. 'As a manager, you can't afford to switch off. It is so easy to get carried away, and then to give a goal away.'

4.34 P.M.: 'THE PREMIERSHIP BECKONS' – WIGAN 3 LEEDS 0

'Roberts despair, Mahon joy,' Stuart Hall begins his report. Jason Roberts strode through the Leeds defence, chipped the ball over goalkeeper Neil Sullivan and ran off at an angle, thinking he had scored, only to see the ball come back off the post. Seconds later it ended up at the feet of Alan Mahon, who hit a stunning 25-yarder into the back of the net. 'For Leeds, honest endeavour isn't enough. For Wigan, the Premiership beckons.' Stuart Hall signs off. For now. Unless Leeds get a grip there may be more goals to come.

4.35 P.M.: THE CHAIRMAN HUFFS AND PUFFS Rob Bradley is turning purple. Try as they might, Lincoln cannot blow Bristol Rovers' ten-man house down. They are pinned back for large parts of the match. The chairman isn't happy. Not after last week's debacle at Kidderminster, when a 1–0 lead was thrown away. Lincoln are ninth; a win would lift them into or closer to the play-off places (fourth to seventh in the table). But a point at home won't be enough.

A volley rasps over the bar. A ball whisked in from the right wing is just in front of us and begs a slight touch but swerves wide. It is one of those days. 'They don't bloody want it enough,' fumes Rob. He doesn't mean it. He knows the players want to win. What they lack, today at least, is the ability to win.

Rob stands and thunderously claps a substitution. Jack Hobbs, sixteen, becomes Lincoln City's youngest ever senior player. He receives a warm welcome, but things don't change. They still can't score.

4.36 P.M.: WREXHAM RATTLE THE BAR Neil Williams's early enthusiasm is slowly ebbing away. He hasn't waved his Welsh flag for some time. He still urges Wrexham forward as the fans behind us grow hostile at their team's relative sterility, but it remains a strange atmosphere. More through empathy with Wrexham rather than animosity to Doncaster, all the neutrals want a home win, but I'm not sure the players can quite meet this demand.

Striker Mark Jones has a header, which Rovers keeper Andy Warrington pushes on to his post, and with ten minutes to go defender Stephen Roberts lets fly with a 30-yarder, which Warrington tips on to his bar. Neil Williams leaps up out of his seat, Josh too. The 6,115 crowd applaud enthusiastically. Wrexham are chasing the game, but can they score?

4.37 P.M.: THE RUN OF THE BALL – EVERGREEN 2 HADLEY 1
Bobbles. They usually go against you. That's life. Like slices of toast that always descend butter-side down. Not today. Well, not for Evergreen anyway.

Their number 7, Phil Otum, a small black kid with plaited, gelled, bleached hair – the works you readily associate with useful, nippy forwards – has darted across to the left. For once the constant urges to 'switch it' have been heeded. Otum turns inside the area and stabs a weak shot with his left foot. We're right in line. The ball looks to be bobbling wide, then in, then towards the post, before kindly diverting back inwards. There are huge celebrations. Has a crowd of 26 ever made so much noise? Everyone laughs except for Hadley, who having dominated the game, having hit the post and bar and seen several scrambles go begging, can't believe their bad luck.

If you have played the game, you know how Otum feels. He hasn't had the best of games, he hasn't been involved much (how could he – the ball has been at the other end mainly), but he has worked tirelessly all afternoon. He has chased lost causes and bundled his way past bigger players. He looks skywards as he troops back. There is a God. Thank you. Question is, will he stay on Evergreen's side?

4.39 P.M.: TOP OF THE LEAGUE AND HAVING A LAUGH – NORWICH 1 CHELSEA 3 Chelsea bag another soft goal, a free header for Ricardo Carvalho from a corner, with eleven minutes to go. It's game over. The match fizzles out, and now the Chelsea fans can celebrate to their hearts' content. They've survived the snow and rain and drizzle and mist in deepest Norfolk.

Neil and I make our way around to the main stand, past the directors' box and the control room. It has all gone off peaceably. And there are no problems anticipated, just talk of poor marking and a foiled fightback. Same as so many other teams against Chelsea in 2004/05.

4.42 P.M.: 'TINNION, TINNION, GIVE US A WAVE!' The singing Bristol City fans love Brian Tinnion now. They want him to wave to them, and he duly obliges. He is the leader of their barmy army; they are 'walking in a Tinnion wonderland'; they even stretch to a 'We love you Tinnion' to the tune of 'Can't Take My Eyes Off You'. Just believe what I say!

I wouldn't. The average gaffer lasts eighteen months. Fans are fickle, popular ex-player or not. But Brian is relaxed now. He has returned to thrusting one hand inside his trouser pocket, and the game is realistically over. 'I think 95 per cent really want me to be successful and be the manager here,' Brian says later, 'and they get behind me, which is great.' Today is fine, but those singing are mainly in the stand behind the dugout. They are literally behind the manager when he is winning, but he can also hear their cutting remarks when Bristol City are losing. It must be a difficult place to manage. And City supporters have expectations beyond the club's current status.

But today there is only one Brian Tinnion.

4.43 P.M.: HADLEY NICK A POINT – EVERGREEN 2 HADLEY 2

Evergreen's resistance is broken. After going 2–1 up and scoring against the run of play, albeit thanks to the kindest of bobbles, they have been pegged back again. Their goal has led a charmed life, but this time they could have done better. Another cross from the right leading to a tap-in at the back post.

Sadly, another fight ensues. The goalkeeper, looking for someone to 'fackin' slap', punches the scorer, Delroy Balfour, who has scooped the ball out of the net, assuming there is time to chase a winner.

4.44 P.M.: A FULL ESCORT – IPSWICH 0 WEST HAM 2

Ipswich have defended poorly all afternoon, and they pay the price near the end. They have had chances to equalise, but in truth not many, and have been kept at arms' length from West Ham's goal. In the final minute Marlon Harewood runs the ball into the corner to waste some time but notices he isn't being tracked too tightly, so turns inside the two defenders. His shot is cleared off the line, but Matthew Etherington follows up to tap in.

The home crowd stream out leaving the West Ham fans to sing 'I'm Forever Blowing Bubbles' on the far side. When Paul Taylor blows for full time he is given a full escort from the pitch amid lots of boos. Noticeably, all the players shake his hand. There is no animosity on their part.

In the dressing room, both managers pop their heads around the officials' door. There are no complaints. Joe Royle jokes that he is going to find out which New Year's party the players went to last night, while Alan Pardew is understandably all smiles. Tongue in cheek, he suggests a first-half headed goal should have stood, but otherwise everything's fine.

4.45 P.M.: 'BRING ON THE ARSENAL' Stuart Hall delivers his brief full-time verdict. He quickly runs through Wigan's three goals, mentions they might have had many more and suggests that on this form they look likely to be playing in the League Leeds departed last season. 'Bring on the Arsenal,' he adds cheekily.

He has just found out that they want a post-match interview with Wigan manager Paul Jewell, a chore to do after his considered full-time report – which, as anyone who listens to *Sport on Five* regularly knows, is always his best, most literary-accented report. It is not to be missed if you are a fan.

The departing fans drift away and say bye to Stuart. He always responds.

4.46 P.M.: LAST-GASP GOAL – GRETNA 2 ELGIN CITY 1 Gretna score from a free-kick in stoppage time to preserve their 100 per cent home record. Derek Townsley heads home from close range in front of their fans at the end where the gates are, to give Gretna a victory that stretches their lead at the top of the Third Division to six points.

The atmosphere is suddenly fabulous. It has been quiet for much of the afternoon. It gets worse for Elgin, though. Andy Roddie, who scored their goal, is sent off in the dying seconds.

The moment the referee blows his final whistle, Paul Barnett pulls back the barrier in the top corner and drives his roller on to the pitch. Selwyn flattens the divots. The reparations have begun.

4.47 P.M.: WAYNE'S WORLD III – MANCHESTER UNITED 2 PORTSMOUTH 1 A goal at last at Old Trafford. Unsurprisingly, it has come from Wayne Rooney. All United's quality moves have done so this afternoon. This time he has once again belied his youth. Van Nistelrooy received a long ball, held off a defender, twisted and scooped the ball to Rooney, who stole a yard, slipped his defender and waited a split second for the goalkeeper to commit himself before sliding the ball into the net. Perfection made to look easy. Streetwise football inside a packed theatre. Simply marvellous.

Time for wild celebrations, and the 'Once a Blue (Always a Red)' chant. It is a cruel sideswipe at Everton, the club that nurtured Rooney but was forced to sell their prize asset. This outrageously gifted performer will surely grace this particular stage as others have before – Beckham, Cantona, Best, Charlton, Edwards. I hope he proves me right and not Gazza-esquely wrong.

4.48 P.M.: BORE DRAW AT WREXHAM The game at the Racecourse Ground is put out of its misery. A heart-warming day sadly not matched by the quality of football. It is a tense, frustrating, largely disappointing affair. A goalless draw that ultimately satisfies neither team. 'Thank you for coming – have a safe journey home' has rarely been so heartfelt. Neil has to drop in briefly to the supporters trust shop but wants to waste no time getting out. He faces the long 325-mile drive back to Cornwall, and there is no point delaying the trek home.

As we leave the ground I glance back at the Racecourse, this proud old home of Wales's oldest football club. I can't believe it is going to be allowed to be bulldozed to suit one man's pocket. I wonder if I will ever return here again. I sincerely hope so.

4.49 P.M.: A LAST-MINUTE WINNER – WORCESTER CITY 2 STALYBRIDGE CELTIC 1 A penalty at Worcester City! The home side have been pressing, and as so often happens when you're at the wrong end of the table, Stalybridge, who have been game throughout but have come increasingly under the cosh, fail to hold out.

It is easy to be harsh on Stalybridge defender Terry Bowker for making a needless lunging tackle on Worcester striker Leon Kelly near the dead-ball line, but that is what happens when you've got tired legs. It is why statistically more goals will be popping in at this stage of games all over the country than at any other time. It isn't all about the voracity of the scorers digging out a result, it's about tired limbs – in this case Bowker's.

In a moment of last-minute tension, some fans, and Worcester City manager John Barton, can barely watch. Up steps defender Les Hines, who coolly slots the penalty hard and low to the keeper's right. It'll be a good night in the bar. Bob Marley jumps up and punches the air. For him, it's the end of three games today: two defeats, and now, one victory.

There is no ugly atmosphere as the ground empties tonight, no 'caging' for the opposition players to endure. Instead, players and fans punch the sky in unison. That's eight games unbeaten now, and City are into the top six.

Bob's celebrations are sweet and short. He has to count a small pre-Christmas gate, and, aside from all the other post-match duties, he also has the fun run to worry about.

4.49 P.M.: A FLATTENED KEEPER The final whistle goes at Sincil Bank, largely to groans of disappointment. Some people applaud, and in the directors' box there are the obligatory handshakes. Bristol Rovers' directors seem quite pleased with their point.

But disappointment and congratulation soon turn to concern. Seconds before the final whistle, Lincoln goalkeeper Alan Marriott was clattered. As most people troop home and the players shake hands, a couple of Lincoln's defenders urge the medical staff to treat the prostrate keeper. Fans start to notice and are slow to leave the ground; they stand near exits waiting for him to recover before leaving. No one leaves the directors' box, though an insensitive voice from the PA asks everyone to go home.

Rob Bradley explodes. 'Shut up! Let 'em see the lad's all right!'

Eventually, after several minutes, Marriott rises gingerly to his feet and is helped off the pitch. He is loudly applauded. The man on the Tannoy will be in trouble though.

4.50 P.M.: WHISTLES AT WALSALL At the Bescot there is panic. Can Walsall hold on to their 3–2 lead? It is so typical of the game. Ralph had predicted Walsall would score four; they ought to have had more. They are worthy of at least a two-goal win and at times have played the sort of exhilarating, expansive football you don't readily associate with the lower half of League One. Then they turn to pussycats and wobbly jelly. Instead of closing in for the kill they start defending and playing keep-ball, which so often results in chaos. Clubs lose the ball more often than not, and usually further back than if they'd carried on attacking.

As was also predicted, Paul Merson is still going strong. He looks knackered, and he lacks the pace to close down quickly, but then that was the case early on too. He never stops doing his little tricks and one-twos and sublime pieces of skill to allow other, younger legs through.

Blackpool try to exert some pressure but other than hoisting a few balls into Walsall's box they are ineffectual. The ref's final whistle blows to huge cheers and relief. Now to check the other scores and, crucially, the table. As for Ralph Rogers, he needs to know if there are any walking wounded to attend to downstairs.

4.51 P.M.: FULL TIME AT EVERGREEN The remnants of the game aren't pretty. Too many scrappy incidents near the dugout and touchline. Too many arms and legs thrust out, and aggressive shouts. A young Hadley defender is felled by an Evergreen forward. 'You fackin' cheat!' shouts Evergreen's coach. 'Get up!' It is ill-judged and unnecessary. This is the unseemly side to grass-roots football, and it is a problem. This has been a good game. Would it hurt to smile?

Bill turns to me and says the ref should call a halt to proceedings. 'There is nothing to be gained from keeping this going.' Bill should know. He has seen the odd game or thousand, many of them at this level, many of them finishing in the same acrimonious manner. He recalls one finishing early when a player had to be treated on the pitch because he couldn't be moved.

Football is about winning and losing. It isn't more important than part-time amateur players missing time off work because they've been nobbled. So the ref duly does as Bill had suggested. He could easily have added on a minute or two's injury time.

Both teams can take something from the 2–2 draw. Evergreen may have been pegged back twice after leading, but they have held the league leaders who pinned them back for long periods. They have worked prodigiously for their point. Literally scrapping for it at times. Hadley will feel satisfied with their late equaliser, and despite dominating the game they know they won't have to suffer such an awful pitch as this most weeks.

As we trudge back to our car, the players remove the goal nets and pull up corner flags. Despite the ill-tempered affair, they all shake hands and will presumably share a pint in the bar. I drop our empty coffee cups back into the clubhouse (another joy at this level of football: we were trusted to drink from our mugs outside). Bill and I then remove hats, gloves, scarves and coats, and I take down notes of the players while he skilfully reverses his car from the awkward position we've had to park in. Time to go home.

4.52 P.M.: SEAGULLS STALEMATE Not much happened at the Withdean to be honest. Not a bad game in terms of tactics and skill, but nowhere near enough excitement. For Brighton it is now six games without defeat. For Forest, this is too little. They need wins.

Attila had hoped to play Seagulls Ska at the end of a rousing win. It didn't happen, so as everyone troops off Attila reads the full-time scores instead. He is keeping a special eye out for his wife's club, Northwich Victoria, who are struggling near the foot of the Conference. Today they have dug out a much-needed win.

Everyone shuffles off fairly happy. A steward comes rushing over as I leave. 'Just wanted to wish you all the best with your book,' he says. 'I hope it goes well for you.' This is a lovely touch. I am genuinely moved. We had only had the briefest of chats pre-match. But people like that, the footsoldiers of football clubs who man the gates and line the pitch, they are the real heart of football. To him, and the many others who have voiced similar sentiments, my thanks.

4.53 P.M.: DANNY COLES HOOFING AND PUFFING One thing I've noticed about Danny Coles: he loves hoofing the ball into the top of the stand. In fact it's something some Bristol City fans seem to enjoy. Where is Danny going to put this one? But I don't understand it as a time-wasting tactic. Not these days. Not with ballboys armed and ready to throw another one straight into play.

Today, Danny is simply trying to earn a breather. Towards the end of the game he is blowing hard.

4.55 P.M.: THE REV LEAVES HIS PEW John Boyers heads home. He doesn't wait to see his flock leave. He is one of them, and once his duties have been carried out he leaves early to avoid the notorious traffic. It has gone to plan. No terrorist alerts, no heart attacks, no abseiling Fathers for Justice campaigners, no players whisked off to hospital.

John has put in a full day. OK, the past two hours have been a breeze, but he has been on hand. He wisely tries to restrict himself to two and a half days' work a week for the club; the rest belongs to SCORE. Tomorrow he will be back at the club first thing, administering faith, asking those present to remember the life of Roy Unwin. He will later perform the funeral service. It is all part of the job.

But unlike too many characters in this book, who are married to the job and to the club – including myself, I fear – tonight John will dedicate some time to someone else who is dear to his heart. His wife Anne, who understands the commitment of her husband to his job, though not necessarily the excesses of the 'beautiful game'. Tonight will be a quiet night in together.

4.55 P.M.: HARRIERS HANG ON 'We don't do much trade at this time,' says Brian Murdoch. No one is taking their eyes off the pitch near the end of the game, not with Kiddy 2–1 up. There are people in front who are unable to watch as the ball is pumped into Kidderminster's box. If you're not a fan, this is a luxurious experience.

'They'll hang on, they look comfortable,' I say with confidence.

The regulars don't agree. A couple of children look at me as if to say, 'Promise?'

Brian is full of belief too. 'A win would send them into Christmas on a high,' he remarks. I know what he's thinking. Boxing Day, a couple of wins, big crowd. Hang on, Kiddy.

There is late drama as a Rochdale substitute, Leighton McGivern, goes for an aerial challenge and leads with his arm. The referee, Paul Danson, bundles him away from angry Harriers players who race around the crumpled heap on the floor. The referee treads on the miscreant's toe (if that had been the other way around I'd like to have seen what would happen) but he does the wise thing: he doesn't send him off. The Rochdale bench are furious about something, but he has saved the player a possible three-match ban. The final whistle blows and there is joy all around. Fans hug one another; a couple of ladies come over and go 'Whhoooo!' to Brian. It is a much-needed victory, and their first under Stuart Watkiss. Can he make the difference?

4.56 P.M.: BOMBSHELL As the final whistle goes at Carrow Road, Neil Doncaster checks a few more rooms. He takes time to text the manager, Nigel Worthington, to say 'hard luck, well done'. He has probably sent that one too many times this season. But he genuinely means it.

Chelsea's players applaud their fans. There is a matter of routine about this. For them it is job done. For Norwich, this was one of those big days they dreamed of last season when they were striving for the First Division title. A learning curve for sure, but disappointing nonetheless.

We chat about family life, and Neil drops a bombshell: his wife and daughter Grace, who is two and a half, a similar age to my son Nicholas, have left him, together with the two cats and the dog. Too many twelve-hour days.

4.57 P.M.: THE ATMOSPHERE AT ASHTON GATE Bristol City's players leave the pitch to enthusiastic applause. They clap back to their fans. Danny Coles is one of the last off the pitch. He is gulping in air and sucking water from one of those outsized drinks bottles. He looks up to the crowd with a beaming smile. This was the positive imagery he was visualising before the match. The happy scenario of an afternoon's endeavours. It is spine-tingling. It is motivational.

Brian Tinnion gets some special cheers. He, too, is happy, and he waves to his family. Crikey, even I feel like waving to someone. Football has that unique ability to touch people. There are few feelings like the elation after a game. It is more than 'job done', it is the culmination of a good week's work. There is nothing like the despair either – something, again, I am all too familiar with. Part of you dies after a match. And it never returns. Matchday is all-absorbing. I love it, but also fear it slightly. Imagine what it must be like for those involved whose jobs depend on it. Those five o'clock fears …

REACTION TO THE ACTION

5 P.M.: BACK-SLAPPING AT THE BESCOT Walsall's victorious players return to their dressing room muddied but jubilant. 'Yesssss! Yahooo!' Dr Ralph Rogers has his fist clenched. 'Well done, man,' he says. 'Hey, that was great, guys.' There are hand claps and hugs all round. Five wins on the bounce. Progress. They can now look ahead to Christmas.

Club owner Jeff Bonser, unusually for a director, is there to greet them. Coach Mick Halsall gets a couple of youth-team players to bring some beer into the manager's office. There's going to be a party tonight. Ralph is part of that team. By now, how many other club doctors, having fulfilled their legal obligation to attend the match in case of emergency, would be on their way home or in a bar upstairs? Ralph is in the engine room.

Neil Emblen comes into the medical room. He recalls that early high ball he had to head clear. 'I thought, fuck, it's going to be one of those days.' He laughs. The sponsors, who won't have known about the injury or pain he has gone through, have named him man of the match. It is richly deserved. 'I'd better give it to you,' he jokes with Ralph. Doc Rogers has booked him in for a massage on Sunday morning, and to see a chiropractor on Tuesday. 'We'll get it sorted, mate, no problem.' Mark Wright, the defender who was clattered in the first half, also limps in. Ralph examines his leg. 'No damage,' he says. 'But call me tomorrow, yes?'

5 P.M.: 'LOOK AFTER YOURSELVES AND WE'LL LOOK AFTER YOU' The Bristol City dressing room is also buzzing. Everyone is pleased with their win. Brian Tinnion is keen to get his troops sat down and to address them straight away. 'Well done. It was a good, disciplined performance,' he tells them. Turning to Danny Coles and his fellow defenders, Jamie Smith, Louis Carey and Mickey Bell, he says, 'We gave them nothing. Brilliant. Terrific focus, effort and concentration.' He has praise for his midfielders too: 'Awesome effort.' Tommy Doherty has run himself to a standstill. He sits motionless, red-faced, breathing hard. As at half-time, his hands are clasped tightly together. He has given his all. Tinnion is also delighted with his forwards: 'Excellent – you took the game to them.'

Assistant manager Keith Millen urges them all to take ice baths, a modern sports medicine theory – the shock of the cold stimulates the skin. They will need to stretch out and have massages too.

Tinnion immediately rams home the importance of the next game – here, on Tuesday, against fellow play-off chasers Bournemouth. 'It's been a hard day,' he concludes. 'Go home. Do nothing. No going out tonight. No drinking. I want you all in fresh and bright tomorrow morning. Ten o'clock. Give yourselves the best chance you can to recover and be fit for Tuesday. You know the rules: look after yourselves and we'll look after you.'

5 P.M.: THE NAKED REFEREE Paul Taylor is pumped up. He is pleased with the way the game has gone for the officials and is standing in the dressing room, disconcertingly naked, running through the finer points of the game. Only Trevor looks weary. It is his last season running the line. He wants a clean break from the game. He doesn't want to be an assessor. He has problems with the system.

A 'bad day at the office for Ipswich' is Taylor's summary as they tuck into a tray of food laid on for them: sandwiches, Pringles, breadsticks, sausages, crudités. Paul hasn't eaten since eight a.m. and is starving. 'Joe Royle has seen it all before,' he continues. 'They'll bounce back.' (And they did, winning 2–1 at Plymouth two days later. West Ham were booed off after losing at home to Sheffield United.)

With amazing frankness and tradition, the officials are paid straight after the game by the home club. There is something refreshing about this. In recreational football it is exactly the same, although I could imagine the look on their faces if a huge envelope arrived.

Taylor jokes about Kuqi losing it. 'He's a big fella, and I thought if he is throwing punches he can get on with it.' I mention the heated Ipswich fans calling him a cheat and getting increasingly irate during the second half. 'Didn't notice,' says Paul. 'I block it all out. I don't count how many fouls I've given or how many in a row to which side I've awarded. I just get on with making decisions. If they want to shout, that is up to them. Nothing I can do about it.'

There is only one downside: the fourth official, Steve Artis, will ask Paul to put in a complaint about West Ham's assistant manager, Peter Grant, who was continually wandering outside his technical area to confront him.

They go for their showers and spray on their smellies. The only part of the referee's day I won't be allowed to see is the post-match assessor's discussion with the officials.

5 P.M.: THE DISTANT ECHO OF FARAWAY VOICES Back in Carlisle, we've been rescued by boat, taken to a community centre, given blankets to warm us, and soup as sustenance (not as good as Brian Murdoch's, but beggars and all that …). Having waded through water our feet are wet and our socks, shoes and the lower parts of our trousers are sodden. Dave has had his updates: Everton and Albion have both won 'comfortably', according to his mate. Defeats would have rubbed the salt in indeed.

There is no power in most of the city, so no other hotels are open. There is no means of public transport in or out of the area either. We are stuck. I am pondering the misery of my predicament while sitting in what is effectively a refugee centre with hundreds of evacuees from the flood when, as if by magic, a faint, familiar sound cuts through the hubbub. It's the Central Band of the RAF playing 'Out of the Blue'. I glance at my watch. It's five o'clock, and I can hear the start of *Sports Report*. Only I can't really hear it, and to be honest I don't have the nerve to wander over to where it's coming from and listen to the scores. It is comforting enough to know that being in Britain at five o'clock on a Saturday evening, regardless of whatever situation you find yourself in, means *Sports Report*.

5.01 P.M.: JAG Back in west London at Television Centre Mark Saggers, as Five Live's anchormen presenters do on any other Saturday, runs through the day's headlines. He then utters those immortal words: 'Here are the classified football results read by James Alexander Gordon.'

Today, James begins, 'The Littlewoods FA Cup …'

You would never guess from the calm authority of his voice the panic that is enveloping James Alexander Gordon as he starts his long march through the day's results. In that small workshop at the end of the Five Live office, Audrey Adams is racing around trying to handwrite the scores as they come in, sometimes even over James's shoulder on the sheet in front of him. It used only to be late kick-offs that finished around this time, but now most games seem to end closer to five o'clock than a quarter to. In the days before needlessly long half-time breaks only unusual incidents like a keeper being kicked hard in the knackers led to games ending after ten to.

As James does his stuff and Aud busies around him, my mind drifts to the millions of punters with their grubby pencils poised over pools coupons. And to fans in cars, or with ears pressed to transistors, or wearing Walkmans on public transport on their way home from games. And to a photographer sitting in a boat on Coniston Water. And back to an errant journalist stuck in a community hall having been rescued from a flood. Oh, the significance and comfort of those classified results.

For 33 years James Alexander Gordon has embodied Saturday teatime. His voice sends shivers down my spine. When he read the results in his inimitable style for the first time back in 1972, former *Sports Report* presenter Peter Jones told him, in his dulcet Welsh tones, 'Good luck, old chap, sock 'em between the bloody eyes with it.' The BBC bigwigs hated his style. 'It shocked them,' James recalls. 'They thought, "Here comes this guttersnipe who has only been here five minutes and he's reading the football scores the way he likes."' But the public loved it. JAG's way of lowering or heightening his voice for an oncoming scoreline is unique. No other results reader comes close to the tension JAG creates. 'I didn't want to throw any lines away. If they lose, you feel sorry for them: Watford nil [he lowers the pitch] Spurs two [he lifts it up]. You're happy for them.' His underlying ethos, fortified by his mentor at the BBC's continuity announcers department, Jimmy Kingsbury, is that he tells the news or scores rather than reads them.

His pronunciation has nothing to do with most modern sports reporting. His voice smacks of home counties stability, middle-class affluence, public-school stuffiness; he's a sort of sporting Lord Haw-Haw. 'What, really?' he asks. 'Do you really think so? That's a bit like Leslie

Phillips saying, "Oh, hellooo!"' It sounds too simplistic to say he is none of the perceived stereotypes, that he is from solid Scottish working-class stock and can reel off the thickest of Glaswegian accents. But it's true. JAG reckons you can detect his Scottish accent most when he pronounces place-names like East Stirlingshire.

He's a perfectionist. Before reading the shipping forecast on Radio 4 he made the effort to find out what each of the phrases actually meant. 'You owe it to the public to get it right.' Same with football. Not just the tone, but the place-names. 'People have emailed from Wales saying, "You're obviously Welsh, or have relatives there – you got our names right." No, I just want to get it right.'

He gets fan-mail from around the world. That's the power of the World Service. You don't have to be in a grim northern town to appreciate those scores, you can hear JAG outside a bar in Zanzibar or halfway up a Himalayan mountain. That is how far the BBC stretches. That is how far our sporting culture travels.

5.05 P.M.: THE GAFFER GATHERS HIS THOUGHTS The post-match press conference is one of the hardest things a football manager does. He is expected to comment at a time of high emotion, straight after a game, when it's easy to shoot from the lip or from the heart. Small wonder so many say things that get them into hot water. Media training – how to respond to questions – might help. So might a few deep breaths.

In his first season in management, Brian Tinnion has developed a simple, sane approach. He goes back to his office and gathers his thoughts. He checks out the scores on Ceefax and Sky Sports to assess the situation. Today's results have, overall, gone City's way. They are up two places to eighth, and have a game in hand over most (until Tuesday). 'I'm just taking a few minutes to think about what I am going to say to make sure I say the things I want to get across and not say anything silly in the heat of the moment,' confirms Tinnion, who, like most managers, early in the season simply sought to get the post-match interviews out of the way. Most feel under pressure to comment immediately. Tinnion says the press can wait a few moments. 'I prefer to be in the right frame of mind. I never go straight from the dressing room to the press area, I always go for a sit down. Then I feel more comfortable.' This is such a simple technique it makes you wonder why so many managers fall for all the same tricks and end up with the same old fines.

Thoughts gathered, Tinnion marches purposefully into the gym which doubles as a press room. On the way he tells me, 'If players see you agitated they don't feel comfortable, so I like to portray an image of calm. There have been times this season when I've had to have a blast, but I try to get my message across in a calm way. Once you start yelling they don't take on board what you are saying.'

5.08 P.M.: ROLLING ALONG Paul Barnett is slowly moving his roller back and forth along the length of Gretna's pitch, flattening it down and levelling out any grooves that might ice over during a cold night and develop into impenetrable ruts that could threaten Monday night's reserve game. 'I like to have the pitch cleaned up,' he says. 'It gets rid of dead grass and bacteria.' He'll be here until 6.30 and will have to return tomorrow to make sure his precious pitch is OK for Monday. There is no rest or peace for the groundsman.

5.10 P.M.: STUART HALL'S POST-MATCH REPORT When my friend Tim and I ran the West Brom supporters coach in the late 1970s *Sports Report* was a must-listen. As fans filed on to the coach, as we exchanged stories and opinions on the game we'd seen, only one voice commanded silence – Stuart Hall's. From the moment the *Sports Report* anchorman said 'Here's Stuart Hall', a coach made up mainly of testosterone-fuelled teenagers fell silent. Those classic Hall-marks – the flow of his narration, the wit, the word-paintings he crafted, the enthusiasm, the deliberately overplayed emphasis of particularly unusual phrases, the liberal sprinkling of literary references (like we ever got any of them!) – would leave us giggling.

'He just seemed to have a knack of picking up small things and making the most of them,' recalls Tim. 'He made us laugh. Most sports reporters can't do that. They are too serious. It was a united thing. We could all laugh along together. I miss that.'

Of course we listen in the car on the way home now, but it's different. The kids think Stuart is a bit mad; they don't know his TV work. We laugh in the front, but you really need a group to appreciate him at his best.

Having listened so often, here I now am, sitting next to the man as he is about to deliver his considered report. The *Grandstand* reporter to my left is feeling pretty smug at his final report, which praised Wonderful Wigan. Hall puts us all in awe.

'Welcome to the pie centre of the world – a feast of football served – a sumptuous filling – Duke Ellington's opener on eleven, a neat finish from a pass spoon-fed to him by masterchef, the rumbustious Roberts …' The Leeds defence are likened to helpless Ikea gatekeepers (one of the Swedish furniture stores had opened to pandemonium in London earlier in the week). But the best is saved until last: 'a rrrrrasping drive from Mahon – promotion beckons – joy, oh joy at the JJB. Wigan 3 Leeds 0.' We all laugh. 'Incredible,' says the reporter from the Asian Network, shaking his head in disbelief. Stuart chortles, a twinkle in his eye. He talks to someone down the ISDN line. They like it too.

Now he'll have to persuade Paul Jewell to come up for an interview. The stadium is empty. It is bitterly cold. But Stuart Hall is still going. One day he will leave the stage. It won't be the same when he does.

5.12 P.M.: TILL TIME AND A TAKEAWAY As the fans file out of Aggborough, Brian Murdoch tells me about his plans to do takeaways. I am bemused. Why? How?

'Simple. You take orders throughout the game, the fans give their seat numbers, and we deliver it to them, or they can collect it if they are standing. We serve it in a foil tray and a plastic bag like you get from a Chinese or Indian takeaway.' Yes, but will they be hungry after scoffing something during the game? 'It might be two or three hours since they've eaten. They have a long journey home so they can eat in the car or on the coach. Or pop it in the boot and eat it later.' At the moment the idea is on the back burner.

Brian's pressing priority now is counting the cash and cleaning up. Some of it he will leave until tomorrow, but he must take back the huge metal trays that carried the cottage pies, and the soup vats. The folk from the other kiosks drift over – Helen, from under the East Stand, and David and his team over by the away fans. Darren, who has been on his own serving at the apex of the main stand and the other corner of the away end, has a huge smile on his face. 'One fan had eight cups of soup,' he announces with a laugh. *Eight.* We let it sink in. It is a lot. 'And he's taken another three home with him. With his mates, they've had the best part of twenty cups between them.' I'm waiting for the punchline. There isn't one. Everyone is ashen faced.

Steve shows me the two pies they've got left and, if scraped together, just enough pork for one sandwich. They are both veggie pies. Can I? Would you mind? 'Be my guest,' says Brian. 'Have it with the missus for supper.' We do. They are excellent.

Brian stays for another hour or so, clearing away, on his own, doing his bit, long after the managers have done their post-match interviews and the laptop-tapping reporters have departed. Yes, he does it for himself – it pays, otherwise he wouldn't do it – but he also does it for Kidderminster Harriers. I ask why. 'It's the appreciation of the customers. These people are friends.' As he said earlier, 'It's personal.'

As we leave, I ask Brian what he'll be having for his tea tonight. 'A sandwich. I like cooking but I never eat my own food.'

5.15 P.M.: SOME MANAGERS' PRESS CONFERENCES

JOSE MOURINHO In the Premier League, post-match press conferences are big events. This isn't Brian Tinnion having a word with a few local scribes and the club website, it's several rows of chairs with microphones and everything.

At Carrow Road, Jose Mourinho comes in first, wearing what has become his trademark grey coat. He is down-to-earth and chooses his words carefully. There are dozens of journalists here. Very few ask questions; most that are posed are banal. A Russian journalist is obsessed by the minutiae of injuries and the percentage chances of players making the forthcoming Champions League clash against Barcelona. Mourinho is asked whether the title is now won, and if he can foresee a situation where Chelsea fail to win the title. These are weasel questions, designed to encourage the Chelsea manager to beat his chest and give ridiculous answers. They can then be pulled apart and portrayed as boastful. Mourinho politely points out that if they draw against West Bromwich (you have to be foreign or very posh to call the Albion West Bromwich) in their game in hand they will go nine points clear – eleven if, as seems likely, they win. 'That is a strong position to be in.' He is further egged on to predict when the title will be won. He blows hard. 'You call me arrogant if I make predictions.' He smiles. He doesn't care when, but would prefer a home game for the fans' sake.

It is obvious stuff, but the journalists continue to fish for more. You can sense his frustration. Mourinho is magnanimous to Norwich who, he acknowledges, deserved their goal. He was pleased, he says, with Chelsea's 'intensity', their response to being pegged back and their technical skills on a cold day.

The press conference is called to a halt by Chelsea's head of communications, Simon Greenberg. A small group follow Mourinho for a few more select words. I look at Neil Doncaster. It hasn't exactly been illuminating. I wonder if continental press conferences are equally bland.

BRIAN TINNION Bristol City hold their press conferences in the gym. This is one step up from the tunnel and various other places where I have interviewed managers and players after games. There is a time-honoured routine: TV usually go first, then radio, then the print media. In reality, everyone crowds around the TV or radio interview and scribbles away.

Tinnion is calm, collected and efficient. He refuses to get carried away with the win but is delighted with the manner in which it was achieved. All thoughts are now on Tuesday's big game against Bournemouth. In each interview he reiterates the same message: he is pleased but also 'relieved' that the players will all be in in the morning. They will start preparing for Tuesday's game with a gym session, a swim and a little loosener to get them all together.

He describes the Phillips save midway through the second half as a deciding factor. If that had gone in it would have been 1–1 and all to play for. 'I thought it was a disciplined performance,' he adds.

NIGEL WORTHINGTON Back at Carrow Road, Norwich's manager Nigel Worthington walks into the press room. He seems less comfortable with the collective attention, although only a quarter of the press corps attend and some tap away on their laptops, backs to him. Slightly nervy and constantly sipping a glass of water, Worthington says he is pleased with his players' effort and their overall performance. The noticeably more local journalists ask plainer questions. Who can live with Chelsea? 'Arsenal, Man Utd maybe, not most of us.' Key moments? 'Bringing Gudjohnsen and Kezman on. I looked over and thought, "Oh Christ."' He smiles. When asked for his views on Mourinho, Worthington is straightforward. 'He is honest, confident and has blended a team together. Not always easy when you have a group of talented individuals.' He describes Chelsea as focused – an overworked phrase in football, but true on this occasion – and insists that Norwich are still smiling despite their defeat.

5.20 P.M.: CHILLI TIMES I like hot food. I'll eat anything hot, but this is ridiculous. I'm standing in the Lincoln City boardroom and they are doling out chilli and rice in the corner. I let the others go first. Like Rob Bradley, I am keeping a keen eye on the scores coming through on the TV.

'I'm just calming down,' Rob says. Lots of things seem to irritate him. He'd make a good grumpy old man – but he'll have to get in the queue behind me and Tim.

He is asked for a response to fans phoning the local radio station to complain about being asked to leave the ground when the goalkeeper was on the floor. 'Tell them we'll issue a an apology,' says Rob.

I saunter over to taste the chilli. People giggle. They've all had some. I dig in with a big fork. The room falls silent. Well, to me at least. It's a bit like being underwater: things are happening but you can't hear anything. Jeez. I reach for my drink. Then, in the insanity that can only apply to men and curry, I decide that by hook or by crook I will finish this hot-as-hell plate of chilli. I fail. Not by much, but by enough. Rob is chatting to the Bristol Rovers directors, and various other people. 'Jesus Christ,' he says, gulping a mouthful. I had warned him.

He does a lot of thanking. In fact, not being someone who has spent a lot of time in boardrooms, I didn't realise how much thanking goes on. Everyone from sponsors and corporate diners to opposition club directors, executive members and people from the supporters club and supporters trust. Lincoln's manager Keith Alexander pops in for a drink. They share the disappointment – not a bad performance, but not good enough. Something is just lacking at the moment.

5.25 P.M.: POST-MATCH RAIN Remember where the park-and-ride driver told me I could get a bus back to my car? 'Here.' He was either lying or confused. Instead, I have to trudge some distance away, which is fair enough, but it is raining hard and getting worse.

When I eventually find the place I realise the full horrors of this temporary situation. The queue is 100 yards long. Stewards try to marshal the bedraggled line as best they can, and try to sift out anyone who has inadvertently joined the wrong queue (there is another park and ride from the town centre), but this does not ease the misery of being drenched. A couple of Nottingham Forest fans who arguably should have known better – the Withdean is, after all, renowned as a largely uncovered ground – are only wearing replica shirts and are getting a dreadful soaking. Water is seeping into all sorts of places. My usually impenetrable bag is letting in water which might damage my recorder. I want to be dry.

Brighton try their best to make this work – by using park and rides, by adhering to their neighbours' wishes, by keeping the political pressure on for their proposed move to Falmer – but nothing stresses the need more than being stuck in a queue for a bus in the rain. There is little romance in this, no throwback to the good old days of public transport when fans would queue and buses duly arrive.

I can't help thinking about the man who will ultimately have to make the decision about Brighton's move to Falmer. The deputy PM, John Prescott, he of 'two jags' fame. One for himself, another for the wife. Both used, allegedly, in this very town during a Labour party press conference to whisk them, separately, a couple of hundred yards down the road on a fine autumn afternoon. I can't ignore the irony of this, of the urgency that would be called for if Prescott was left to soak. You begin to understand how Brighton & Hove Albion fans must feel, out in the cold, unable to go a single step forward, as if everything is against them – the way you feel when you are waiting for a bus and it's pissing down. You just want to go home.

5.30 P.M.: A BEER IN THE MANAGER'S OFFICE We're standing around the TV in Paul Merson's small office at Walsall. The Saddlers have moved up five places to tenth – the first time they have been in the top half of the table all season. Perhaps more importantly, they are just five points off the play-off places. Just a month earlier they had been dumped out of the FA Cup by non-Leaguers Slough Town, and the talk had been of Merson's imminent departure. Walsall held their nerve, and the future on this midwinter's evening looks bright.

I chat to coach Frank Barlow about Merson's on-field contribution, how he conducts Walsall's play. 'You've been watching from the stands,' says Frank. 'Down at pitch level it's just a sea of arms and legs. He makes it look simple. He's a genius.'

Colin Hendry joins us. He is full of praise for Walsall but so disappointed with his players. They are just lacking focus. He has a moan about a referee from a game a few weeks earlier. 'Do you know you've just ruined everything we've worked for all week?' he apparently told him.

'Wonder what Jimmy Walker was doing here,' says Ralph Rogers as we leave. A move back from West Ham possibly? They would love that here. Walsall have been fielding an on-loan goalkeeper, Joe Murphy, from West Brom. Walker was popular.

5.30 P.M.: GOING HOME, CHILLING OUT Danny Coles wants to go home. He has had his ice bath and shower, and surprisingly, given that sportsmen like to retain body heat after endurance events, is just wearing a club polo shirt, tracksuit bottoms and trainers. 'I feel very tired to be honest,' he says. 'The heat took it out of me. There wasn't a lot of air out there today.' This is the fickle British weather throwing its spanner in the works. It has been cold during the week, then suddenly it warms up on matchday.

Danny feels the game went well. 'I was delighted with the result,' he says. His confrontation with his old mate Lee Matthews was 'good experience. I clipped him a couple of times – nothing heavy, but he did react. It was just frustration because nothing was going right for him.' I suggest that even the gaffer, Brian Tinnion, is happy. 'We gave a good performance, but the staff gave us the right information to win the game. That has to be good, and it was today.'

Danny starts to sniff a lot. 'I just want to get home, get my feet up and do nothing really, but it is so much nicer going home on the back of a win.

If we had lost 2–0 you'd want to have a drink, whereas we know it was a good win and I can chill out and enjoy it.'

His working day is over. His only requirement is to go home, relax, have something sensible to eat and go to bed early so that he is refreshed in the morning. Tonight, he'll have a Chinese takeaway, 'chill out' watching TV and chat to a couple of mates on his mobile phone until the adrenalin of the match leaves his body and he can sleep. Alas, this won't be until around midnight.

Of all the people involved in matchday, the players seem to have it relatively easy. They certainly have the shortest day compared to those who make it all happen. They are also likely to earn the most. Yet they are also the people who can influence things the most. It is their ability that shapes the future of clubs. They have to shoulder that responsibility and sometimes the blame. Danny, like all players, has lots of time to ponder that. Too much time, arguably. It is small wonder some players fill it with bad habits and go off the rails.

5.35 P.M.: GLUM FACES AT AFAN LIDO The Afan Lido bar is busy. Phil Robinson is snowed under, and one of the beer taps has decided to throw a wobbly. But there is also despondency. Those who peer at the television can see the full horror: Lido are one place above the relegation zone. They have two games in hand, but if they lose them they are right in the thick of it.

Phil looks disappointed. He has a furrowed brow. When you care as much as he does, it's hard not to take it to heart. 'Should have won today,' he observes. 'Missed chances when we were on top, you see. Then we let in a silly goal. Story of our season.'

So many other teams will tell similar tales. It is why some do well and others struggle, why some survive and others go down. Afan Lido have it all to do.

5.40 P.M.: THE AFTERMATH AT ST GEORGE'S LANE The scores come in at Worcester City as directors start munching their post-match meal of curry and rice. Bob Marley, though, is still busy – this time making sure the student who is videoing their games is happy with things. He also checks with the supporters trust committee to make sure they've got enough stewards to help marshal the fun run in the morning, and he ropes me in for duty. It is a headache, and Bob rarely relaxes. But he has that knack – you want to help him.

5.40 P.M.: HEADING HOME TO CORNWALL It is often hard to be positive after a disappointing result. Wrexham didn't lose, but a 0–0 draw is little use to them at the moment. Neil Williams has to ponder this on the long drive home to Cornwall. 'The ten-point deduction is a real killer,' he says. Without it they would be clear of the relegation zone.

We recall happier times at the Racecourse, like arguably the most remarkable victory in Wrexham's history, a 2–1 win over Arsenal in 1991, who won the championship that year. Wrexham finished 92nd in the Football League, bottom of the old Fourth Division, but luckily for them the team that won the Conference couldn't go up so they survived. Mickey Thomas, who had played for Manchester United and a host of other clubs, struck a glorious free-kick to equalise for Wrexham, and five minutes from time Steve Watkin scored the winner. 'It was fantastic – what football is all about,' says Neil. 'It summed up what being a lower league supporter can be like.'

When Neil wants to cheer himself up he puts on the video of the game. He has been watching it a lot lately. I have a few West Brom videos, mainly from the Ron Atkinson era, but I find watching Cyrille Regis, Laurie Cunningham, Bryan Robson and the rest a bit depressing. It's not them – they didn't actually win anything, but they came close, they played some fantastic football, and our merry band of teenage mates on the coach from Worcester were there every step of the way with them. It's just that, well, I don't like harking back because it reminds me of how poor, by comparison, the present is. And that just leaves me feeling sad. But then not as sad as being the supporter of a club in crisis.

Time for an awkward question for Neil. 'What would you do if the worst happened, if the club actually went under?'

'I wouldn't know what to do,' says Neil, pausing for thought. 'Maybe I would support one of the clubs who have helped us, like Brighton – their fans have been brilliant. I wouldn't feel comfortable supporting a bigger club. It wouldn't be as personal; you wouldn't feel like you belong. Wrexham is the only club I want to support, but it is being taken away from me.' This is a big issue to ponder during long journeys home on nights like these.

5.45 P.M.: TINNION ENTERS THE BOARDROOM There are lots of time-honoured traditions football people are supposed to observe on matchdays. Brian Tinnion has had a drink with his opposite number, Martin Foyle. Now there is another ritual – having a drink in the boardroom.

Tinnion admits this can be difficult. For starters, how it goes depends on the result. 'It can be an intimidating place if you've lost and they aren't too happy with you and the team,' he says. 'You can tell by the atmosphere that they aren't enthralled with the afternoon's work, but you've got to be strong enough to handle that.' Then some of the directors or their colleagues may have had a drink, and they may talk a little too freely at a time when the manager least wants to hear this sort of thing.

'There are invited guests and sponsors who put in valuable money, but sometimes they are not judicious with their comments,' says Brian, picking his own words carefully. Glad-handing is a necessary part of the job. 'They want success, and if they've put a lot of money in they are disappointed. You've got to expect that. The fact is they've got more money than you, and at the end of the day if they're putting money up, they expect results. You have to stand up and take the criticism if they feel it is necessary to give it. My chairman is very supportive – he has been 100 per cent behind me and always tries to pick out the bright parts of performances even when we haven't played well. He understands the job and the financial restrictions, and he appreciates the hard work I am doing.'

In reality, Brian is just like most guys. He wants to meet up with his family and go home. Later, they will go out for a bite to eat.

5.45 P.M.: ALL DARIO GRADI'S FAULT I haven't included all the post-match press conferences in this book, but at the JJB, basically, Paul Jewell, Wigan's manager, was delighted while Leeds boss Kevin Blackwell was magnanimous but disappointed.

I leave via the main entrance, where another cluster of Leeds fans is hovering, though slightly thinned out. Unperturbed by what they have seen – even twelve months ago the result would have been highly unlikely and big news – some are still milling around for autographs.

I walk past a familiar face but can't place the name. I hear a voice as I walk through the glass doors. 'Seth's signing.' Ah, Seth Johnson, a midfielder Leeds splashed out £7 million for in their 'living the dream' days. Johnson's career began at Crewe, one of several players who, under the careful tutelage of Dario Gradi, progressed to Premier League football – in Johnson's case to Derby for £3 million before joining Leeds in October 2001. These now seem unfeasibly large sums for a player languishing on the bench in a mid-table Championship side. At 26, he ought to be at the peak of his career.

The person excitedly proclaiming Seth's availability for autographs is at least 50, probably older. It still seems something of a shame for people of that age to be spending winter evenings scurrying around outside what, in old-money terms, are Second Division football grounds trying to obtain the signatures of footballers. But if that turns you on, so be it.

I strike up a conversation with a Leeds fan on my way back to the car. 'I bet Seth Johnson never thought he'd be playing in the Championship at this stage of his career,' I venture with a smile. The reply is a tirade against Dario Gradi, whose reputation for polishing rough diamonds and selling them on is apparently ill-deserved because he cons everyone by selling crap players on to innocent clubs like Leeds (even though Johnson came via Derby, but don't let that worry you, mate). That's why Leeds are in the position they're in, 'because of fucking wankers like that'. It is hard to bite your tongue, because what Gradi has achieved is unparalleled by any other small club. A man who has carefully nurtured players, developed them, kept or sold them on, and ploughed the money back into youth development. But now I know the truth. He is part of the great Leeds conspiracy. The age of this embittered fan? Oh, you don't want to know …

5.50 P.M.: (GROUND) HOPPING HOME Two minutes after leaving Evergreen's ground we are back on the A41 heading for Broadway. 'Should be back for half-six,' says Bill, who has guests for dinner and is so much more relaxed now that his football thirst has been quenched. Another ground ticked. Another programme for the collection.

I imagine the thousands flocking home elsewhere, the traffic outside the grounds, the numbing, soggy toes. But we're warm and on our way home, through the Cotswolds, through another slice of English life. And no less earthy an experience than at the Hawthorns or elsewhere. Come Monday, Bill will plan next week's journey. Somewhere within two hours of home, which from Broadway leaves plenty of options. Ann will do whatever she wants, as usual.

We talk about the psychology of being a supporter. We're so often told it's all about being a one-eyed fan, about wearing the shirt and following one club for your entire life, about passing it on to your kids, being diehard. But what exactly is wrong with variety, I wonder? 'It is equally valid,' says Bill. 'But they don't seem to get it.'

6 P.M.: ABUSING THE REF It is more than an hour after the final whistle. Paul Taylor left me in the friends and family lounge at Portman Road while the officials had their confidential meeting with the assessor.

When Paul appears, he says a brief goodbye to everyone and we leave. Referees, unlike just about everyone else in the football business, do not stay behind after games. Fraternisation isn't encouraged. It isn't a good idea because it could lead to allegations. 'Most of the time we aren't invited anyway,' says Paul.

It has been a long day, and Paul wants to get home to his family. As he lugs his gear into the boot of his car a fan shouts at him. 'Oi ,Taylor, you were shocking today.' Paul says nothing. The fan wants him to react, but he doesn't. I wonder what might have happened if there hadn't been two of us. This is more than an hour after the game has finished. The fan has either waited for him or it is coincidence – which, given the area we are in, seems unlikely. 'I've got a choice,' says Paul, getting into the car. 'I can either engage in conversation, I can come back with a witty rebuke, perhaps levelled at how his team has performed, or I can just ignore it. That is what I did. There is no point getting worked up about it.' He has to wear his referee's tie and blazer. 'They know where our cars are. Usually it's in a secure compound, so we're OK.' Paul whips off his tie and blazer as soon as possible. 'We could be any couple of people on our way home now,' he says, joining the slowly chugging queue leaving Portman Road. 'Best to disappear into the night to avoid confrontation.'

I ponder this deeply tragic statement. Match officials have to vanish into the ether. It is a matter of routine that they cannot stop on their way to or from games; that they aren't welcomed to stay behind for a drink afterwards; that they can't stay in the same hotel or even, as Paul suggests, the same town or city as the away team. They have to travel incognito and can't always walk safely to their cars after games. Other than that it's OK.

AT THE END OF THE DAY

6.01 P.M.: A STRANGE PASSION It is time for Rob Bradley to go home. He chats to a couple of supporters trust folk before he leaves Sincil Bank. He is their representative on the board and is on the trust committee, so he is honour-bound to reflect their views.

His working day as a football club chairman is over. Yet, as we trudge back to his car parked down a side street, he tells me Lincoln City never quite leaves him. His passion to do right by this club causes him sleepless nights. He lives with one of his sons since splitting up from his wife, Polly, a few months earlier. She understands his interest in Lincoln City – she comes to the games herself sometimes, though she isn't here today – but football can take its toll. 'It takes you over. You might do a couple of hours in a day or spend all day on it but you are always thinking about it. It is a passion. When your head is spinning morning, noon and night, you can't contribute much as a husband.'

We drive up through the city centre and around Lincoln Cathedral, which is partially lit and surrounded by mist, and looks magical – a true emblem of the 'throbbing metropolis' Rob Bradley saw as a boy when he first went to matches with his red-and-white scarf tied tightly around his neck, carrying his metal milking stool to stand on. He loves this beautiful city and its football club, but I wonder if it is to a fault?

'I'm separated from my wife because it has changed me as a person,' Rob says. 'I can't do the couples thing any more – looking around shops and things like that. The kids have grown up and left home. I have been an absolutely useless partner, not even wanting to go on holidays, and we have drifted apart.'

He hasn't seemed to have derived much pleasure from the game today. He has moaned throughout, but then I do frequently too. Tim's reaction to West Bromwich Albion winning a play-off final at Wembley in 1993 was 'Thank God that is over.' Relief rather than joy. Football is a strange passion.

Rob has spent many, many hours with some of the people we have seen today. They are his football family. 'You end up spending as much time with them as your own family, don't you? Football binds you together. The first thing you speak about when you see people is football.' He pauses to consider this unique social context. 'Football is totally and utterly pointless if it is just 22 blokes kicking a ball about. The whole point about football is what happens on the sides around that football pitch. It is a fantastic community thing. It can bond a whole city together. When you get to Cardiff for a play-off final, even if you get hammered 5–2 there are 30,000 people on the streets waving at you on the bus. What could be better for Lincoln the city, let alone Lincoln City?'

No one makes Rob Bradley do what he does for Lincoln City. There is an air of the reluctant hero about him: he came to the club's rescue during their hour of need and has helped to steer them away from relegation and administration to safety. Indeed, they are now a thriving community football club. Rob Bradley hasn't been the only person involved, but he has played a significant part. But as I drive home across the Midlands I still can't help wondering whether he has paid too high a price. On the other hand, where would Lincoln City and clubs like them be without the likes of Rob Bradley? Dead.

6.10 P.M.: AN HOUR OF NEED Back in Carlisle, there is no doubt about it – I'm stuck. No accommodation, no means of making my own way home; there is no public transport in or out of Carlisle, and the petrol stations have been commandeered for use by the essential services. My only option is to persuade someone to come and get me out of this Godforsaken place. But who? Teresa is at her mum's; our son, Nicholas, will be upset if she leaves. Tim could come, but not until his wife returns the car after eight o'clock, so given that I reckon it will take four hours to reach Carlisle, that means after midnight.

Then Bob Marley, the Worcester City director, calls. 'Anything I can do to help?'

'Er, well, Bob . . . it's a big ask, but I don't suppose . . .'

It is Bob's son's birthday party, but yes, he'll come when that breaks up at 6.30. 'I'll be straight up.'

'But hold on, Bob, it's Carlisle – 250 miles. Are you sure? You don't even know where I am.'

'I'll call when I'm close.' And then he was gone.

6.20 P.M.: THE 'NECESSARY EVIL' ON HIS WAY HOME Aside from the attentions of a lone nutter, Paul Taylor is pleased with the way things have gone today. 'The players were very responsive,' he says. 'We were all talking to each other. There wasn't much silliness out there, very little dissent. Decisions were accepted so it was a good game to be involved in. We haven't affected the result. I can't imagine too many people are going home talking about the officials, and when I read the reports in the papers tomorrow I can't imagine we will be mentioned at all. Job done.'

Unlike the players, whose performances will only ultimately be judged by their managers, Paul's decision-making has been officially analysed. 'The match assessor reports privately on my performance, but I think we are often our biggest critics and are the best assessors because I can come home from a game thinking "That went particularly well", or I'll want to have a look at incidents on the video and think, "Why did I do that?" But if nobody notices me I've had a good game.' Referees are often accused of being attention-seekers, and there have certainly been some down the years who have courted publicity in a way that is probably unhealthy for the overall image of the profession. What they are rarely credited with is self-analysis.

Today, although he may have blanked it out, Paul Taylor has been the target of sustained abuse. 'You don't know what you're doing!' 'One-nil to the referee!' 'Who's the bastard in the black?' Even in the gentile area where I sat he was called a fascist and likened to Hitler. OK, these might be generalisations, and if football is theatre then referees are only pantomime hate-figures. At best Paul admits they are viewed as 'a necessary evil'. 'You get a series of fouls which go one way and their team are under-performing and are getting beat, and I become an easy scapegoat,' says Paul, who is sneezing and constantly blowing his nose.

Expecting football fans not to moan at referees is like asking them not to gulp air – it is the reason some people go to football. I have seen fans who don't holler a single word of encouragement to their team but moan incessantly at referees. That's football. Paul doesn't have a problem with this: they've paid their money, they're entitled to their opinions. Some of the banter can be quite funny as well. But, as we drive home in the dark, it seems to me there are so many quantifiable differences between referees, who are so universally hated, and players, who are so widely adored. The players will not be officially reprimanded if their performances are not good enough. They are not subject to that sort of detailed scrutiny. The boss might bollock them, but he can't get them removed from a list of footballers able to play at a specific level of the game.

The number of key decisions a referee has to give in a game is mind-numbing. 'I have to make a decision on every tackle,' Paul tells me. 'In the course of a game I may give up to 30 fouls, a few dozen throw-ins, a dozen or so corners, some goals and a few other bits and pieces. Today, you've probably seen me make 50 key decisions, but there are probably another 250 that you haven't seen because nothing has happened. So I've made 300 decisions in the course of a game. If I've got 295 of those right, I haven't done bad, have I? My problem is making sure those five others are the smallest decisions possible – a throw-in on the halfway line or something. During the course of a game you might have three or four really big decisions to make. Getting those right is vital.'

It is assumed they don't care about these decisions. The reality, as Paul has already told me, is far different. They mull over their mistakes. 'You beat yourself up over it. I feel dreadful sometimes driving home alone. It can be a lonely existence.' He recalls a game earlier in the season, Cardiff v. Plymouth, which the away team won 1–0. He turned down a penalty appeal from Cardiff. 'Neither myself or my assistant had a particularly good view so I couldn't give it. You've got to be pretty certain because it's a big decision, and we didn't give it. When I looked at the video, and when you've seen sixteen different angles of the same incident, I could only find one that favoured my position. But that is just the way it was: I couldn't give it. So then you start to think, should I have done this or that to get myself into a better position.'

The media? Well, I guess we are to blame too. Listening to sports talk programmes like Radio Five Live's *606* won't help. It is full of fans moaning about referees who've 'lost the plot'. Paul prefers to listen to soothing music instead. TV is no better. 'They watch an incident from twenty different camera angles and shape an opinion. I see it once. Until I see the video, I won't know if a West Ham player was offside or not when they claim they scored. I've got faith in my assistant who made his own decision. For Christ's sake, we are human beings. We get as many things right in the game as we can.'

Paul is nursing a cold, which gets worse as we chat. Tonight he will have a meal and switch off from the game, but he still has a report to write and the video to watch. Paul often has to fight the temptation to scan the match video the moment he gets in. 'Sometimes I want to put it straight on and can't wait to see if I have got things right or wrong. Today, I'm fairly relaxed about it. I will probably watch it on fast forward and stop it for the key incidents within the next 24 hours. I love the game, I love being involved at the level I'm at, and I provide a good-quality service. If it wasn't good enough I wouldn't be allowed to continue.'

How many players, I wonder, will take home a video of the game to analyse their performance? How many players who will have made many more bloopers than the ref will already be out on the lash? Then look at the difference in the earnings of the respective parties.

For all the preparation, insults, pressure, hostility, debriefing and analysis, a Football League referee is paid £235 a game plus 40p-per-mile expenses, and hotels if needed. Get two games a week and it is a decent enough living, but it doesn't begin to measure up against the wages of the players and many other people in football. In fact, it seems like thin gruel indeed.

6.30 P.M.: GOING HOME Brian Tinnion leaves Ashton Gate with the match video tucked under his arm. Other than referees, managers are the other folk to paw endlessly over the games with a fine-toothed comb. Brian will watch his in detail tomorrow. 'It's great when you've won, hell when you've lost,' he says.

When I wrote my previous book, *The Sack Race*, about football management, I found that many managers refused to go out on Saturday evenings when their team had lost. It hurt so badly, they didn't want to be seen in public or listen to some diatribe from a drunken fan telling them where it was all going wrong. Brian Tinnion isn't like that. Tonight his family will go out for an Italian meal. 'You have to be fair to your family, and anyway, if you see a few supporters and they come over and chat, so what? They care. I'm very well known, so there is no escaping. You have to listen to some, as long as they don't say silly things.'

This seems such a sane attitude to football management, and to life. Maybe the job has yet to hurt him? Maybe he has a lot to learn about the role and its complexities? It changes people in many ways. Maybe, though, he is just getting it right from the start.

6.40 P.M.: MUD AND GOLD I pin Bob Marley down for a few words to sum up our day together. Add the massive work commitments to his various football activities – is it all worth it? Has he ever thought of relinquishing his role and easing back? 'No. I'm one of those people who needs to be busy. I don't watch telly as such. I don't actively read books, only a few pages at a time. The hour-and-a-half football bit is the least rewarding part of it for me. It's not high up there in terms of self-rewards.' So what is? 'Tomorrow, having a thousand people dressed up as Father Christmas earning the football club a lot of money; being perceived as a "good egg" in the community; developing community links; bringing people here to the football club. That is more important.'

More important than your marriage?

'No, of course not, but it wasn't just football that screwed my marriage up. I'm not the kind of dad to fall asleep on the sofa on Sunday afternoons. I haven't asked my sons if they want to run the Santa Fun Run tomorrow. But they are. That's great news because they are healthy lads and they want to do it. They are already showing signs that they want to be involved, to be community people. If part of me being here has rubbed off on them, then that has to be good.' However, Bob accepts there are downsides, like having to send out 2,000 letters telling people he is going to have to shut the roads tomorrow. 'My name is at the foot of that letter. That isn't going to make me popular, is it?'

Our day together has witnessed other abuse, from parents and from fans. It is a sad reflection of what people think of Bob and his fellow directors. So why do it? 'Because you love the game. You don't do it for ego because you get nothing out of it. You don't do it for financial gain because it is the other way around: it costs you money. You certainly don't do it for thanks because you don't get much of that either, and if you are doing it for that, you're going into it for the wrong reason anyway. You do it for the love of the game. You hope to make the game better, and that is important. I've no real affinity with Worcester. I've only lived here for twelve or thirteen years. Hednesford is my home town. Wherever I ended up I would have wanted to help the local team. Worcester is secondary; football is first for me.'

Suspecting that I already know the answer, I ask Bob which thing has given him the most pleasure today. The little blond-haired seven-year-old flying into a tackle, or that last-minute penalty being stroked in? 'The seven-year-old tasting his first football,' Bob replies. 'Unless as a country we provide football for that seven-year-old that penalty in the last minute wouldn't have happened.' Tears well up in his eyes. They aren't crocodile ones. This is genuine, and I am wary I have pushed him into uncomfortable territory at an energy-sapping time of day when emotions are high. He is about to take both his boys out for the evening. 'We've got it wrong,' he continues. 'If we got more seven-year-olds playing properly, educated right, eating and drinking right, living right, it has got to help.'

So much mud, so many connections with differing levels of grass-roots football, from a country field with enthusiastic eight-year-olds to a directors' room full of optics. 'That's non-League football – mud and gold together. You've seen me out with the groundsman at 9.30 this morning, and tonight marking out the lines for the start and finish of the Santa Fun Run. It covers a wide expanse of football. From a seven-year old who has just played his second football game to a lifelong Worcester City supporter who has handed his details over for the AGM, who must be 75 at least – it covers a huge age and social range. But they're all doing their bit, from the dad who is putting up the nets through to the groundsman here. They're all doing something, and I have to thank them for it.'

And then he has gone. To pick up the kids and go out to the basketball. The day isn't yet over.

7 P.M.: WHERE HAVE ALL THE PINK 'UNS GONE? When we used to run our coach to West Brom, or indeed when I used to travel on the Midland Red bus back in the early 1970s, one of the highlights was getting back to Worcester and buying an evening sports paper. We had a choice: the pink *Sports Argus*, which covered the West Midlands clubs, including Albion; or, more locally, in Worcester we had the attractively titled Green 'Un, which you could generally get from about 5.30 p.m. onwards. Tim and I disagree about this. He reckons you could only buy a Green 'Un back in the seventies, that the *Argus* established its hegemony only after the Green 'Un disappeared. I reckon a newspaper stall outside Foregate Street station sold both.

Every town, city and region in the country had an evening sports paper. Oh, I know in the age of the internet, email, texting and Ceefax and with the growth of local radio they serve little purpose; I know that they wouldn't be of much use now when kick-off times vary so much. But if you can remember the dampness of the paper as you read it from cover to cover – including the detailed chronological description of your team's victory (did you bother if they lost?) – on a bus, in a pub, in the chippy, in your armchair, with the newsprint blackening your fingers, then you'll know how important these papers were.

Now, alas, although it still sells well in Brum, you can only get the *Sports Argus* on Sunday mornings. Tim, as a married man with kids, had a Saturday-night ritual: walk to the shop, buy an *Argus*, order a takeaway, have a pint while reading his paper, return to collect his curry. But sadly, papers like these are dropping like flies around the country. It is inevitable, but they were an essential part of the evening matchday experience, and I mourn their passing.

7.15 P.M.: THE REF LOST THE PLOT Paul Taylor arrives home. He is no longer a 'bastard in black', pantomime or otherwise; he is just a regular guy who loves his wife and family like any other. He has put a quarter of a century's work into football and hopes to carry on until he has to retire at 48.

I wonder if, like some of the other matchday people featured in this book, he brings some of the anger aimed at him back home? 'I try to separate it out,' he says. 'If you have a bad day it's not your family's fault. You have to switch off. I worry about it, I need to put it right, but that is down to me.'

It is time-consuming. Paul, of course, offers himself for this stick during other people's leisure time. He tells the tale of when his son, Joe, was two and a half years old and 'Mel sat him down to watch me referee a game live on TV to show him where Daddy was. He thought I had another family somewhere which took me away from him. How do you explain that to a two-year-old?' You can't, of course. Or to the partners of football people who are married to the job.

I take my leave and get into my car. The sports stations are full of fans espousing their views. It's only right, of course – the fans are at least as important as any other element of the game – but the debate is tedious and repetitive, its scope narrow. On TalkSport, four out of five callers I listen to moan about the referees. Mike Riley is accused of a howler at Anfield for not giving Liverpool a penalty. Spurs lash in five goals, but rather than share the joy of their team handing out a thrashing, a couple of callers complain about trivialities regarding the ref. I retune to Five Live's *606*, and it's the same stuff. Southampton fans (why is it always Southampton fans?) drone on about their game at St Mary's. Guess what has annoyed them today? Yep, the ref. Oh, and one of his assistants. Same at Watford. It's the same boring stuff – rants largely about managers who should be sacked, incompetent referees and clubs that 'lack ambition'.

True, this has been the stuff and nonsense fans have moaned about since time immemorial, but what about the bigger picture? Where is the wit? Where are the real issues – clubs in crisis, abject catering, pricing, toilets, tactics? All of this takes a back seat to ref-bashing. I'm not saying referees are always right (me?), but the sport is using them as scapegoats while other things we should talk about are threatening to ruin the fabric of the game we love.

7.30 P.M.: DINNER WITH THE DOC Back at Ralph Rogers's flat in Birmingham with his partner Liz, over a glass of wine and superbly seasoned salmon, we ponder many football issues: qualifications, the role of club medics, and footballers spending their Saturday nights (and large amounts of disposable income) at all-night lap-dancing clubs. Ralph knows – he's seen them. 'It just ain't on,' says Ralph. 'Wouldn't happen in America. Sportsmen just don't do that sort of thing.' Liz wonders why, earlier in the afternoon, she saw two top footballers in town buying expensive Gucci accessories when their club was playing. The only feasible answers are that they either don't care or don't see it as an essential part of the professionalism that goes with being a top player. Or both.

For years it has been easy to manage the biggest clubs in the land, England too, without having taken a single coaching qualification. It is laughable. All you've needed to do if you want to be a football manager is find a chairman mate who'll give you a job, prove you can shout a bit louder than your team-mates, and charm the press. That's it.

Things are changing, though. Managers wanting to coach Champions League teams will soon need a Pro Licence, a super-duper qualification for the best head coaches around that many continental countries adopted decades ago; we've only had it in England since 2001. And without qualified coaches there is little chance the game will seek to employ the best qualified medical staff. It is a problem the FA are keen to address, and Ralph is at pains to praise the efforts of their medical chief Alan Hodgson. But highly qualified sports medics like Ralph are still thin on the ground. Walsall are lucky to have him – and they know it.

'I'm not bragging,' Ralph says, 'but I don't see many people like me outside the top few clubs. I'm here for the players seven days a week, 24 hours a day. That is my philosophy about sports medicine: you have to be there for the athletes, and that is what I choose to do. If you are a GP you won't do it the way I do it because you haven't been educated that way. I trained in the USA so I have a different perspective to the way I do the job and the way I believe it is right to do the job.'

In this mood, Ralph Rogers is a different person to the ultra-smart, neat, professional person all and sundry will have seen at Walsall. Leaning back with his legs over the arm of a chair, wearing a tracksuit and white sports socks, and having drunk a couple of glasses of wine, he offers more impassioned pleas for football to respect sports medicine. At times he is genuinely witty, at others there is a gallows humour: he readily recognises he is condemned by many every time he opens his mouth. He is American and black. Look around English football clubs: how many (or few) black managers and coaches are there? Just three of the 92 Premier/Football League managers at the time of writing, whereas 25 to 30 per cent of the players are non-white. An enormous disparity. Stretch that out to coaching and support staff and the stats are just as grim. Ralph is the only black doctor he knows of in English football.

I leave content, but confused. It has been a fascinating day, one that has given me a different perspective. Many of the things we have talked about make sense, but they are simply ignored.

8 P.M.: AN EVENING AT AFAN LIDO The Afan Lido club bar has thinned out. The post-match drinkers have largely disappeared, and Phil Robinson is preparing for the evening. Tonight, like most Saturday evenings, is Cabaret Night at Afan Lido. A local singer will entertain the 30 or 40 regulars who turn up to enjoy a few drinks at their local football club. Many – most, in fact – are linked with the club in one way or another, as players, coaches, parents of children involved, or simply those who know someone who has a connection. 'It's a regular crowd,' says Phil, who enjoys the odd drink these days but not many. 'I'm no trouble. Three pints and I'm pissed.' He was teetotal in his bodybuilding days. His wife, Linda, is still here too, making more sandwiches and serving drinks during busy periods.

Matchday is a long, punishing schedule for Phil. I wonder what drives him on. After all, when he started this remarkable club it was little to do with pulling pints, more about playing and coaching. 'It is what I started,' Phil replies. 'I have had so much enjoyment out of it I just want to continue doing it. I wouldn't want to do it if I didn't enjoy it. I have had one or two ailments as I've got older, but I want to carry on for as long as possible.'

It has been suggested that Phil should take a step back. As he admits, he has had a couple of minor health scares, but Phil reckons it has nothing to do with age. 'People say it is because you are old. That pisses me off, because you are as old as you feel – and I don't feel old. I have always been fit and have always kept myself fit. I still look after myself, and I'm under doctor's orders now to make sure I look after myself.'

Occasionally, as he goes about his work, I catch Phil glancing up at the photographs of the 200 faces with their Welsh international caps smiling back at him. He has had a hand in the development of all of them. They serve as a reminder of what Afan Lido is all about, and what football ought to be about. They are a constant reminder of what can be achieved through hard work and honest endeavour, if players are coached properly and have the right spirit ingrained in them.

Phil Robinson is simply dedicated to the club he has created, to the game he has served so splendidly, to his family whom he so loves so dearly, and to the community of Port Talbot, where he has offered sporting opportunities to thousands of boys and girls. His work has earned him a service to sport award from West Glamorgan County Council, but, you know what? I'd knight him if I could.

8.30 P.M.: WORKING LATE AT THE OFFICE At Carrow Road the press conferences have long since finished, the fans have drifted home, Chelsea are swanning back to the capital and the floodlights are being switched off. After a couple of post-match meetings, including a private conversation with Nigel Worthington, Neil Doncaster, coat and jacket off, returns to his office to deal with more paperwork, check his incoming emails and other messages, and liaise with other members of staff. Grace, his two-year-old daughter, smiles back at him from a photograph to the left edge of his desk.

He leans back and decides to call it quits. He has been here for eleven and a half hours after all. He heads off to the boardroom for a debrief. He'll be back in tomorrow, and on Monday at 8.30 a.m. sharp. There are few days off for a busy football club chief executive, or at least for someone as hands-on as Neil Doncaster. He is well paid and he has had offers of other posts, but none of them appeals. Just look at the unpredictable boardrooms and owners elsewhere, then look at the stability of Norwich's board, who have readily bought into the idea of creating a large, community-focused football club (Charlton Athletic were their role models) and have the mettle to see it through. And look at the quality of life in Norfolk. All are sound reasons for staying put.

I do wonder, though, as I do with so many other men in this book, whether Neil is married to the job. Those six or seven twelve-hour days and giving your all to a football club may sound an honourable thing to do, but is it healthy?

9 P.M.: NIGHTMARE JOURNEYS? Neil Williams pulls in at Sedgemoor services on the M5 in Somerset. I thought stopping for something to eat would mean a cooked meal. Instead it is a sandwich, a packet of crisps and a Coke. He needs a break but doesn't want to waste time.

Motorway service stations are miserable, often solitary places on dark winter matchday nights. I know – I've stopped at enough of them on my way home from reporting on matches and writing this book. But at least I am being paid. For football fans, they are pretty hopeless places. The food is overpriced, and at this time of night there is limited availability. Yet there are thousands of football fans travelling home from games who could be catered for.

Sat here, chewing a chilled sandwich, the concerns of Wrexham FC suddenly seem far away. Neil is summoning up one final effort for his eleven-hour road journey – there are still at least one and a half hours to go – and this is now becoming a mind-numbing chore. (And all for a nil–nil draw.)

I'm not sure if this is the right time to raise this, but, 'Ever had any nightmare journeys?'

Neil looks at me as if I am mad. He screws up a 'where to begin?' face which melts into a disturbing giggle. 'The worst one was when we drew Man Utd in the FA Cup in 1995. I was lucky enough be one of the 7,000 Wrexham supporters to get a ticket for the game at Old Trafford. So I set off on a real miserable night in January [planning to stop over in Wrexham]. It was pouring with rain and blowing a gale and I got fifteen miles away from home on Friday night and a fox ran across the road in front of me. I carried on, but about twenty miles further on I got up to Bodmin Moor, near Jamaica Inn, and the car overheated. Radiator gone – the fox had hit it. I had to get towed back home, so I couldn't get to Manchester for the kick-off. I still have the ticket to this day.'

I'm just hoping he doesn't break down on the infamous Bodmin Moor tonight.

9.30 P.M.: FORGING LINKS Sixteen hours after he woke up, Bob Marley is still foraging. He is at University College Worcester with his sons Seb and Sam, ostensibly for a lads and dads night out together at another sport he enjoys – basketball. Worcester Wolves are in British basketball's second tier, the National League Division One. But it is also a chance to press the flesh and meet some faces. Worcester City are trying to forge links with the college in order to sponsor a few players who can jointly study at the college and play for City. It is a chance to tap into the few talented players who value their higher education and want the best of both worlds, and it is realistically the only chance Worcester are going to get to sign high-quality players cheaply. It is another brick in the wall for Bob.

10.30 P.M.: MATCH OF THE DAY AND FRIED ONIONS I'm glad *Match of the Day* is back on BBC1. If you have Sky you can choose your game on *Football First*, but there is nothing quite like *MOTD*. It's not Lineker, Hansen and co. for me, but the music. It takes me back to Jimmy Hill and the mid-1970s when there were some great games. My mum used to cook hot dogs and fried onions, which sizzled and caramelised and tasted wonderful. The juice used to drip down the rolls they were served in and I would further drench them in brown sauce. *MOTD* was a family thing, although by then my brother would be out drinking somewhere. So Mum, Dad and I would sit down and munch while watching some long-haired souls playing football on indescribably muddy pitches. And it was great.

10.35 p.m. – In Bristol City manager Brian Tinnion has an early night.
10.40 p.m. – Reverend John Boyers says goodnight to Anne before switching off the bedside light in Sale.

10.40 P.M.: BACK HOME Neil Williams reaches Helston at last, the small Cornish town he left at half-past six in the morning. He has driven for eleven of the last sixteen hours, collected more shirts for his appeal, seen Wrexham pick up a precious point but fail to score, and enjoyed the warmth of other fans who have rallied to Wrexham's cause in their hour of need.

He unpacks his jacket, Welsh flag, toy sheep, huge hat and scarf, and still wearing his Cornish Red replica shirt slumps into an armchair clutching a mug of Ovaltine. He has a final glance at the club programme and a quick stare at *Match of the Day*, then heads upstairs to bed. Knackered.

He has given his all for Wrexham FC today, the club he so dearly hopes will survive. He switches off his bedroom light wondering how many more times he will be able to make this journey, this 'pilgrimage' back to North Wales to cheer on the team he supported as a lad, when he walked five miles home from the bus stop after watching them play. If his devotion counts for anything, they will make it.

10.45 p.m. – In Lincoln Rob Bradley calls it a day.

10.50 P.M.: DREAMING OF SANTA Bob Marley arrives at his mate's house where he is kipping. He's just dropped his two sons off with his estranged wife Mandy. Some people count sheep to sleep; Bob counts the number of entrants for tomorrow's fun run. He'll be up at 5.30 again, laying into some 'work work' before going down the Lane with all the irrepressible enthusiasm I had when I first ventured down there as a little boy. My dreams were about seeing the City win, Bob's are about raising some much-needed cash. He switches off his bedside light.

10.50 p.m. – In Birmingham Dr Ralph Rogers takes a final look out on to the busy Bristol Road before drawing the blinds and creeping into bed.
10.55 p.m. – In Dumfries Paul Barnett yawns, switches off his sidelight, and prays for a quiet night from three-month-old son Jack.
11 p.m. – Stuart Hall in Cheshire and James Alexander Gordon in Berkshire turn in.
11.10 p.m. – So does Bill Berry in Broadway.
11.20 p.m. – Then WPC Alison Geddes follows suit in Birmingham.
11.25 p.m. – And Phil Hamilton in Aston.

11.30 P.M.: TIRED OF WAITING I'm still in Carlisle, waiting for Bob Marley. I haven't heard from him. I hope he hasn't broken down or got lost. I am tired and bored.

11.30 p.m. – Danny Coles switches off the bedside light in Bristol.
11.35 p.m. – Paul and Mel Taylor climb into bed in Cheshunt.
11.40 p.m. – Brian Murdoch hits the sack in Kidderminster.
11.45 p.m. – Tim Lewis in Worcester puts his West Brom worries to bed.
11.50 p.m. – Neil Doncaster in Norwich turns in.
12 a.m. – John Baine, aka Attila the Stockbroker, heads off for some shut-eye in Brighton.

12.30 A.M.: TAKE ME HOME I am now seriously worried about Bob Marley. Where is he? Why hasn't he called? I am starting to feel guilty. What if he's had a crash?

Waiting. It reminds me of Saturdays of old. Waiting for buses, waiting for trains, waiting to get to a match, waiting to go home . . .

Suddenly, Bob breezes in. As only Bob Marley could do, he has managed to pick up a couple of girls on their way home. No, don't get me wrong – not in a 'ladies of the night' or suave James Bond kind of way. They flagged him down and he offered them a lift home in exchange for directions to the community centre. Dodgy, but smart.

1 A.M.: PHIL ROBINSON CALLS IT A DAY Phil Robinson has closed the bar, paid the cabaret singer, moved the pool table, locked up, bottled up, washed up and checked everything is as it should be in the Afan Lido bar. He is finally ready to go home. Phil has been at Afan Lido for seventeen hours. Tomorrow is his day off, but he'll be back at the club on Monday morning, sorting, organising, fixing and doing what needs to be done for the sake of this small club on the South Wales coast he started in 1967. He takes one final look around, then switches off the light. Time to go home.

4 A.M.: FLOODS OF TEARS Bob Marley and I approach Worcester. We have chatted all the way home – we could talk our way to Land's End (or to Neil Williams's house at least) about football. Typically, he won't tell me his address so I can send a cheque for the petrol. I don't really know what to say. I feel humble. It is typical of this man's generosity – someone I met through football, whose grass-roots efforts are notable. It takes a very special, considerate person to make a 500-mile round trip like that, at night. What more can I say? Thanks, Bob.

It had to be me. Just as I had intended, but failed, to start this book with someone fully committed to matchday, so I had fully intended to finish this book with the last character to switch off the light. A dedicated fan like Neil Williams, maybe? Or Rob Bradley, no less a fan but in recent times a concerned chairman of Lincoln City too. Or Bristol City manager Brian Tinnion, wearing the carpet thin with worry. Or Paul Barnett, hearing that whistling wind and wondering what the elements might do to Gretna's ground. It is hard to top the fabulous efforts of Phil Robinson at Afan Lido, or the wonderful work Alison Geddes and Phil Hamilton do in inner-city Birmingham. Or the services given to the game by the likes of Paul Taylor,

Neil Doncaster, Ralph Rogers and Brian Murdoch, not to mention the spiritual support of John Boyers – all people who love their work and do it well. Maybe the day would end on Attila the Stockbroker making his way back from a gig, or Bill Berry, heading home from some far-flung ground he has hopped to? Or Danny Coles unable to sleep, suffering one of his night-time attacks of cramp?

No, it had to be me. Though I wish it had not been in such a dramatic manner.

My matchday is finally over. All these people, and millions more, contribute to the rich tapestry that is our national game. It has been an incredible journey with so many memories: prayers at Old Trafford, the majesty of Lincoln Cathedral, a fans parade at Wrexham, Chelsea showing their championship worth, Brian Murdoch's food, Wayne Rooney's genius, Paul Merson's guile, Neil Emblen's arse, Tommy Doherty's retching ability, Roy Unwin's death, Phil Hamilton's and Bob Marley's tears, floods, snow, ice, showers and sunshine . . . and that little blond-haired boy playing for Hadley Rangers U-10s.

I ponder these images and more as I creep upstairs and sneak into bed. Home at last. I cuddle Nicholas, our gorgeous two-year-old who is snuggled up next to his mother. Dreaming of, well, whatever toddlers dream about (animals mainly, according to psychologists). Sweet dreams, I hope.

Football is a game of passion, enthusiasm, skill and expertise. It has unique intensity and beauty, and is above all else a marvellous cultural experience. Saturday, matchday, is its special day. I learned to love football, and I hope Nicholas will too.

I squeeze him a little tighter and rest my head against his. Yes, I hope sport gives this sweet little fella a smidgen of the joy it has given me down the years – and none of the despair! God bless, little man. God bless.

THE PEOPLE

ATTILA THE STOCKBROKER – BRIGHTON'S PA ANNOUNCER
John Baine, aka Attila the Stockbroker, is a self-proclaimed 'sharp-tongued, high-energy, social-surrealist poet and songwriter' who mixes medieval music and punk. He is also Brighton & Hove Albion's poet-in-residence and their PA man, who has played an eclectic mix of music on matchdays ranging from the Sex Pistols to the Scissor Sisters. In September 2005 Attila, 47, celebrated 25 years as a performer.

PAUL BARNETT – GRETNA'S GROUNDSMAN 'Barney' became the Football League's youngest groundsman when he was handed responsibility for the pitch at his hometown club, Scarborough, at the tender age of nineteen in 1988. He left the club in 2002 and was briefly on the staff at Sunderland before moving to Gretna FC to renew his acquaintance with former Scarborough director Brooks Mileson, who is Gretna's MD.

BILL BERRY – THE GROUNDHOPPER Former civil servant Bill Berry runs a weekly magazine called the *Football Traveller*, a must-have read for groundhoppers or anyone else in need of an up-to-date list of the forthcoming weeks' British football fixtures. A Londoner from Putney, Bill now lives in Broadway, Worcestershire, and has been a groundhopper for more than 30 years. He has watched matches at about 1,500 grounds.

REV JOHN BOYERS – MANCHESTER UNITED'S CHAPLAIN John Boyers is a Baptist minister and the national director of SCORE, a registered charity specialising in sports chaplaincy. He has been club chaplain at United since 1992 having fulfilled a similar role at Watford for fifteen years. Born in Grimsby in March 1949, he is a keen supporter of Grimsby Town FC. (SCORE can be contacted at PO Box 123, Sale, Manchester, M33 4ZA.)

ROB BRADLEY – THE CHAIRMAN In 2001 Rob Bradley, a self-employed architect and lifelong Lincoln City fan, became the first head of a supporters trust to be elected as the chairman of a Football League club. Lincoln were heavily in debt at the time and went into administration in 2002. During season 2004/05, Rob's fifth in charge, they posted record profits of £735,000.

DANNY COLES – BRISTOL CITY'S CENTRE-HALF Danny Coles is a six-foot-tall central defender with his hometown club, Bristol City. He was a virtual ever-present during the 2004/05 season, making 41 appearances (plus two as sub), and by the end of the season had played 150 games for the club overall. He was placed on the transfer list at his own request midway through the season.

NEIL DONCASTER – NORWICH'S CHIEF EXECUTIVE Neil Doncaster was appointed chief executive of Norwich City FC in 1997. Born in Honiton, Devon, in May 1970 but raised in Croydon, Surrey, Neil is a trained lawyer. At Norwich he has been part of a management team that has squashed the club debts of £8 million (in 1997) to break even by 2002 and established Norwich City as a community club in Norfolk.

ALISON GEDDES – COMMUNITY POLICE OFFICER AND YOUTH WORKER Alison Geddes is a community police officer in Birmingham, where she set up the Handsworth Youth and Community Project in 2003 offering sport and recreational facilities for local children and youths aged between eight and eighteen. In March 2005 the scheme expanded to include a Positive Futures football programme run under the guidance of local coach Kevin Brookes.

JAMES ALEXANDER GORDON – THE CLASSIFIED RESULTS READER James Alexander Gordon has read the football scores on BBC Radio's *Sports Report* since 1972. He worked in music publishing before joining the BBC as a continuity announcer. He was raised in the Scottish town of Grangemouth and overcame polio as a child to achieve a lifelong goal of reading the news on BBC radio.

THE PEOPLE

STUART HALL – SPORTS REPORTER Stuart Hall has reported on football matches in northwest England for BBC Radio in his own inimitable way since 1959. His distinct style – irreverent, witty, erudite – has stood him apart from other sports journalists. He is the former chuckling presenter of BBC TV's *It's a Knockout* and regional TV programme *North West Tonight*.

PHIL HAMILTON – THE GRASS-ROOTS COACH Phil Hamilton is a 45-year-old youth worker in Aston, Birmingham. He runs two junior football teams, coaches dozens of kids each week and has steered hundreds of boys on to a lifelong path of sport and health. He works for an urban regeneration scheme called Groundwork.

BOB MARLEY – THE NON-LEAGUE CLUB DIRECTOR Bob Marley has been a director of Worcester City FC since 2000, in particular running the club's junior development programme. Born in Hednesford, Staffordshire, in May 1967, in 2004 he established and became the first chairman of the Midland Junior Premier Football League. He is a director of a business-to-business mobile phone company, the Phoneworks.

BRIAN MURDOCH – THE CATERER Brian Murdoch has been the award-winning caterer at Kidderminster Harriers FC since 1962. Having started as a street vendor selling burgers and hot dogs from vans, he now owns a hotel, wine bar and restaurant in Kidderminster.

PHIL ROBINSON – THE DOGSBODY Phil Robinson was a gym instructor at a local sports centre when he founded Afan Lido FC in Port Talbot in 1967. The club has risen from the Port Talbot and District League to the Welsh Premier League and has competed in the UEFA Cup. Phil has been secretary throughout – and player, manager, coach and development director. He even runs the club bar.

DR RALPH ROGERS – THE CLUB DOCTOR Dr Ralph Rogers is a Birmingham-based doctor of sports medicine and exercise physiology. He runs his own clinic MOST (Medical Orthopaedic Sports Therapy) in the city and is club doctor at Walsall FC and Warwickshire Country

Cricket Club. Born, raised and educated in the USA, he has also trained and practised medicine in continental Europe and the UK.

PAUL TAYLOR – THE REFEREE In 1989, aged 29, Paul Taylor became the youngest person to become a Football League referee. He lives in Cheshunt, Hertfordshire, and works for BT in London. Season 2004/05 was his sixteenth on the Football League officials list.

BRIAN TINNION – THE MANAGER Brian Tinnion was appointed as manager of Bristol City in June 2004. A midfielder who made 497 appearances for the club, 2004/05 was his first season in football management. His previous clubs were Bradford City and Newcastle United.

NEIL WILLIAMS – A DEVOTED FAN Neil Williams is a Wrexham fan who lives in Helston, Cornwall, where he works for a scuba diving company. He makes regular 650-mile round-trip journeys to watch his hometown team. In 2004/05 Wrexham were threatened with extinction: their owner sought to evict the club and sell their ground, and they were placed in administration early in the season and subsequently docked ten points by the Football League. This only made Neil love his club all the more. As a keen member of their supporters trust, Neil engaged in several fund-raising schemes in 2004/05.

THE MATCHES

AFAN LIDO 1 LLANELLI 1
1 April 2005
Vauxhall Masterfit Retailers Welsh Premier League
Attendance: 221

BRIGHTON & HOVE ALBION 0 NOTTINGHAM FOREST 0
22 January 2005
Coca-Cola Championship
Attendance: 6,704

BRISTOL CITY 2 PORT VALE 0
2 April 2005
Coca-Cola League One
Attendance: 10,284

EVERGREEN 2 HADLEY 2
12 March 2005
Hertfordshire Senior League Premier Division
Attendance: 26

GRETNA 2 ELGIN CITY 1
5 February 2005
Bell's Scottish Football League Division Three
Attendance: 809

HANDSWORTH POSITIVE FUTURES LEAGUE
19 March 2005
Results not applicable

IPSWICH TOWN 0 WEST HAM UNITED 2
1 January 2005
Coca-Cola Championship
Attendance: 30,003

KIDDERMINSTER HARRIERS 2 ROCHDALE 1
10 December 2004
Coca-Cola League Two
Attendance: 2,337

LINCOLN CITY 1 BRISTOL ROVERS 1
15 January 2005
Coca-Cola League Two
Attendance: 3,929

MANCHESTER UNITED 2 PORTSMOUTH 1
26 February 2005
Barclays Premiership
Attendance: 67,989

NORWICH CITY 1 CHELSEA 3
5 March 2005
Barclays Premiership
Attendance: 24,506

WALSALL 3 BLACKPOOL 2
17 December 2004
Coca-Cola League One
Attendance: 5,476

WIGAN ATHLETIC 3 LEEDS UNITED 0
19 February 2005
Coca-Cola Championship
Attendance: 17,177

WORCESTER CITY 2 STALYBRIDGE CELTIC 1
3 December 2004
Nationwide Conference North
Attendance: 849

WREXHAM 0 DONCASTER ROVERS 0
29 January 2005
Coca-Cola League One
Attendance: 6,115

WHAT HAPPENED NEXT?

AFAN LIDO were relegated from the Welsh Premier League on the final day of the 2004/05 season. They were docked three points for unwittingly fielding a player in a game against Airbus UK in March – defender Leigh Shrimpton, who had picked up a suspension playing Sunday football. Without the three-point deduction Lido would have finished just out of the relegation zone on goal difference. An appeal failed, so in 2005/06 they will compete in the Motaquote Welsh League Division One. **PHIL ROBINSON** continues as their secretary and director of football. **LLANELLI** staved off the threat of relegation and finished fourteenth in the Welsh Premier League.

BRIGHTON & HOVE ALBION finished twentieth (two places above the relegation zone) and preserved their Championship status on the final day of the season with a 1–1 draw at home against Ipswich. Defeat would have seen them relegated. The club has been granted permission to stay at the Withdean Stadium until June 2008 and can increase capacity to 9,000. The Office of the Deputy Prime Minister has told them a decision on their new ground proposal at Falmer will be made by 31 October 2005. **ATTILA THE STOCKBROKER** is still their PA announcer and poet-in-residence. **NOTTINGHAM FOREST** finished 23rd in the Championship in 2004/05 and were relegated to League One.

BRISTOL CITY finished seventh in Coca-Cola League One, one place and one point outside the play-off spots. **DANNY COLES** is still with the club. Manager **BRIAN TINNION** has asked for an experienced coach or director of football to join him at Ashton Gate. **PORT VALE** finished eighteenth in the League One table.

EVERGREEN FC finished seventh in the Hertfordshire Senior League. **HADLEY FC** won the league by five points.

GRETNA were the first club in any British league to be promoted. They ended the season with a 100 per cent home League record, had a massive goal difference of 101, beat their nearest Division Three rivals Peterhead by twenty points and were a whopping 47 points clear of third-placed Cowdenbeath. Striker Kenny Deucher was named Bell's Scottish League player of the season; he scored 41 goals, including an amazing six hat-tricks. PAUL BARNETT is still their groundsman. ELGIN CITY finished in sixth place.

IPSWICH TOWN finished in third place in the Coca-Cola Championship. They lost their play-off semi-final to West Ham, who beat them by the same score, 2–0, as they did in the League game at Portman Road featured in this book. Ipswich have played six times in the play-offs in the past ten seasons but have triumphed only once. WEST HAM were promoted to the Premiership after a 1–0 win over Preston North End in the Championship play-off final in Cardiff. They had slipped into sixth spot, the final play-off position, on the final day of the season with an away win at Watford. Referee PAUL TAYLOR will carry on refereeing in the Football League. He has eight grounds to complete before he can claim to have officiated at all 92 Premier/ Football League grounds in England.

KIDDERMINSTER HARRIERS were relegated from Coca-Cola League Two, ending a five-year spell in the Football League. BRIAN MURDOCH continues to do the catering for spectators at Aggborough. ROCHDALE finished ninth in League Two.

LINCOLN CITY finished sixth in League Two and briefly threatened to earn automatic promotion. They reached the play-off final for the second time in three seasons but lost to Southend 2–0 after extra time. ROB BRADLEY stepped down as Lincoln City chairman and as chairman of the Lincoln City Supporters Trust at the end of the season. BRISTOL ROVERS finished twelfth in League Two.

MANCHESTER UNITED finished third in the Premiership, some eighteen points behind winners Chelsea, and will have to qualify for the

2005/06 European Champions League for the second season running. They also lost the FA Cup final to Arsenal on penalties after extra time. In May 2005 US tycoon Malcolm Glazer launched a £790 million takeover of the club by increasing his shareholding to 75 per cent. The future direction of the club seems uncertain. JOHN BOYERS is still the club's chaplain. PORTSMOUTH hovered near the Premiership relegation zone but finished safely in sixteenth spot.

NORWICH CITY finished nineteenth in the Premiership and were relegated on the final day of the season having lost 6–0 at Fulham. Until then they had hauled themselves up the table by winning four of their previous six games. NEIL DONCASTER remains their chief executive. CHELSEA won the Premiership, finishing twelve points clear of nearest rivals Arsenal. They lost just one League game all season and conceded a miserly fifteen goals.

WALSALL'S win against Blackpool hoisted them up into the top half of the Coca-Cola League One table, but it was the high point of their season. A dip in form took them back close to the relegation zone, and serious questions were asked about Paul Merson's future, but they won their last five games to finish fourteenth. RALPH ROGERS remains their club doctor. Blackpool finished in sixteenth place.

WIGAN ATHLETIC were promoted to the Premiership for the first time in their history after a final-day 3–1 win over Reading. LEEDS UNITED finished fourteenth. STUART HALL remains a BBC matchday sports reporter.

WORCESTER CITY won just one of their next ten games after the Stalybridge win and drifted into the relegation zone. But under a new manager, Andy Preece, they won seven of their final eleven games to finish seventh in the Nationwide Conference North table. BOB MARLEY is still a director of the club. STALYBRIDGE CELTIC fought their way from the foot of the table to finish nineteenth.

WREXHAM were relegated from Coca-Cola League One in the final week of the season. The ten points they were docked for going into administration effectively did for them. Had they not received the punishment they would have had enough points to stay up. The club was £4 million in debt. Talks are ongoing about the sale of the club, but at the time of writing it seems they will remain at the Racecourse Ground for at least one more season. It wasn't all bad: in April Wrexham won the LDV Vans Trophy at the Millennium Stadium in Cardiff, beating Southend 2–0 after extra time. NEIL WILLIAMS'S shirt auction raised £13,500. DONCASTER ROVERS finished tenth in League One.

Finally, my beloved WEST BROMWICH ALBION secured their Premiership status with a remarkable final-day win on what was dubbed 'Survival Sunday'. With Norwich City and Southampton losing, and Crystal Palace only drawing, West Brom clawed their way off the foot of the table with a 2–0 win at home against Portsmouth to finish seventeenth – just one place above the relegation zone. And I was there!